WELSH GO

SERIES PREFACE

Gothic Literary Studies is dedicated to publishing groundbreaking scholarship on Gothic in literature and film. The Gothic, which has been subjected to a variety of critical and theoretical approaches, is a form which plays an important role in our understanding of literary, intellectual and cultural histories. The series seeks to promote challenging and innovative approaches to Gothic which question any aspect of the Gothic tradition or perceived critical orthodoxy. Volumes in the series explore how issues such as gender, religion, nation and sexuality have shaped our view of the Gothic tradition. Both academically rigorous and informed by the latest developments in critical theory, the series provides an important focus for scholarly developments in Gothic studies, literary studies, cultural studies and critical theory. The series will be of interest to students of all levels and to scholars and teachers of the Gothic and literary and cultural histories.

SERIES EDITORS

EDITORIAL BOARD

Welsh Gothic

Jane Aaron

UNIVERSITY OF WALES PRESS
CARDIFF
2013

www.uwp.co.uk

British Library CIP Data
A catalogue record for this book is available from the British Library.

ISBN   978-0-7083-2607-7 (hardback
            978-0-7083-2608-4 (paperback)
e-ISBN   978-0-7083-2609-1

The right of Jane Aaron to be identified as author of this work has been asserted in accordance with sections 77 and 79 of the Copyright, Designs and Patents Act 1988.

Typeset in Wales by Eira Fenn Gaunt, Cardiff
Printed on demand by CPI Group (UK) Ltd, Croydon, CR0 4YY

CONTENTS

Acknowledgements

This book owes its origins to those undergraduate students of English at the University of Glamorgan who in the mid-2000s were failing to sign up in sufficient numbers for an optional second-year module on Welsh writing in English. Though the first- and third-year modules on more contemporary Welsh writing were well supported, the second-year option, which dealt with the so-called 'first flowering' of Anglophone Welsh writers, and included on its syllabus such luminaries as Caradoc Evans, Dylan Thomas and the 1930s industrial novelists, failed to appeal, and as a result was threatened with closure. As I sought to find ways of increasing the allure of the material, I noticed that those optional modules offered by the department which featured the Gothic genre were in each year regularly oversubscribed. It proved surprisingly easy to reshape the original module, broaden its chronological scope, and submit it for approval as a new course entitled 'Terror and the supernatural in Welsh writing in English'. Under that title it served to draw sufficient subscribers to satisfy the student numbers requirements of the university for the rest of my time at Glamorgan, but its teaching was somewhat hampered by the fact that there was little secondary critical material available on the topic. This book has been written with the aim of helping to fill that gap; it is dedicated, with gratitude and appreciation, to those students whose lively responses made my years of teaching at Pontypridd so pleasurable.

In preparing the volume for publication I have been much supported by John Koch and Diana Wallace, who both read through the first draft and made many very useful suggestions for amendments; I am much indebted to them both. I should also like to thank those friends and colleagues with whom I discussed various aspects of the book in progress, in particular Helen Phillips, Sarah Prescott,

Katriona Mackay, Kirsti Bohata, Huw Walters of the National Library of Wales, and the editor of the Gothic Literary Studies series, Andy Smith. The staff of the University of Wales Press, particularly Sarah Lewis, were also enthusiastically supportive of this project, and I much appreciated their professionalism and diligence.

For kind permission to quote from her poem 'The Zombie-makers' I am very grateful to Ruth Bidgood. Though they have since been revised, parts of the first chapter of this book first appeared in 'Haunted by history: Welsh Gothic 1780–1800', in Stewart Mottram and Sarah Prescott, eds, *Writing Wales, from the Renaissance to Romanticism* (Farnham: Ashgate, 2013), and are used here by permission of the publisher.

To the class of EL2S013

Prologue

'A Long Terror'

'A long terror is on me' grieves Gruffudd ab yr Ynad Goch in his thirteenth-century 'Lament for Llywelyn ap Gruffudd, the Last Prince'. Llywelyn's fall in 1282 marked the close of the Welsh struggle to maintain independence in the face of the Anglo-Norman conquerors. The poet represents his prince's death as a trauma of such magnitude that it shatters his world, leaving no place of safety: 'There is no refuge from imprisoning fear / And nowhere to bide – O such abiding!' (*'Nid oes le y cyrcher rhag carchar braw; / Nid oes le y triger; och o'r trigaw!'*). Every aspect of his environment has been defamiliarized; even the diurnal cycle of nature seems in disarray: 'See you not the sun hurtling through the sky, / And that the stars have fallen?' (*'Poni welwch-chwi'r haul yn hwylaw'r awyr? / Poni welwch-chwi'r sŷr wedi'r syrthiaw?'*). Terror is the only appropriate affective response to such a traumatic loss of security and identity as the death of Llywelyn and the conquest of Wales entailed: 'When that head fell, men welcomed terror,' says the poet (*'Pen pan las, ni bu gas gymraw'*).[1] Early Welsh poetry is a long litany of such terrors: before the coming of the Normans, bards from the sixth century onwards recorded the invasive onslaughts of the Saxons. The anonymous ninth-century poem 'Stafell Gynddylan' ('Cynddylan's Hall'), for example, laments the sacking of Cynddylan's hall Pengwern, near modern-day Shrewsbury, and the slaughter of the chieftain and his retinue. Written in the voice of one of the few survivors, Cynddylan's sister Heledd, the poem describes Pengwern as 'dark tonight, / with no fire, no candle', and asks, 'Save for God, who'll keep me sane?' (*'Stafell Gynddylan ys tywyll heno, / Heb dân, heb gannwyll; / Namyn Duw pwy a'm dyry pwyll?'*)[2]

It is no coincidence that early Welsh texts like these were re-discovered, published and translated into English for the first time during that epoch which also saw the birth of the Gothic as a literary genre. After the era of Enlightenment with its emphasis on rationality and its valorization of classically influenced literature, writers and scholars of the turbulent second half of the eighteenth century, rebelling against what was perceived as the emotional aridity and repressiveness of the 'age of reason', actively sought to re-engage with, and create, a literature capable of arousing strong affect, be it sentimental, sublime or terror-ridden. In 1765, Horace Walpole published *The Castle of Otranto*, hailed as the founding text of the Gothic genre. A year earlier when Evan Evans (Ieuan Prydydd Hir) published *Some Specimens of the Poetry of the Ancient Welsh Bards Translated into English* (1764) he was participating in a parallel new movement popularized by the immense success of Thomas Gray's 'The Bard' (1757), an ode supposedly sung by the last poet to survive Edward I's alleged extermination of the Welsh bards in 1282 after Llywelyn's fall. Within this Celtic revival movement, early Gaelic and Welsh poetry was seen as illustrative of the unrepressed vitality of pre-Enlightenment culture and as evidence that the Isle of Britain too had once been inhabited by 'noble savages', free of the artificial constraints of modern civilization. In Gray's ode, the Plantagenet conquerors are roundly cursed: the bards slaughtered by Edward rise again, 'a grisly band', to 'weave with bloody hands . . . / The winding sheet of Edward's race'; even the very landscape of Wales, its 'giant oak and desert cave', swear eternal revenge against the king.[3] From the last decades of the eighteenth century on, the un-dead voices of the pre-conquest past are frequently to be heard in Welsh and Anglophone writing from Wales, castigating not only Wales's conquerors but also their own descendants, the modern-day Welsh, found wanting in the appropriate spirit of resistance to foreign rule. The 'long terror' of ethnic annihilation persists in such texts, which constitute the core materials of Welsh Gothic as a specific branch of the Gothic genre – or so, at any rate, this book argues.

In recent years Gothic literature referring to the history of imperial conquests and resistance to such conquests has been categorized as participating in the expanding oeuvre of what has been termed 'postcolonial' or 'imperial' Gothic, first labelled as such in Patrick Brantlinger's *Rule of Darkness: British Literature and Imperialism 1830–1914* (1988).[4] To what extent it is appropriate to categorize Welsh culture in general as 'postcolonial' is a question which has by now been debated at some length, and the outcome is still undecided, particularly amongst historians.[5] Within literary circles, however, it has been accepted that the literatures of all countries which have been invaded, but have resisted absorption into the dominant imperial culture, are appropriate subjects for interpretations based on postcolonial theory. As William Hughes and Andrew Smith put it in their introduction to a special issue on 'Postcolonial Gothic' of the journal *Gothic Studies*,

> The rather simplistic and restrictive notion of what it is to be postcolonial that is still occasionally encountered in some circles – namely a blinkered consideration of nations and cultures only after the departure of the invasive power source – has thankfully been eclipsed for the most part by a broader reading that situates the onset of the postcolonial at the point in which the indigenous culture, with its power structures, has its integrity violated by external (cultural or physical) interference.[6]

When that primary experience of violation remains alive as a central trauma in the cultural memory of a people, postcolonial theory is considered a suitable tool with which to assess its impact and its cultural affects. Within a British Isles context, it is nowadays customary to analyse the rich wealth of Irish Gothic materials in terms of the long conflict between Ireland and England,[7] and by now Kirsti Bohata, Darryl Jones and others have already embarked upon the process of extending such interpretations to Welsh Gothic writing.[8] Such an approach also frequently draws on psychoanalytic theory, and in particular on Freud's analysis of 'the return of the repressed', to explore the way in which the past colonial trauma, never fully surmounted, emerges in the text to 'uncanny' effect.[9]

While the insights afforded by postcolonial and psychoanalytic theory underpin this book throughout, the dominant methodology employed in the pages which follow is, however, more historical than theoretical. In mapping out the terrain of Welsh Gothic over two centuries in an introductory study of this type, maintaining a historicist perspective helps to keep in view the specificity of the Welsh experience and thus of the literature to which it gave rise. Recent criticism has argued for the importance of a historical approach in assessing Gothic literature. In *A Geography of Victorian Gothic Fiction*, Robert Mighall defines the Gothic as 'a rhetoric', 'an attitude to the past and the present'. 'Epochs, institutions, places and people are Gothicized, have the Gothic thrust upon them', he argues; 'That which is Gothicized depends on history and the stories it needs to tell itself.'[10] The history that an imperialist, colonizing culture needs to tell itself often involves representing the indigenous people of a conquered domain as darkly 'other' and barbaric in order to rationalize their domination. The colonized can, however, retaliate by themselves making use of the Gothic mode to protest against the barbarities of their subordination. Alternatively, rather than resisting the powerful invading culture they can identify with it, interiorizing its representations and portraying their own people as primitive and demonic. But in a reverse swing, writers of the imperial culture can also rebel against its dominant values and 'go native', changing sides ideologically and identifying with the colonized. As we will see, all four of these fundamentally opposed but often unstable perspectives, which can shift within a text as well as from author to author, find representation within that body of literature which uses Gothic materials and is located in Wales.

In the first part of this book, four chapters explore Welsh Gothic writing from its beginnings in the last decades of the eighteenth century to the date of the second Welsh devolution referendum in 1997, with two chapters devoted to the nineteenth century and two to the twentieth. The first chapter focuses on the Romantic period, during which a shared preoccupation with history, whether it be in the form of national or familial history, or the story of ruined castles, abbeys and ancient remains, characterizes texts located in Wales. In particular, the focus is on past and present relations between the Welsh and the English, though the manner in which that history is Gothicized varies according to the national perspective of the author. Welsh novelists tend to present their Welsh heroes and heroines as vulnerable innocents whose native virtue and integrity are threatened either by invading English gentry or by their enforced residence across the border in the 'devil's parlour', that is, London. But Welsh locations during this period also frequently provided the settings of so-called 'first-contact' Gothic novels,[11] written from the perspectives of travellers who on their first encounter with Wales were startled and sometimes alienated by its threatening landscapes, ruined castles and abbeys, and the perceived barbarities of its inhabitants whose very language spoke of a more primitive world.

That shock of otherness, particularly in relation to the language difference, was sharply felt in the middle years of the nineteenth century when the growth of industrialization brought to the attention of the entrepreneur and capitalist the fact that their potential workforce in Wales spoke little English. Education regulations which banned the speaking of Welsh in schools, along with the flood of incomers coming into Wales to labour in the new coal mines and iron and steel works, resulted in a 20 per cent drop, from 70 to 50 per cent of the population, in the number of Welsh speakers during the second half of the century. Many took it for granted that the Celt had entered the twilight zone, that the Welsh language would die and that Welsh culture would became merely a plaintive echo within English culture. The second chapter of this book argues that such assumptions incited the publication of a number of Gothic fictions prophesying the doom of the Welsh. But the threat to Welsh survival, along with the activating influence of the mid-nineteenth-century national independence movements in Europe and in Ireland in particular, challenged some of the Liberal leaders of Welsh life, who came to ascendance after the Liberal landslide of 1868, to establish in the 1880s a Welsh Home Rule movement, *Cymru Fydd* or Young Wales. Though it proved short-lived, the political movement was accompanied by a Welsh literary renaissance, some of whose members also evinced in their fictions an interest in clairvoyance and the occult movement, then burgeoning in Britain and the United States. Within that movement, certain aspects of traditional Welsh culture, such as Druidism and the association of the Grail legends with the early Celtic Christian church in Wales, acquired new lustre. A culture previously presented as primitive and barbaric now featured as a source of transcendent light, particularly in the later fictions of Arthur Machen, to date the only generally acknowledged Welsh Gothic writer, whose work is also discussed in chapter two.

The popularity of the occult movement at the *fin de siècle* was related, of course, to the decline in Christianity following from the long-term effects of the revolution in ideas incited by the theories of Darwin and Marx. In the Welsh context the most striking changes of the first decades of the twentieth century included the rapid rise of socialism and the concomitant attacks on Welsh chapel culture. Both developments found expression in the literature of the period, some of it employing the Gothic mode. In the case of the chapels, the use of Gothic tropes for their disparagement was not a new development. During the second half of the eighteenth century, in the same period as that which saw the birth of the Gothic genre and of the Celtic revival, a series of Methodist religious revivals transformed Welsh communities, but faced Anglican disparagement, as a superstitiously primitive and barbaric form of worship which encouraged in its congregations over-enthusiastic and even licentious behaviour. In part as a consequence of this persecution, the preachers and deacons who led the chapel communities, which by the 1850s included 75 per cent of the Welsh population, defensively tightened their control on their congregations, initiating a system which began to be experienced as so oppressive by some of their members that, in the struggle to free themselves from the chapel's grip, they found it necessary to demonize Dissent. The third chapter of this book, on 'Haunted communities', examines early twentieth-century 'chapel' Gothic.

The second half of the eighteenth century also witnessed the dawn of the industrial era in Wales, with the development of the iron, slate, coal and, later, steel industries. The flare of the furnaces, the blackened landscapes, the miners descending in cages down the deep pit and the omnipresent possibility of sudden death became part of the image of Wales and lent themselves very readily to Gothicization. In the south Wales coalfield in particular the lack of opportunity to find employment as anything other than a coalminer (or his wife) created the sense of a doomed or haunted community, sacrificed to the needs of Westminster and the British Empire. Chapter three also investigates those texts of the 1930s and 1940s in which the conditions of labour in the coal industry, and the very pits themselves, are represented as daemonic powers that drain the lifeblood of the workers and their families.

At the same time, as the census figures decade by decade inexorably registered the decline in Welsh-language speakers, the fate of the Welsh language and its culture remained a dominant concern. The horror of living through one's own cultural death is imaged in texts whose protagonists are represented as haunted by the princes and warriors of pre-conquest Wales risen from the dead to castigate the modern Welsh for their heedlessness and neglect of their language and culture. The fourth chapter of this book, 'Land of the living dead', explores the development of this postcolonial theme in an array of exemplary twentieth-century and contemporary Welsh- and English-language Gothic fictions. There is a grim vitality to these texts' use of the Gothic, a vitality in part drawn from and contributing to modern, global developments in the genre. But they had a specific political message for their first readers in twentieth-century pre-devolution Wales, warning them to heed their heritage and respect their distinctive ethnicity, lest the spirits of their forefathers return to haunt them.

In texts located in Wales but not necessarily written with Welsh readers in mind, such preoccupations with the past are often represented as but part and parcel of the characteristic superstition and backwardness of the indigenous population. Stressing the primitiveness of the Welsh in this manner allows Wales to feature as a suitable site for an array of Gothic extravaganzas, and it would be a failure of inclusion in a book on Welsh Gothic not to make some attempt to trace the literary history of at least a few of the figures drawn from Welsh folklore and superstition which are omnipresent in the genre. Accordingly, in the second part of this book, on 'Things that go bump in the Celtic twilight', the focus switches from Welsh history and the concerns to which it has given rise in Gothic writing to the evolution in literature of four such figures: the druid, the Welsh witch, the hounds of Annwn and the sin-eater. Witches are of course an ubiquitous and international feature of folklore, but their close association in Celtic myth with ancient mother goddess figures renders them potentially more powerful and more ambivalent figures within Welsh Gothic than they are elsewhere: chapter five follows the literary representation of the Welsh witch in fiction, from the early years of the Gothic genre to the present day. Since the Romantic era, the druid has featured as an emblem of Welshness, closely associated with the Welsh bard, and living on as cultural leader through the institution of the eisteddfod; the continuing resonances of this enigmatic figure are also explored in this chapter, along with another phenomenon more specific to Welsh mythology, *cwn Annwn*, the hounds of the underworld that hunt the souls of the damned and herd them to hell.

The sixth chapter focuses on the arguably historical figure of the sin-eater, whose activities were first recorded in the seventeenth century. Through eating and drinking bread and beer passed to him over a corpse, the sin-eater was believed to take upon himself the sins of the dead; but as soon as the ritual was over, he was reviled as a scapegoat and driven away with curses and blows to live in isolation on the fringes of his community. From his first fictional appearance in the 1830s the Welsh sin-eater has featured in literature as an emblem of guilt and abjection, bearing in enforced solitude the crimes of others. Like the vampire, he later became deracinated, and the texts in which he currently appears are more likely to be American than Welsh. The Gothic element, however, still strongly predominates; the international sin-eater moves through his or her community isolated by the same aura of supernatural dread as that which surrounded him in his first Welsh appearances. His abjection has also been connected with postcolonial themes; his community projects upon him the self-hatred it experiences as a subjugated people.

In the post-devolution twenty-first century, however, some of the bitterest aspects of Welsh history have been healed. The conquered princes of the past less frequently haunt the pages of contemporary Welsh Gothic, in which the tropes of the genre are often humorously played with, to evoke laughter rather than horror. At other times more sombre themes prevail, as the Gothic is used to give expression to the contemporary fears of the post-industrial communities of south Wales and the continuing decline of the rural communities of the west and north, the Welsh-language heartlands.

In its epilogue, this book investigates such post–devolution strains within twenty-first-century Welsh Gothic.

A curious aspect of Welsh Gothic is its previous lack of critical recognition: according to the *Handbook to Gothic Literature* (1998), for example, Wales has contributed virtually nothing to the wealth of world literature in the Gothic genre.[12] Similarly, the 2002 *Cambridge Companion to Gothic Fiction*, while it includes a chapter on 'Scottish and Irish Gothic', makes no reference to Wales. With the sole exception of Arthur Machen (who is categorized as 'British' in the *Cambridge Companion*),[13] no Welsh authors of the nineteenth or twentieth centuries, it is claimed, concerned themselves with the task of reflecting in literature the national abundance of dark myth and folklore. Yet, the fact of the matter is that a trawl of relevant bibliographies and library catalogues will with relative ease result in a rich haul of literary materials that could arguably be categorized as Welsh Gothic. Why these texts have been ignored is in part due to the general neglect of Welsh writing, particularly of the nineteenth century; also, most of the critics previously active in the field have been more concerned with issues of identity, or with the need to develop a specifically Welsh literary history and canon, than with generic criticism. Yet, a focus on the Gothic by no means precludes explorations of national identity. A culture tends to Gothicize that which it most fears, and many of the fears encoded in Welsh Gothic are specific to the history of Welsh people. This book as a whole aims to demonstrate the fact that Welsh Gothic writing exists in abundance and that it has much to tell us about the changing ways in which Welsh people have historically seen themselves and been perceived by others.

PART I

Haunted by History

1

Cambria Gothica (1780s–1820s)

૭

In Ann of Swansea's *Cambrian Pictures* (1810), the Honourable Captain Maitland, quartered with his regiment near Caernarvon, suffers a rough introduction to the terrors of wild Wales. While ostensibly courting Eliza Tudor, the heiress of Tudor Hall, his eye falls upon one of the household's domestics, the pretty dairy-maid Gwinthlean, whose virtue he covertly assails 'with all the united artillery of vows, promises and flattery'.[1] At length Gwinthlean promises to meet him at a red barn in the neighbourhood, but arrives there in a state of some affright; a suicide once hung himself from its rafters and since then local legend has it, she tells him, that the 'tefil haunts the parn'.[2] Reluctantly, she allows him to draw her into the building, but

at the very moment the captain supposed himself on the verge of accomplishing his wishes, she burst from his arms with a loud shriek, and flew out of the barn. Captain Morland, astonished at this action, would have flown after her: but between him and the door stood a huge terrific black figure, with cloven feet, fiery eyes, and tremendous horns, which seized him in its strong grip, pinioned his hands behind him with an iron chain, threw him on his face, fastened his legs together in the same way, then swinging him across his shoulders, flew with him to the stables behind Tudor Hall, and stuck him up to his neck in a dunghill.[3]

Rescued from this predicament by Eliza and her father, 'the dis-appointed captain exhibited a most deplorable spectacle of mud and terror'; he protests to all and sundry that 'the devil himself in proper person' had 'caught him up and flew a long way with him in the air' and insists that two men from his regiment watch over his bed each night 'for fear of the devil paying him another visit'.[4] But once he has recovered, Maitland is inveigled into attending a local wed-ding where to his mortification he witnesses 'the rosy Gwinthlean' married 'to a tall, athletic fellow whom he had no doubt was the person who had performed the part of the devil at the red barn'.[5] After the ceremony Gwinthlean makes it public that it was at her husband Hoel Watkin's instigation that the assignment in the barn took place. 'He would wrap himself up in the hide of an ox, and cure you of trying to ruin innocent country girls', she tells the captain, who leaves Wales in some haste, and subsequently has to change regiments too, 'the unfortunate story of the devil and the dunghill' having 'pursued him to the parade and the mess-room'.[6]

Wales's reputation as a haunted land has in this fictional case served its inmates well by helping to rid them of an unscrupulous would-be exploiter. Encouraging the spread of local tales of terror in order to frighten away potentially threatening incomers was, apparently, in reality common practice in many areas of Wales at this time. Ghosts proliferated in particular in coastal spots frequented by smugglers or wreckers who had good reason to discourage strangers from lingering within sight of the coves and caves in which they operated. The Blue Lady of Dunraven and the ghost of the 'wrecker lord' Thomas Wyndham were both said to haunt Southerndown in Glamorgan, notorious as a wrecking village; the murdered Lady Stradling and the witch Mallt-y-nos inhabited nearby St Donat's Castle from which the Stradling family reputedly operated a flour-ishing smuggling trade; a witch called 'Old Moll' haunted the pointedly named Brandy Cove near Caswell Bay on the Gower peninsula, and a tribe of witches protected Llanddona in Anglesey, another reputed haven for smugglers.[7] In Wales as a whole, the abundance of folkloric tales of witches, devils, wizards, death por-tents, cursing wells, hell-hounds, haunted castles and the like suggests the possibility that what they represent may not simply be the super-stition of the inhabitants, but their not necessarily conscious tendency to discourage possible exploiters from entering their territory by portraying it as steeped in supernatural horrors. However, if that was indeed the case, by the close of the eighteenth century the device had backfired; the rising popularity of the Gothic genre meant that the darker elements in Welsh folklore were by now more likely to attract visitors to the country than to repel them. This chapter on the representation of Wales in Gothic writing from the 1780s to the 1820s begins with a section on the ways in which Wales was depicted by its late eighteenth- and early nineteenth-century visitors, before moving on to examine the manner in which Welsh authors, in their turn, made use of Gothic devices to explore their relation with the ruling state, as visitors to England and as partners in the Wales-England union. The texts discussed in these first three sections are primarily concerned with the Wales of their time, but in its final section the chapter closes with an account of Gothic historical fictions located in Wales and written during the Romantic period.

Romantic tourists in Gothic Wales

Their taste fashioned by the prevailing vogues of the era, travellers to Wales at the close of the eighteenth century enjoyed the sublimity of its mountain scenery, the eerie majesty of its ancient ruins, and the picturesqueness of its unsophisticated inhabitants who according to their visitors still adhered to pagan superstitions. In *The Abbey of St Asaph* (1795) by the Anglo-Scottish writer Isabella Kelly (1758–1857), Lady Douglas, on a month's tour of Wales, informs her children as the Cambrian mountains rise 'with bold magnificence' into view striking the mind 'with pleasing awe' that these are the 'reputed regions of inspiration'. Formerly, she says, they were inhabited by druids who

> studying nature, and the effects of plants and herbs, completed many surprising cures; which in that darkened age were imputed miracles; in the more remote countries, the people still retain a large portion of their ancient superstition, attributing to certain springs very miraculous influence.[8]

The Abbey of St Asaph is a contemporary novel – Lady Douglas is the widow of an army officer who fought for Britain in the American War of Independence, but lost his life in a subsequent military campaign in the East Indies – but the superstitiousness of the Welsh peasantry is integral to the plot of this full-blooded Gothic fiction. The abbey, 'a Gothic, noble piece of architecture', fronting not only 'stupendous mountains' covered with forests of 'wild magnificence' but also the ruins of a castle 'tottering in superb decay', is reputedly haunted by at least two troubled ancestors of its proprietors, the Trevallion family. In former days when the castle yet stood 'strong' and 'fortified',

> Owen of Trevallion, the first of the race, and invested with it by one of the princes of Glendower, returning from a signal victory, found his wife Bertha folded in the arms of a lovely youth; and in a transport of jealousy plunged his sword in her bosom, and completed his vengeance by the death of the stranger, who with his parting breath exclaimed, 'I am her brother!'[9]

In bitter remorse, Sir Owen is said to haunt the scene of his fatal error, accompanied by his much later descendant Sir Eldred Trevallion, the brother of Sir Hugh, the present owner. Sir Eldred had reportedly committed suicide by 'dashing himself with fury' from one of the windows of his 'ancient pile' when his wife perished in his arms, two days after his return from an East Indian campaign in which he was mistakenly reported killed: his wife, prostrated by grief at the supposed loss, was too weak to endure the shock of his sudden return.

Though she is warned by the abbey's domestics and tenantry that its ruins echo to the 'groans and moans' of undead Trevallions, the novel's heroine Jennett takes pleasure at nightfall in wandering through the 'solitary mouldering' castle. Jennett is in service at the abbey as a companion to Sir Hugh's daughter, but – not entirely surprisingly – it is eventually disclosed that she is in fact Sir Eldred's long-lost daughter, Rodolpha Trevallion, the true heiress of St Asaph. On one of her moonlit rambles, 'enrapt by the sublimity of the scene', she loses herself in contemplation of the abbey's past. 'These are the haunts of meditation,' she thinks:

these the scenes where ancient Bards the inspiring breath extatic felt;
and from this world retired, conversed with Angels, and immortal
forms on gracious errands bent, to save the fall of virtue struggling
on the brink of vice, – to wake in whispers, and repeated dreams, – to
hint pure thoughts, – and warn the favored [*sic*] soul, for future trials
fated to prepare.–[10]

It is well that Jennett is thus warned and prepared for at this point
her musings are interrupted by the sudden appearance, as if sprung
from the earth in front of her, of a male figure whose 'features
appeared distorted by internal agony' and who cries out in torment,
'"Guilt! – guilt! – oh, guilt!"' Staggered, Jennet falls on 'the still
agitated earth' which immediately opens wide before her and an
apparition ascends from it 'to a stupendous height, – the extended
arms lengthened in proportion, and forming a circle totally enclosed
her'. On the front of its head 'something like a countenance appeared
but horrible beyond imagination; the eyes seemed globes of fire;
and the gaping jaws emitted sulphurous flames' while 'a vesture
which floated loosely around the spectre, represented by pale gleams
of light, the forms of every noxious reptile'. The apparition hails
her:

> Rash, obtruding daughter of mortality, wherefore com'st thou to
> these unfrequented paths, and blood distain'd retreats? . . . learn, that
> nightly escaping from the burning seas of purifying fire, my anguished
> spirit troubles this sequestered spot, and mourns the murderous deeds
> that close the gates of everlasting peace and mercy . . . until the ocean
> renders up its long forgotten dead, and yawning graves give up their
> sleeping charge; and the bright morn of resurrection dawns, never
> shall the once famed Owen of Trevallion find repose.[11]

But Jennett, for whom 'darkness had no horrors' for 'she knew
the all pervading eye of heaven, powerful in the deepest gloom as
in the mid-day light', is not long daunted. Soon, she is exploring
the castle's dungeons once more, and this time she has the happiness
to discover entombed within them not another spectre but a living
prisoner, Sir Eldred Trevallion, soon to be revealed to be her father,
who has been held captive in the ruins for nineteen years. His

wicked brother Sir Hugh had plotted his death in order to inherit St Asaph, but the doctor commissioned to do the deed had scruples and imprisoned Sir Eldred in the dungeons instead. It was the doctor who with great ingenuity, through his knowledge of the underground passages with which the abbey grounds are riddled, had for years impersonated the ghost of Owain of Trevallion. He confesses that he has 'artfully encouraged the tale of the ignorant, respecting unquiet spirits disturbing the Abbey, till at length they became a general tradition, which staggered even the enlightened, and at the same time effected my purpose', that is, of keeping prying eyes away from Sir Eldred's prison.[12]

With its spirited heroine, Isabella Kelly's novel reads entertainingly, but already, though a comparatively early instance of the Gothic, it is riddled with clichés. The sudden startling appearance of violent and apparently inexplicable supernatural phenomena, along with the idea of the past as exerting a fatal influence on the present, had been central to the genre since its conception with the publication of *The Castle of Otranto* in 1764. But *The Abbey of St Asaph*, unlike Walpole's novel, includes within the text rational explanations accounting for all its supernatural phenomena. For example, during her dungeon wanderings Jennett encountered a skeleton which seemed to bow towards her, then to throw its own skull down at her feet with piercing shrieks, but she discovers later that all she had in fact disturbed was a large rat which had made its nest in the skull and accounted for its shrill agitations.[13] This device of first thrilling the reader with supernatural horrors before providing natural reasons for the apparitions is also borrowed, from Ann Radcliffe's *The Mysteries of Udolpho*, published to great popular success in 1794; Radcliffe makes a point of providing rational explanations for all of the apparently supernatural manifestations in her novel. In this way Gothic writers – and their readers – could both enjoy the illicit thrill of supernatural horror and condemn it virtuously as superstition at the same time. *The Abbey of St Asaph* follows Radcliffe's innovations closely; in its second volume, Jennett delivers a lengthy tirade against Gothic superstition, telling her supposed family (that is, the Welsh peasants who found her and gave her a home when she was left by her wicked uncle and his henchman, the doctor, as an abandoned infant on the mountainside),

let not your judgement be perverted by such ridiculous superstition; we scarce ever hear of an ancient Abbey or Castle, but what
is reputedly haunted by some discontented spirit; we frequently hear
of horrible figures, and unnatural sights, but they exist only in a
gloomy or disordered imagination . . . As for noises I admit them,
but they are perfectly innocent and natural. The interior of our Gothic
structures being generally very lofty and vaulted, causes an echo, so
that a single pin falling in one part will reverberate the sound thro'
the whole building; and striking the listening ear, busy fancy, ever
fond of the marvellous, and perhaps tainted with superstition, magni-
fies the harmless echo to deep and horrid groans . . . The tale is
related, made a standing topic, gathers strength from each repeating
voice, till the tinkling pin is exalted to a shriek more terrific than a
peal of thunder: and thus the silly tradition becomes established.[14]

Even parents dismayed by their offspring's enthusiasm for the new
fashion in horror fiction could but approve of such a speech.

Isabella Kelly, then, shows herself to be an author very aware of
contemporary developments in popular fiction and the type of
literary device likely to appeal to her readers. I have dwelt on her
book in some detail here because it serves as a characteristic example
of early Gothic novels set in Welsh locations and written from the
point of view of visitors to the country. In one sense it is atypical,
however, in that its heroine's infant years were spent amongst the
local peasantry; in most of these novels little interest is shown in the
locals except as stereotypically superstitious domestics or as ghosts
from Wales's dark past. But Jennett is also to some degree a visitor
to Wales: as a child she had attracted the attention of the visiting
Lady Douglas, who had taken her back to England as a companion
to her own children, and had there educated her in the good sense
which permits her later, at the age of nineteen, to withstand local
superstitions on her return to Wales virtually as a stranger. At any
rate, the 'sublime' wild landscape in which *The Abbey of St Asaph*
is set, its ruins, its superstitious peasantry, its allusions to ancient
bards and druids whose influence is still active and its passing references to Wales's turbulent past (e.g. those inaccurately plural 'princes
of Glendower' in whose wars the Trevallions had fought) are all to
reappear in subsequent Gothic texts located in Wales. There is very
little necessary connection between this novel's plot and its Welsh

location, and yet much of the colour and atmosphere of the tale comes from its setting: this is Cambria Gothica, wild country of a myriad ghosts and their haunted and debased present-day descendants. And Isabella Kelly, with her keen eye for what was fashionable, was by no means the only writer to believe that such a context was likely to have popular appeal at the end of the eighteenth century.

In 1798, Sarah Lansdell, from Kent, for example, published *The Tower; or the Romance of Ruthyne*, which opens on 'one of the most gloomy and uncomfortable nights of a very stormy winter' with 'Matilda and Augusta pensively ruminating in a dreary apartment of Ruthyne Tower', while 'a tremendous gust of wind drove the rain with violence against the casement, and added to the solemnity of the gloom by deeply howling through the irregular passages of the decaying Tower'. '[I]t seemed a spot of all others the most calculated to inspire horror and despondence,' says the narrator.[15] The sisters Matilda and Augusta have been abruptly dispatched to Wales from their English home by their wicked stepmother and are virtually imprisoned, in rooms separated only by a secret doorway from a Black Chamber, furnished with an occupied coffin and inhabited by their long-lost aunt Seraphine, for nine years a captive in Rhythun Tower. Wales is an appropriate location for such dark deeds, not only because of its isolation and ancient ruins, but because its inhabitants are a dark race apart, incapable of understanding or questioning the activities of their English visitors. David, Matilda and Augusta's local servant, 'whose travels had never extended beyond the next market-town, at eight miles distance', is apparently so surprised by 'the soft tone of Matilda's voice, when she ordered him to fetch the wood . . . that he could scarcely believe they were of the same order as the females he had heretofore seen'.[16]

An 'old abbey on the borders of Wales' also becomes a chamber of horrors for the unfortunate heroine of Ann Howell's 1796 novel *Anzoletta Zadoski*. Anzoletta, the disgrace of her unmarried Polish mother, is abducted by her enraged grandfather and held captive in the 'Abbey of T-'. The features of the surrounding landscape are 'bold and romantic' but Anzoletta is given little opportunity to enjoy their charms; rather, she is made acquainted with the abbey's dungeons.[17] There she perceives tell-tale signs – 'an old palet-bed, a broken pitcher, and a heap of rags' – indicating that the dungeons had previously served as a prison, and gives up all hope for her own liberation:

> 'My fate is decided,' said she . . . 'this dungeon will probably be my tomb!' . . . A thousand vague and terrible suspicions now rushed on her mind, and her reason overpowered, gave way to all the distracted impulses of fear; she shrieked aloud.[18]

Little is known of Ann Howell, née Hilditch; her surname suggests that she may have married into a family of Welsh descent, but she was apparently living in Portsmouth when she wrote *Anzoletta*. For her, however, as for Isabella Kelly, it seemed appropriate to locate in Cambria Gothica a tale of persecuted innocence incarcerated in the haunted ruins of a strange and barbaric land, far removed from the light of civilization.

A year later, in 1797, M. G. Lewis, riding high on the phenomenal popularity of his Gothic novel *The Monk* (1796), produced on a London stage his play *The Castle Spectre* which was also to prove a fashionable success. The play begins with a 'Prologue' explaining why it is set in Wales: apparently, a picturesque ruin appeals to the sensibilities of the spirit of 'Romance' – that 'moon-struck child of genius and of woe' – because of the potential wealth of story connected with its 'time-bow'd towers'.[19] Accordingly, the 'bright enthusiast' Romance responds promptly to the invocations of an aspirant to her creative favours who is loitering with poetic intent in the environs of Conway Castle, and the result is the play, which recounts the gory history of two aristocratic brothers, the earls Osmond and Reginald. Both love the same woman, Evelina, whose preference for Raymond, whom she marries and by whom she has a daughter, leads to her accidental murder by Osmond; he had intended the blow for his brother. Later, Osmond transfers his affections to her daughter, only to find Evelina, as a ghost, interfering with his intentions once again, in the most horrifically dramatic of the play's many horror-laden scenes (and 'Monk' Lewis's spectres are not explained away).

There is little historically to link this family tragedy with Conway Castle in particular, and yet its location is unlikely to have been a haphazard choice. That Lewis was very aware of the importance of appealing to the tastes of his audience is evident from the manner in which he defends in his notes to the play his inclusion in this purportedly medieval Welsh saga of Osmond's African servant, Hassan:

> That Osmond is attended by Negroes is an anachronism, I allow; but from the great applause which Mr. Dowton constantly received in Hassan . . . I am inclined to think that the audience was not greatly offended at the impropriety. For my own part, I by no means repent the introduction of my Africans: I thought it would give a pleasing variety to the characters and dresses, if I made my servants black; and could I have produced the same effect by making my heroine blue, blue I should have made her.[20]

The inclusion of an African servant in a 1797 play would interest the audience, and hence Hassan's presence was desirable whether or not it was credible in historical terms. Welsh castles as a backdrop to supernatural tales of terror must also have had known appeal at this time, or they were unlikely to have featured in a play by Lewis.

The popularity of 'Monk' Lewis's play appears to have further encouraged the vogue for Welsh settings: Charles Lucas, curate of Avebury in Wiltshire, makes reference to 'The Castle Spectre' in the notes to his mock-Gothic novel *The Castle of Saint Donats* (1798), before proceeding to inhabit his Glamorganshire castle with a whole family of spectres. Given its Welsh location,

> in so rude, so wild, and romantic a spot as the rocky cliffs of St. Donats . . . it is not to be wondered at that those demi-inhabitants of the other world should think proper to take up their residence here. There was scarcely a room in the house that had not had the credit of a visitant of this sort.[21]

In another 1798 novel, *Ianthé, or the Flower of Caernarvon* by Emily Clark, apparently the granddaughter of the illegitimate son of Theodore, king of Corsica, 'Ruthlin [*sic*] Hall' 'furnished . . . in a truly Gothic taste', becomes the ominous abode of Ianthé when she tours Wales with her parents Sir James and Lady Claremont. Scorning local superstition she takes as her bedroom an apartment which 'led by a private door to the haunted rooms in the tower', only to find herself listening with dread one night to

> footsteps in the adjoining apartment; she was not suffered to remain long in suspense: the secret door immediately opened, and discovered four men in masks, who, advancing towards her, carried her off in their arms, without resistance; her senses having fled, from the horror their first appearance excited.[22]

Such scenes of castellated horrors proliferate in the thirty-six Gothic novels located in Wales and published during the Romantic period which are listed in Andrew Davies's bibliographical article "'The Gothic novel in Wales" revisited'.[23] Davies's list is not intended as definitive and only includes materials available in Cardiff libraries; of the four novels referred to above, for example, only the last is listed within it. Yet, it serves to underline the fact that, as Davies says, 'a sizable body of fiction' which can be categorized as Welsh Gothic was published during the period, most of it emerging from the pens of tourists to Wales rather than Welsh-born authors. 'Wales has of late years become the fashionable tour of the man of fortune' reported Richard Colt Hoare in 1806,[24] and there were practical as well as aesthetic reasons for the country's popularity at this time. Prevented by the wars with France from taking the continental Grand Tour, the British gentry looked for fashionable experiences of the sublime, the picturesque and the horrid closer to home. The publications of the Celtic revival, particularly Gray's 'The Bard', alerted them to Wales as a location equipped to deliver such affects. What is more, historians and critics analysing the social and cultural making of 'Great Britain' after the 1707 Act of Union between Scotland and England have argued that these novels and indeed the Celtic revival itself were the product of a political as much as cultural process. The enthusiasm for all things Celtic reflected in the travel books, poetry, drama and fiction of the period helped to construct an enlarged and re-'imagined community' of 'Great Britain', which required regeneration after the debilitating loss of America.[25] According to Linda Colley's arguments in her influential *Britons* (1992), the Welsh antiquarian societies, such as the Cymmrodorion and the Gwyneddigion, when they commissioned and published for the new mass audiences of the printing presses Welsh grammars, dictionaries, histories and bardic 'specimens' in translation, were contributing primarily to a newly expanded consciousness of British rather than Welsh nationhood. 'Ancient Britons', that is, the Welsh, were reconfigured as colourful ancestors to modern-day Britons; though they might be poor relations – countrified and unsophisticated – they were nevertheless part of the family. Tourism to Wales was both encouraged by this process and helped to further its ends: the more Wales was visited the less alienatingly 'other' it became.

Some of the fictions already discussed in this chapter clearly illustrate this process. In *The Abbey of St Asaph*, for example, Jennett, whom the reader first encounters as a Welsh peasant, ends her career not only as Rodolpha Trevallion, heiress to the abbey and educated in the ways of the English gentry by her patroness Lady Douglas, but also wedded in a love match to Lady Douglas's son Lionel, thus emblemizing the happy marriage of Wales to England. At the same time, for all the political significance of such unions of the British nations within the expanded United Kingdom, the more characteristic insistence in these fictions on representing Wales and the Welsh as wild and primitive compared to the civilized sophistications of their visitors underlines differences rather than similarities. And in the few Gothic novels of the period penned by Welsh-born authors, the sense of dissimilarity between Welsh and English locations and inhabitants is often further stressed, though, interestingly, the pattern is now reversed. In these texts the innocents who suffer persecution are Welsh and the locations in which they are terrorized and lose control of their lives are generally in England, or, if the trauma occurs in Wales, then their virtue is assailed not by Welsh spectres or villains but by unscrupulous incoming marauders. It would appear that the Gothic genre, here as elsewhere, is to some extent at any rate rebelling against the political exigencies of its day. Wales and the Celtic fringe generally were supposed at this time to be in the process of being drawn closer and closer into social, political and economic integration with the English power-base,[26] but in Welsh Gothic fictions the reverse is more frequently the case: the shock of the encounter with the 'other' often leaves representatives of both countries fleeing back to the safety of their own habitats rather than embracing any notion of belonging to a Greater British whole. The next section of this chapter examines a few Welsh examples of this phenomenon.

In the Devil's parlour

In the earliest novel to appear on Andrew Davies's list, *Ellen, Countess of Castle Howel* (1794), published by Anna Maria Bennett (*c.*1750–1808), the daughter of a Merthyr Tudful grocer, Wales is consistently presented as the abode of peace, innocence and civilized democracy, in contrast to the savage barbarities of English high society. Though Code [*sic*] Gwyn, the Welsh birthplace of the heroine, can apparently from an architectural point of view be described as 'a large Gothic mansion', not only Ellen but all its inhabitants experience it as a site of civility, culture and democratic good order:

> The hall appeared to be the bond of union between the heads of the family and the domestics – there the harper had his seat, and there the avocations and labours of the day constantly closed with a dance, in which all the youngest part of the inmates mingled, without a frown on the brow of pride, or presumption in the bosom of poverty.[27]

But this felicity is soon interrupted by the return of the soldier son of the house who brings with him as a guest an English lord: 'the Lieutenant had no sooner introduced Lord Claverton by name, than Griffiths [the butler] hurried the domestics out of the parlour'. The old Welsh way of life cannot be maintained in the presence of one who represents the much more strongly polarized English system of rank, and the scene seems to critique the rigours of England's social hierarchies.

Code Gwyn is debt-ridden, however, and all it represents is under threat; in order to save the estate and its dependents, Ellen, the young orphaned granddaughter of the house, agrees to marry a wealthy elderly neighbour, the anglicized Lord Castle Howel, who soon removes her from Wales to his town house in Regency

London. There she succumbs to the lure of fashionable English upper-class pursuits:

> When women of the first fashion, were so anxious to fill up every moment of *their* time . . . in dressing, public amusements, and gaming, the three grand pursuits of the superior women of the age; how was it possible *she* could be so stupid, as to prefer any of the obsolete amusements, which had filled a long summer's day and winter's evening in the mountains of Wales?

Though Ellen in fact manages to protect her chastity, such is her appearance of impropriety once she has become a habitué of the card tables that her horrified lord, wrongly convinced that the child she is carrying is not his own, drives her out of his house as a fallen woman. Her only protector on her subsequent imperilled journeying is her Welsh maid from Code Gwyn, Winifred Griffiths, who laments, "'Aye, aye, I see how it is, Satan has set his clofen foot on my poor lady . . . Oh, my poor aunt Griffiths always said, "London was the tifel's drawing room!"'"[28] Ellen finds no peace until after a series of Gothicized vicissitudes she returns once more to Wales, only to find her old home impoverished and its order broken up. Sarah Prescott, writing of Bennett's novels in her volume *Eighteenth-century Writing from Wales*, argues that *Ellen* is a novel concerned with the disinheritance 'not only of Ellen's son but of Wales's gentry as a whole'; 'although nostalgia is expressed for the feudal past of "Ancient Britain" the continuation of this past is seen as untenable'.[29] The culture in which Ellen was reared has already receded into the past, but its loss is lamented and the closer connection with the English power-base – London, that den of vice, the Devil's drawing-room – is a matter of horror rather than compensation.

Wales is as much a zone of ruins in the novels of writers with Welsh connections as it is in the tourist novels, but for these novelists even Welsh ruins can be places of solace and security for their characters, compared to the dangers which threaten them in more fashionable circles. In the epistolary novel *Angelina* (1796) by Mary Robinson (who was married to the illegitimate son of Thomas Harris, brother of the Welsh Methodist leader Howel Harris, and also claimed Welsh descent from her mother), English upper-class society, given the threats it poses to a woman's reputation, proves far more destructive to Welsh heroines than their native circles: Sophia Pengwynn, another Welsh – or, in her case, half-Welsh – innocent, is nearly undone by its entrapments. After a happy upbringing with her aunt Miss Pengwynn in the wilds of Wales, Sophia is brought to England by her tyrannical father, who plans to marry her off to the corrupt and would-be bigamist Lord Acreland, but she has spirit enough to flee from him. On her flight she is befriended by the apparently sympathetic Madame Dorelle, and invited to make her home in her new friend's fashionable residence, only to be informed by a client not entirely lost to dishonour that she has in fact been lured into a high-class brothel. Lord Arranford warns her,

> [I]f you remain beneath this roof another hour you are lost for ever
> . . . The woman under whose protection you came hither, is the
> most infamous of her sex! Her constant practice is dissimulation,
> and her means of living the destruction of unguarded innocence .
> . . [E]very moment that you continue here will add to the ruin of
> your reputation, which nothing could retrieve, if you were once
> seen in the society of Madame Dorelle.[30]

It is the modern English class and gender system, with its sexual double standard and the barbarities of its marriage market, that destroys women in these novels, and not the old Welsh way of life. This repeated plot device within Gothic novels written by authors with Welsh connections – of the powerful English entrapping and ruining the vulnerable Welsh – can be read as representative of a haunted Welsh fear of betrayal and destruction at the hands of the more powerful neighbour.

The fear of forgetting the indigenous culture and succumbing to the loss of Welsh identity haunts travellers to England in many of the Welsh-authored texts. Very little is known of Robert Evans who published *The Stranger or Llewellyn Family: A Cambrian Tale* anonymously in 1798 and *The Dream, or Noble Cambrians* (a lost text) in 1801, but the mass of authentic Welsh detail in *The Stranger*, as well as his surname, strongly suggest that Evans was Welsh in origin. Connected through his mother to the landed Llewellyn family of the old Welsh gentry, but reared in obscurity in a Welsh village, Charles Marmaduke, hero of *The Stranger*, arrives in England as an impoverished Oxford student. His gender does not save him from being, like Bennett's and Robinson's heroines, nearly undone in London, the Devil's parlour: in the metropolis he is tricked into visiting what he takes to be a fashionable gentleman's house only to be much taken aback by the free behaviour of its female inmates. Disingenuously his hostess 'gently chid his want of attention in not reflecting that the manners of the town were more easy, free, and liberal than those of the country . . . Its greatest privilege was, that it permitted every one to live without restraint.'[31] But what is in fact on offer in this house of ill repute is not true liberty but entrapment in corruption and the abandonment of earlier values. Marmaduke, at last, recognizes the nature of his surroundings, and the recollection of his upbringing in Wales arms him to resist its temptations: 'He gazed on the Syren with a mixture of astonishment, anger, and pity. The image of his father seemed to rise before him, clothed with indignation, and urging his departure – "Fly, Charles, or thou art undone!"'[32]

The reader, however, knows even better than Marmaduke that he has in fact very nearly already been undone. For the young Welsh student's every move, including his unwitting brothel visit, is being watched by a 'stranger'. From the moment Marmaduke first left Wales,

[T]he stranger in all his walks became . . . his inseparable companion. Whithersoever he went, he followed him. If he walked fast, the other accelerated his pace; if slowly, he shortened his step; and whenever he stopped, the other posted himself at a convenient distance. Thus, in all his perambulations . . . his motions were watched by the prying eyes of the stranger. Often he would endeavour to force the intruder to an explanation of his conduct, but in vain; he seemed conscious of its impropriety, and carefully avoided all conversation. But however he might decline speaking to Marmaduke, he made him the frequent subject of his discourse with others: the manner in which he passed the hours of each day; the time spent in studying; the company he kept; his time of rising and retiring to rest; and even the form and quality of the clothes which he wore, were the objects of his observations and enquiries.[33]

The presence of this shadow perpetually at the hero's heels gives to Robert Evans's novel the same haunted quality as William Godwin's *Caleb Williams* (1794) or James Hogg's *Confessions of a Justified Sinner* (1824). But at the close of the novel, after his return to Wales, Marmaduke finally learns that the stranger was in fact no stranger at all but a fellow Welshman, employed to spy on him by Madame Llewellyn, the formidable head of his family. It is only while Marmaduke is in England, however, that surveillance is required. He can apparently be trusted to be himself in Wales, but under testing and potentially corrupting English conditions he must be watched. Will he remain true to the values of his Welsh upbringing in England, can he carry Wales with him even when besieged by a series of temptations and vicissitudes, including at one point incarceration in a debtor's prison? Throughout his troubled journey, the stranger uncannily follows him: though Marmaduke wishes to shake him off, and 'pass' as the same as his fellow English students, the stranger is always there, at his back, a Welsh shadow from which he cannot separate himself. In effect, he operates as the exterior embodiment of Marmaduke's conscience, split off from his ego and functioning as his 'double', in a manner that Freud characterized as of the essence of the uncanny.[34]

Madame Llewellyn, the source of that haunting influence and the strongest character in the text, is an archetypal Welsh matriarch, accustomed to a semi-divine dominance over her clan: 'She was thought to be the last of a very ancient family of the name of Llewellyn . . . The parish being entirely her own, she assumed a patriarchal authority over all its inhabitants.'[35] She is fiercely opposed to the anglicizing processes of modernity; rather than give way to English fashions she uses her influence to persuade the neighbouring gentry to adopt the simple life of their peasantry, and engage in such tasks as spinning their own wool: 'spinning she universally promoted. In a corner of her library was placed her wheel . . . that the whole family might witness, and emulate her exertions. She would moreover encourage the smart daughters of her wealthier tenants to pursue this, their *proper employment*.'[36] She maintains the traditions of herbalism too and is 'the great physician of the neighbourhood . . . Her caudles were uncommonly rich and nourishing.' Not surprisingly, she is also rumoured to have supernatural powers: 'her wiser neighbours went so far as to say, she understood the black art, and astrology.' Vigilance, however, rather than witchcraft, is the main instrument of her rule:

> No young man who was not fixed in his intentions of honourable courtship, would carry a damsel's milk-pail, or even give her an arm in coming from the fair, if within a mile of her house . . . through a dread of Madame Llewellyn, who heard and saw every thing, and who, to give her her due . . . was *a woman of a very active and vigorous mind.*[37]

And it is that vigilance she wields by remote control over Marmaduke in England until he finally returns to Wales, tested and found true, and she claims him as her own, a worthy heir of those dominions which through her insistence have managed to retain their Welsh character in the face of encroaching anglicization.

No such happy ending befalls Henry Mortimer, the adopted son of Sir Owain Llewellyn in *Cambrian Pictures*, the author of which, Ann of Swansea (Ann Julia Hatton, 1764–1838), herself endured a life beset by vicissitudes. Born in Worcester to the theatrical family of Roger and Sarah Kemble (Sarah Siddons was her older sister), Ann spent some of her childhood years in Wales when her parents starred in John Ward's travelling theatrical company.[38] At nineteen, in London, she made an unfortunate marriage to a bigamist, and subsequently was employed for a period as a model in Dr James Graham's notorious Temple of Health and Hymen in Pall Mall, an institution which professed to offer help with sexual potency and fertility problems. After a very public suicide attempt, in which she attempted to take poison in Westminster Abbey, her exasperated family granted her an allowance of ninety pounds per annum on condition that she reside at least one hundred and fifty miles from London. In later life, she settled in Swansea, and after the death of her second husband William Hatton, maintained herself by publishing popular fictions in which her adopted country, Wales, is represented with strong partisanship.[39] In *Cambrian Pictures*, her hero Henry Mortimer is also an adopted Welshman, reared in happy seclusion in Dolegelly Castle in north Wales, but when he becomes a student at Cambridge his good looks have the misfortune of attracting the eye of Dowager Dutchess [*sic*] of Inglesfield, now in her fiftieth year but still predatory. Undeterred by Henry's refusal of her offer of marriage she arranges for his capture and transport by sea to 'the dark towers of Raven-hill Castle' in Cumberland, 'a grand specimen of Gothic architecture' on whose 'high and ponderous walls . . . were placed ravens sculptured in black marble'.[40] The Dutchess's two daughters are already incarcerated in the castle, as their mother, in the grip of her 'diabolical passions', is plagued by jealousy of their suitors and cannot endure the possibility of having her age exposed by a grandchild. Julia, the eldest of the two, had secretly wed her tutor but once their marriage was discovered, he was imprisoned and died of grief in the same cell as that in which Henry is now confined; his young widow has become a maniac who haunts Henry, mistaking him for her dead Nevil. She is also a thwarted poet, against the wishes of her parents, who thought a 'female of rank sufficiently learned, if she can read and write a visiting-ticket'.[41] Her Gothic verse, hidden in a secret recess in his cell, entertains Henry's prison hours; he is particularly affected by her 'Eda, or the Bridal Night' in which the spurned Eda speaks from the grave to warn her unfaithful lover,

> When deep the midnight bell doth toll,
> Expect thy buried bride.
> . . . .
> And thou shalt see the grave worm draw
> Across my neck its trail
> And thou shalt see the black toad gnaw
> My cheek so sunk and pale.[42]

Henry himself is later on the verge of expiring after the failure of his thwarted attempt to escape Raven-hill Castle; his illness provokes the Dutchess's remorse but such is her 'burning passion' for his person that it is only her death that eventually brings about Henry's release and return to Wales.

In both *The Stranger* and *Cambrian Pictures*, young men brought up in Wales are represented as blushing innocents abroad. '[Y]ou blush like a miss just led forth from the nunnery, and exposed for the first time to the rude gaze of man,' says the Dutchess to Henry at the commencement of her assault on his virtue, to which he responds by explaining 'that he had but just escaped from the mountains of Wales, and that as yet he had not got his feelings in subjection'.[43] To be Welsh in these texts entails artlessness in comparison to the more mannered English; such lack of sophistication is represented as a virtue in a young man as in a young woman, but it leaves its innocents vulnerable and open to abuse. The inability to control one's feelings, or at any rate their display, suggests that one may all the more easily be controlled by others. The fact that both of these ingénues are male is unusual; generally in early Gothic fictions, particularly in the so-called 'female Gothic' texts which characteristically concern young women besieged by threatening assailants of their virtue, such vulnerability is the province of females only. But Jim Hansen in *Terror and Irish Modernism: The Gothic Tradition from Burke to Beckett* notes the occurrence of such unexpected gender patterns in Irish Gothic writing too and suggests that they represent 'the feminization of a colonized people' as a 'standard component of imperial and capitalist assimilation strategy'. Whatever their gender, the Irish are the less powerful and therefore female partners in an unhappy act of union in which England is the dominant groom. In cartoons published in Dublin periodicals in 1800, the Act of Union between England and Ireland 'took on the character of a Gothic marriage' suggests Hansen; he argues that the Irish Gothic genre as a whole sought to symbolize the destructive nature of that 'marriage' from the Irish, or female, partner's point of view.[44] Similar arguments can be made with regard to Welsh Gothic writing too; in the next section of this chapter a number of attempted acts of union between dominant English predators and vulnerable Welsh victims are assessed, as they feature in texts written by Welsh-identified authors, where the 'happy marriage' of England and Wales which provides closure in many of the English tourist fictions is re-imagined. More often than not, though, in these texts the Welsh victim who has the misfortune of attracting the predator's gaze is, as one would expect, female.

Acts of union

The so-called Act of Union between England and Wales of 1536 was more the ratification of conquest than the 'marriage' of two independent if not equal partners, for all its use of the language of love. By its means Henry VIII,

> of a singular zeal, love and favour that he beareth his subjects of . . . Wales, minding and intending to reduce them to perfect order, notice and knowledge of his laws . . . and utterly to extirpate all the singular sinister uses and customs differing from the same . . . established that this said country . . . of Wales shall be . . . incorporated, united and annexed to and with this realm of England . . . [F]rom henceforth no person or persons that use Welsh speech or language shall have or enjoy any manner of office or fees . . . unless he or they use and exercise the speech or language of English.[45]

His Majesty's Welsh subjects will be forgiven their 'sinister' difference as long as they give it up forthwith and submit to full incorporation within England, leaving their difference as a repressed ghost haunting the realm's fringe. The language of conquest, with seduction rather than marriage as its goal, also characterizes many of the attempted acts of union that feature in early Welsh Gothic texts. Both of Anna Maria Bennett's novels include British imperial soldiers who turn from pillage abroad to attempted seductions in Wales. In *Anna: or Memoirs of a Welch Heiress: interspersed with anecdotes of a Nabob* (1785), Colonel Gorget, the nabob of the subtitle, just returned from the making of his fortune in India, tries to rape Anna when she refuses to respond to his advances. According to Bennett, his years of imperial service had accustomed Gorget to such behaviour for, amongst the British colonialists, 'cruelty and carnage were called bravery and justice, and an unbounded greediness . . . bore the respectable name of prudence'.[46] Similarly, in the first chapters of *Ellen, Countess of Castle Howel*, Lord Claverton, also just returned from the colonies, announces to his servant 'I'll have that girl' as soon as he sets eyes on Ellen. But marriage is not his goal either:

his Lordship very deliberately began to play the plan of his future
establishment, in which, however, he considered it as *too* great an
honour for a little country rustic to be included, and therefore
intended to keep her for his hours of relaxation, in a small box, near
the metropolis.[4]

To speak of 'boxing' or annexing Welsh country rustics, as a sup-
plementary property adjoining one's main establishment, effectively
parallels the language and purposes of the 1536 Act of Union,
though it is unlikely that Anna Maria Bennett herself made any such
connection.

Another English lord who enters Wales with the manifest purpose
of buying it up for 'his hours of relaxation' is the chief villain of
Ann of Swansea's *Cambrian Pictures*, Lord Clavering. Having announced that 'if any estate within a few miles of Canarvon [*sic*] was
to be disposed of he should like to become a purchaser,' he is asked
'has your lordship any notion of residing in Wales?' He replies, 'not
absolutely of residing . . . but there is plenty of game in the country,
and as I am a sportsman, I should like to have a hunting-lodge'.[48]
However, the game Lord Clavering is hunting seems to be human
as much as animal: he leaves a trail of ruined rustic maidens behind
him before finally coming up against a passion for Rosa Percival.
Rosa is not as 'comeatable' (to use a slang term of the period) as his
former victims, because she is the legitimate daughter of his English
friend Sir Edward Percival: Sir Edward was persuaded to marry
her Welsh mother, whom he had initially seduced, by the dowry
offered by her rich tradesman brother Gabriel Jenkins. Although
Sir Edward abandoned both mother and daughter immediately after
the marriage, leaving Rosa to be reared in Wales by her uncle, his
interest in her is renewed by Lord Clavering's offer of a substantial
sum of money for her hand in marriage. But Rosa resists her titled
suitor, much to her uncle's satisfaction: she says, 'Lord Clavering is
my aversion.'

'Tol der lol,' sung Gabriel Jenkins, capering about the room, and
kicking his wig before him, 'gad, but this is nuts for me to crack; a
mountaineer, as your father calls you, to have spirit enough to refuse
a lord; but come along, Rosa, I long to let them see a bit of Cambrian

blood, pure and honest, neither ashamed nor afraid to refuse the gingerbread gilding of title . . . your father would have sold you without pity, just as if you had been timber on his estate, to this Lord Clavering, and this noble would have bought you: very decent proceedings truly, just as bad to the full as if you had been a negro slave in a West-India plantation.'[49]

In 1807, three years before *Cambrian Pictures* was published, the abolitionists finally succeeded in their aim of putting a stop to Britain's involvement in the slave trade, after two decades of well-publicized campaigning. To equate the situation of Welsh women, and by implication of Wales generally, with the slave question was therefore strongly to emphasize the moral rightness of saying no to the buying up of people and lands by English wealth and influence. Her refusal does not save Rosa, however, from another scene of kidnap and claustrophobic incarceration, in which Lord Clavering, with the connivance of her father, arranges for her imprisonment in an isolated farmhouse. The episode includes an archetypal nightmare sequence in which Rosa, having struggled to escape but still in ignorance as to why she was imprisoned, unwittingly hails with relief Lord Clavering's carriage on the lonely road, and pours out to him her tale of woe, with which he appears to sympathize as he takes her inexorably back to the very farmhouse from which she had just escaped. Only very gradually does she recognize that 'she was entangled in the net wove for her by Lord Clavering'.[50]

Another visitor to Wales achieves his aims of union with considerably greater ease in 'The Prediction', one of the four novellas collected in Thomas Richards's anonymously published *Tales of Welsh Society and Scenery* (1827). Born in Dolgellau in 1800, the son of a local solicitor, Thomas Richards (1800–77) was educated at Christ's Hospital in London and qualified as a surgeon, before going out to Tasmania in 1831 as a surgeon on the convict ships; there he pursued two careers as a journalist and doctor, and won fame before his death in 1877 as 'one of the first and the most substantial of early colonial short story writers'.[51] Because of internal connections and repetitions between *Tales of Welsh Society and Scenery* and a later volume, *Tales of Welshland and Welsherie* (1831), published under the name Edward Trevor Anwyl, recent biographers have suggested that Edward Trevor Anwyl, who also published a historical novel, *Reginald Trevor; or the Welsh Loyalists. A Tale of the Seventeenth Century* (1829), was the pseudonym of Thomas Richards.[52] 'The Prediction' is set in 'woods of almost primeval antiquity . . . on the eastern side of the vale of Clwyd', in Denbighshire.[53] The peace of this rural idyll and its residents, the Kynaston family, 'lineal descendants of Griffith ap Cynan, the founder of the Five Royal Tribes of North Wales', is shattered by the sudden advent in their midst of Sydney Conyngham, a Gothic anti-hero par excellence, or so at least his appearance would suggest:

> A complexion so pale as to appear absolutely unnatural, with hair as dark as the wing of the rock-raven, formed too abrupt a contrast to convey an agreeable impression to the spectator, although it was impossible not to regard with interest the extraordinary expressions which they displayed, when their possessor was influenced by feelings more than commonly intense and agitating. This power of interesting others was much augmented by the brilliance of a full rich dark eye, which, like that of the fabled basilisk, sparkled with the most piercing lustre, when every other feature of his remarkable countenance was reposing, apparently, in the most unruffled tranquillity.[54]

Conyngham is a Byronic villain of seductive charm and soon he holds in thrall the head of the family, Oliver Kynaston, and his daughter Lucy. But their servants are far more suspicious; on her deathbed the old domestic Margaret warns Lucy to 'shun this wily stranger – shun him, my child, as you would shun the Evil One himself', and after her death her son Evan becomes more than ever sure of the truth of her words.[55] 'My old mother . . . always said, that mischief would come of this foregathering with English strangers,' he tells his fellow servants while assuring them that 'it shall never be said that Evan of Garth deserted the place where he has been fed for thirty years and more, because a strange Saeson [Englishman] has come to play the devil in it'.[56] Evan does his best to warn Lucy during a key scene in which Conyngham proposes marriage to her in the garden, which he has entered, 'notwithstanding his assurance of inevitable success, with the stealthy caution of a cat who is about to pounce upon the innocent and unconscious redbreast'.[57] Of course Lucy accepts him with an overjoyed excess of feeling, but

> While she was weeping on his bosom, a raven, which had built her nest on a ledge of the rock under which they sat, began to croak her vespers . . . the harsh sound thrilled now through Lucy's heart, and caused an involuntary shudder. Scarcely had the tremor subsided, before the report of a gun caused both lovers to start, and look upward. The raven had been shot . . . she fell lifeless into the well, staining its pellucid water with her blood. In her descent she passed so close to Lucy, that her white dress was sprinkled with the blood of the poor bird; and she thought of this afterwards as an omen that it would have been better for her not to have despised.[58]

The hunter is Evan, who now appears to warn Lucy that 'There is other vermin in the woods beside this dead raven . . . beware of them, Miss Lucy, and take care they do not rend you.'[59]

But the marriage plans go ahead although throughout the neighbourhood 'Every one blamed the Squire for throwing away his child upon an English stranger . . . From Conyngham's first arrival at Bryntirion he had been looked upon as an interloper, and regarded with a jealous eye by the honest, but irritable, Cambro-Britons.'[60] For his part 'he had always considered the bumpkins, by whom he was surrounded, as utterly beneath his notice'.[61]

Lucy and Conyngham are to plight their troth in a picturesque ruined chapel but just before the taking of the vows, in an episode strongly reminiscent of the wedding scene in *Jane Eyre*, galloping hooves are heard approaching the secluded building. 'Conyngham bade the priest, who had paused, proceed, in a tone so fierce, that the holy man . . . trembled like a child', but too late – Charles, Lucy's brother, rushes in, just returned from military duties in Calcutta, and denounces Conyngham as an already married man.[62] Unfortunately, though, Lucy has neither Jane Eyre's personal resources nor her moral strength; while she is carried out of the chapel senseless, never indeed to recover her mental balance, Conyngham tells her brother that 'she is mine, body and soul; and she had better be my wife than my –'.[63] It transpires that revenging himself upon the brother had been all along Conyngham's aim: as a fellow-soldier in Calcutta, he had introduced the young Charles to the pleasures of gambling, only to have Charles denounce him publically as a cheat after catching him using loaded dice. The botched wedding leaves Lucy mad and her father seized with a fit of paralysis which he does not survive; Conyngham's vengeful cup is full, particularly given that before the wedding he had succeeded in persuading Oliver to disinherit his son and leave all the family property to Lucy and himself. Through a usurping act of union Charles Kynaston, descendant of Griffith ap Cynan, will not now inherit the land of his fathers, just as a prediction had once foretold.

According to the myth *Hanes Taliesin* (the History of Taliesin), the bard Taliesin had also once foretold the first Anglo-Saxon conquest of the Ancient Britons and their disinheritance;[64] these early Welsh Gothic texts seem intent on re-enacting the traumas of Welsh history, in the distancing romanticized form of the fateful marriage plot. As yet, however, the novels discussed in this chapter have all been set in the authors' contemporary Wales. Not surprisingly, though, given its connection with the Celtic revival's antiquarian movement and the popularity of Gray's 'The Bard', the Welsh Gothic genre from its outset also included historical fictions. The final section of this chapter continues the exploration of the representation of Cambria Gothica during the Romantic period through examining an exemplary array of historical fictions.

Gothic histories

In 1796, the first number of William Owen Pughe's journal *The Cambrian Register*, published with the aim of bringing 'to light what may be deemed most rare and valuable' amongst 'the hidden repositories' of Wales's 'ancient memorials', featured as its frontispiece Richard Corbauld's etching 'BRITTANIA directing the attention of HISTORY to the distant view emblematical of WALES'.[65] History, it is implied, had hitherto neglected to pay due attention to Wales but Brittania was now eager that it should make amends. The caption to the illustration draws attention to those aspects of Wales's past deemed of particular interest, that is, 'the ruined castle and bardic circle' duly featured in the frontispiece. Of interest they

certainly were to one London Welshman, William Earle (1781–
c.1830s), the son of a London-Welsh bookseller and the author of
The Welshman, a Romance (1801), a novel set at the time of the
thirteenth-century conquest of Wales.[66]

The Welshman delineates in some details the atrocities of the
conqueror Edward I and the devastated state into which he thrust
Wales, leaving it inhabited by outlawed rebels, plotting revenge in
caves, and manic widows, wandering the countryside with their
infants in their arms, in hopeless quest of their lost spouses. At one
point after the death of Llywelyn, Madoc, the novel's hero, a general
in Llywelyn's defeated army and a wanted man, disguises himself as
'an insane' and braves Edward in his court to harangue him for his
crimes. 'When you came with mighty force to Wales, you found
her like a full ear of corn; rich in her native worth,' he reminds
England's king, but 'you did pursue her sons with fire, rapine, and
the sword: – slaughter obeyed your nod – the blood of thousands
was split for your pleasure.' Madoc dwells with insistence on the
horror of English rule; as a result of it Wales has become 'a barren
wilderness – a ravished country'. The vengeful spirits of the butchered
Welsh prince and his followers will, however, forever haunt their
conquerors; Madoc assures Edward that, '[T]he blood of Llewellin,
and those slaughtered in the fight, fades not in the cold marble tomb;
– it lives – and breathing, lives – calling aloud for vengeance.'[67] The
king retaliates by persuading the Pope to excommunicate as rebellious subjects all Welshmen who resist his rule, and the army of
freedom fighters Madoc has gathered about him lose heart and
disperse. Although he is attended by an anachronistic druid, Molcar,
whose attempts at exorcising his chief from the spectres that haunt
him contribute to Earle's novel much of its Gothic flavour, Madoc
too succumbs to the fear of excommunication. Finally he becomes
an actual 'insane' and dies a prolonged and agonizing death after a
bungled suicide attempt, impaled on a rock for two days 'while the
surrounding hollows echoed with his groans'.[68]

Earle employs an epigram from *Macbeth* to head his last chapter:

> Alas! poor country,
> Almost afraid to know itself! It cannot
> Be called our mother, but our grave

> . . . where violent sorrow seems
> A modern ecstasy: the dead man's knell
> Is there scarce asked, for whom? and good men's lives
> Expire before the flowers in their cups,
> Dying ere they sicken.

The 'poor country' to which the quotation is here taken to refer is Wales of course rather than Scotland, but its use is a reminder of connections between the history of Wales and that of the other countries which made up the British 'Celtic fringe'. In a chapter on 'Scottish and Irish Gothic', David Punter argues that within those genres 'the dehumanising force in Gothic generally is brought into alignment, direct or indirect, with that power which reduces or dismembers the national narrative of a people operating under a sign of subjugation'. 'Throughout Gothic,' he says,

> one can sense . . . a mingled yearning and terror for a set of simpler verities, an unquestioned legitimation. This nostalgia goes through a further twist of intensification in Scottish Gothic, for that supplanting, real or imagined, is forcibly juxtaposed by the native Scots with the destruction of a 'national way of life'.[69]

A similarly complex nostalgia also makes itself felt in many of the texts discussed in this book. At the close of the eighteenth century, the Welsh middle and upper classes, like the Scots, seemed 'set on an inevitable trajectory that would eliminate national difference', leaving it behind as 'force of powerful feeling' associated only with the peasantry, who retained closer ties to a pre-conquest, Welsh-speaking identity. A yearning for that lost authenticity is evinced in the end pages of *The Welshman*, on which Earle advertises another production, *Welsh Legends: A Collection of Popular Oral Tales*. The advertisement announces that the 'Editor' of the legends was 'originally from Wales', and that he had collected his materials 'not in the well-built house' but in 'the thatched cottage, among, we may say, the *primitive* Welsh, who have carefully preserved and transmitted from generation to generation, from grandmother to grandchild, every tale, story, legend or ditty, which they had received from their ancestors'. It is there, says the advertisement, 'that *authentic* information can be gathered, and it is from these genuine sources that the Editor has, in an intercourse of several years, been enabled to obtain the collection which he now offers to the Public'.[70] Modern bibliographers have recently attributed to Earle himself the author-ship of the anonymously published *Legends*.[71]

Welsh Legends, however, does not so much fictionalize actual Welsh legends as invent a few Gothic tales of its own and attempt to recapture in prose the popular appeal of Thomas Gray's 'The Bard'. Throughout it, Earle's patriotic zeal is as evident as it was in *The Welshman*, though in one of the tales, 'The knight of blood-red plume', the relation between the Welsh and their conquerors is represented as more complex, with the Welsh portrayed as complicit in their own downfall. According to the tale's narrative frame, a lost traveller, who had tried to take shelter within the ruins of Rhuddlan Castle only to flee from it traumatized by the cries of its spectral 'tormented spirits', is befriended by a local inhabitant and regaled with the castle's ghost story. In the twelfth century, after the Norman invasion but before the Welsh conquest, Sir Rhyswick, lord of Rhuddlan Castle and 'the friend and favourite' of the prince of Wales, betrothed his only child, Erilda, to Morven, the prince's son and the heir apparent of Wales. But before the marriage was con-secrated she fell under the spell of a demonic stranger, the 'Knight of the blood-red plume', who gave his name as Wertwrold, a specifically Saxon appellation. Having succeeded not only in winning her love, but in tricking her into killing her father inadvertently when he attempted to prevent them from eloping, Wertwrold exults at the close of the tale: 'And is Erilda mine?' he cries,

> Why, this, indeed, is triumph – she is mine, voluntarily mine – she has fled her paternal roof for me, an *unknown* – she has rejected Morven, the heir apparent to the crown of Wales, who came to her with heart full of love, and proffered the wealth of his country at her feet, to share her smiles, for me, an *unknown*.[72]

Erilda has allowed herself to be seduced away from all that she should hold dear by the allure of the 'other', the unknown stranger. Wertwrold points out that even had she not unwittingly stabbed her father, the shame of her act of treason would have destroyed

him anyway: 'you scrupled to commit an immediate murder, yet
planned a lingering death for the parent who had nurtured you . . .
You bid him who gave you life, live for a time in agony, to reflect
on his daughter's infamy.'[73] She has betrayed not only her father
but also her country; she was 'proffered the wealth' of Wales but
spurned it for the stranger, leaving its representatives stricken and
dying behind her as she fled. Frustrated by the fact that 'Morven's
father had restored Wales to prosperity and peace', Wertwrold had
been seeking an opportunity to sink the country into unrest once
more and had found it in her susceptibility.[74] Hers are the tormented
cries which disturb the peace of Rhuddlan's ruins, eternally lament-
ing her crime of betrayal. Earle's tale effectively employs its demonic
seduction plot to Gothicize cultural assimilation, exploring in particular what it means voluntarily to acquiesce in the process of
estrangement from the indigenous culture under the allure of the
apparently more glamorous 'other', and the subsequent sense of loss
and guilt.

The final tale in *Welsh Legends*, 'The mountain bard', recounts
the story of Jolo Golch [*sic*][75] who joined the bardic circles in his
youth:

> In the Snowdon mountains dwelt a bardic band, whose customs
> nearly approached the druidic order, but divested of their barbarisms
> and Gothic idolatries: with these, young Jolo would associate, and
> join in their patriotic song . . . smooth and flowing was his verse,
> extempore composed – and soon he was elected the chief of the
> Snowdon bards.[76]

Jolo's history is told from an explicitly Welsh point of view, which
presents Wales as the 'sister kingdom' of a tyrannous and greedy
England, who approached 'our' lands intent upon pillage: 'Edward,
whose great object was to subjugate and oppress the sister kingdom,
advanced his thousand warriors to our native mountains.' At this
crisis point Jolo asserts his powers as leader of his people in a military
as well as metrical capacity, rousing them to opposition: '"Countrymen and soldiers!" cried the chief Bard of the Mountains . . .
"protect those rights and privileges which your forefathers have
enjoyed, and which from you your children should inherit."' But

in the heat of the attack his proposed strategy is neglected, with fatal consequences: 'The Britons . . . forgot the instructions of the intrepid Jolo, and were routed . . . by the English . . . The signal was given for the slaughter of the bards; and up each craggy cliff the eager soldier flew.' Jolo himself, however, escapes capture and death: 'High upon the Wyddfa's lofty summit sat Jolo Golch . . . Thrice had the enemy attempted to tear him from his seat, but as often met with repulse.' And he continues to versify, even in defeat; the song of the intransigently loyal fighting bard is hailed as eternal, ever haunting the ears of its Welsh audience: 'Jolo Golch mixes not with the world: in the lofty mountains of Snowdon he dwells . . . his song will ever please – his patriotic spirit ever be admired.'[77] Jolo Golch's patriotic spirit surely could not easily be appropriated by Earle's contemporary English readers; in this text, as in *The Welshman*, the imagined reader is positioned as a sympathizer with those Ancient Britons who still relate to England and the English as 'other' and inimical. And it is very much the English whose behaviour is Gothic and barbaric here; amongst the Ancient Britons, not even the druidic bards have anything that smacks of the 'Gothic' about them.

'The mountain bard' clearly feeds on the popularity of Gray's 'The Bard'; another lengthier fiction based on the same source was published in 1809, Evan Jones's *The Bard; or, The Towers of Morven. A Legendary Tale.* Little is known of Evan Jones, who announces himself on the frontispiece of his book as of the 'Royal Navy'. In the prologue to his book he informs the reader that 'the legends which are introduced in the course of the tale, are strictly true as to the facts', but the tale which follows is a curious, over-heated combination of Gray's 'The Bard' and 'Monk' Lewis's *The Castle Spectre*, with a versified paraphrase of Earle's 'legend' 'The knight of the blood-red plume' thrown in for good measure as one of the bard's recitatives. Evan Jones's romance takes Gray's Bard as the starting point of a complex saga in which Mysanwy [*sic*], the wife of Hoel the last Bard, is kidnapped by his enemy Ithel, who murders her when she resists his sexual advances only to find himself some years later equally besotted by her daughter Elfleda. Kidnapped and held prisoner in Ithel's castle Caer Cerrig, Elfleda is spared the worst possible consequence of his ardour by the intervention of an apparition:

the unpitying wretch prepared to gratify his worst desires, when a soft strain of seraphic harmony stole over his astonished senses. The distant vacuities of the chamber were filled with a bright radiance, dazzling to the imperfect vision of mortals; and disclosed to his strain-ing eyeballs a pallid form of celestial mould, attired in garments of the purest white. With one hand pointing to a deep ghastly wound in its bosom, and the other extended towards the portal, it solemnly exclaimed: 'Forbear.'[78]

This angelic spectre is of course that of the dead mother, Mysanwy, or rather it is a copy of 'Monk' Lewis's ghost in *The Castle Spectre*, who also sported pure white garments, a deep wound to the bosom and accompanying lights and harmonies, and who also, as in this case, successfully prevented the violation of her daughter. Evan Jones's apparent desire to please his audience with a happier ending than that allotted to the protagonists of his source materials interferes somewhat with the expected politics of his tale, however. Though denounced in the orthodox fashion by Hoel at the opening of the tale as the 'despotic' and 'cruel' slaughterer of his bardic brethren, Edward I, 'struck with the miraculous interposition of Providence for their deliverance and safeguard', shows an unexpected sympathy for Hoel's child and her betrothed Rhuallon at its close, and bestows upon them 'the wide domains of Ithel . . . as a token of his admir-ation of their tried virtue and unshaken fortitude'.[79] As befits one who so proudly announces himself as of the Royal Navy, Jones in this final scene is painting his Ancient Britons as grateful recipients of the English monarch's bounty.

But that Evan Jones should presumably feel a loyalty towards the Hanoverian monarchy which affects his portrayal of earlier English kings is not in fact of course as much a contradiction of the spirit of Gray's 'The Bard' as might appear. At the close of that poem the last Bard prophesizes the ascendancy of the Tudor kings, and acclaims them as 'Britannia's issue' and the redeemers of Welsh humiliations; it is they who will finally avenge the slaughter of his prince and his bardic brethren and bring peace of mind and renewed pride back to Wales. He summons the 'great Taliessin' to admire a vision of Elizabeth Tudor, whose 'eye proclaims her of the British line', and to know his nation avenged of its Plantagenet violators.

For later Welsh bards, however, no such easy resolution of the sense of Wales's wrongs was available. Take, for example, the poem with which Richard Llwyd, the bard of Snowdon (1752–1835), made his name in 1800. *Beaumaris Bay* is a profoundly patriotic poem, and the object of its patriotic devotion is very much ancient rather than modern Britain. Describing the castle built by Edward I at Beaumaris, the bard of Snowdon laments that

> Here earth is loaded with a mass★ of wall,
> The proud insulting badge of Cambria's fall,
> By haughty Edward rais'd; and every stone
> Records a sigh, a murder, or a groan.
> The Muse of Britain, suffering at its birth,
> Exulting, sees it crumbling to the earth.
> Ah! what avails it that the lordly tower
> Attracts the thoughtless stare and vacant hour
> If ev'ry Bard with indignation burns,
> When to the tragic tale the eye returns;
> If for his haunted race, to distant times,
> There's still reserv'd a vengeance for his crimes.

The notes appended to the poem substantiate the case against Edward, and read like a contemporary, twenty-first-century argument for the concept of Welsh colonization:

> ★So effectually did English policy operate to the exclusion of the natives from these strong holds, and the towns which gradually grew near them, that in a rental of the borough property, taken so lately as 1608, I find but seven British names . . . The history of these fortresses is a continued series of oppression and irritation.[80]

For the bard of Snowdon, 'Britain' (as in the 'muse of Britain') and 'British' (as in 'British names') clearly signify an ethnicity whose modern-day representatives are the Welsh and whose historical oppressor is that England which excluded their ancestors to the rural outskirts of post-conquest castle towns like Beaumaris. And the poem suggests that this past history is still haunting contemporary Britain: the castle's crumbling walls still echo to the groans of old atrocities and endure as a monument to horror and oppression. But that leaves 'Great Britain' a divided state, with its differing peoples haunted in opposing ways by these massed stones: Edward's 'haunted race' fears retaliation for past crimes while the bard's descendants are haunted by loss and a bitter sense of injustice.

It was the antiquarian movement with its rediscovery of the work of the medieval Welsh bards which fuelled such representations; its publications also added local colour to the numerous Welsh tour books of the period, the best-known of which remains Thomas Pennant's *A Tour in Wales* (1781). Pennant's volumes, in their turn, served as a direct source for some of the Gothic historical novels, most strikingly, Nella Stephens's four-volumed *The Robber Chieftain, or, Dinas Linn* (1825), a fantastic elaboration of one passage from the *Tour* which describes Pennant's journey to Dinas Mawddwy in Meirionethshire. On the road he

> was informed of the place, not far from hence, where *Lewis Owen*, vice-chamberlain of *North Wales*, and baron of the exchequer of *North Wales*, was cruelly murdered in the year 1555, by a set of banditti, with which this country was over-run. After the wars of the houses of *York* and *Lancaster*, multitudes of felons and outlaws inhabited this country; and established in these parts, for a great length of time, from those unhappy days, a race of profligates, who continued to rob, burn, and murder, in large bands, in defiance of the civil power . . . To put a stop to their ravages, a commission was granted to *John Wynn ap Meredydd*, of *Gwedir*, and to *Lewis Owen*, in order to settle the peace of the country, and to punish all offenders against its government. In pursuance of their orders, they raised a body of stout men, and on a *Christmas-Eve* seized above four score outlaws and felons . . . and punished them according to their deserts. Among them were two sons of a woman, who very earnestly applied to *Owen* for the pardon of one: he refused; when the mother, in a rage, told him (baring her neck) *These yellow breasts have given suck to those who shall wash their hands in your blood.* Revenge was determined by the surviving villains. They watched their opportunity, when he was passing through those parts to *Montgomeryshire* assizes, to waylay him, in the thick woods of *Mowddwy* . . . and left him slain . . . This race was distinguished by the titles *Gwyllaid y Dugoed* and *Gwyllaid Cochion Mawddwy*, i.e. *The banditti of the Black Wood*, and *the red-headed Banditti of Mawddwy*.[81]

The tale has since been revivified for generations of Welsh children by I. D. Hooson's stirring ballad 'Y Gwylliaid Cochion' in which the mother's curse and the bandits' revenge is memorably described: the brothers of the bandits hanged by Baron Owen 'wash their hands in the Baron's life-blood – while yet he lived' (*'A brodyr y deuddyn a grogwyd / . . . A olchodd eu dwylo yng ngwaedlif / Y Barwn – ac yntau yn fyw'*).[82] Nella Stephens takes as the name of her bandit tribe the first of Pennant's titles, calling them the Banditti of the Black Forest, but otherwise follows the dating and location of his account closely. Strangely, though, she appears to consider Pennant's supposition that the bandits' origins dated from the Wars of the Roses as justification for making them English-speaking. They are led in her novel by an Englishman, Otho of Heavingham, the robber chieftain, who preys upon a monolingual Welsh-speaking neighbourhood. When the mother (or rather the grandmother in Stephens's novel) utters her curse she is not understood; the object of her vilifications hears it as 'gibberish'. But one of his followers has been educated in England and is able to act as her translator: '"It is the English language in which she does converse," returned sir Leolyn, addressing lord Owen, who was wholly ignorant of any other dialect than his native Welsh, "and she speaks it most correctly."'[83]

The tale Stephens goes on to tell is an extraordinary farrago of revenge, abduction and betrayal; Otho is finally poisoned by his own mother whom with his dying strength he in turn slaughters. These events take place deep in the subterranean caverns underneath the banditti's hideout, the fortress of the Black Forest, a tower of immense height built upon both 'a worn-out mine'[84] and a Druidic burial chamber, for '[t]he Druids, it is well known, selected gloomy, interminable forests, as the theatre best suited to their horrible incantations and religious sacrifices'.[85] The fortress can be entered only through a hollow oak leading down to an abyss which petrifies the novel's heroine Adeliza when she is kidnapped and brought thither by the banditti:

> Poor Adeliza's terror, on first perceiving the yawning gulf beneath her feet, had not been excited without some great reason, for nothing could appear more frightful than this perpendicular abyss; and the

termination of its extreme depth would not have been discernible, had it not been for the light emitted from a couple of glaring torches, that were borne in the hands of two black human figures, stationed at the bottom of the pit, and who, with uplifted faces, grinning horribly a ghastly smile, appeared as if watching for the descent of fresh victims, brought thither to contribute to their horrid sacrifices.[86]

But a wooden platform on a pulley system ascends from the depths to take down the captive, and the black figures are revealed to be mechanized marble statues, which operate the platform's machinery. Adeliza is the betrothed of Sir Leolyn, the son and heir of the baron of Dinas Linn, Sir Owen's accomplice in the attempt to eradicate the banditti and Otho's sworn enemy; Adeliza herself, fortuitously enough given the linguistic limitations of the banditti, is an English noblewoman from St Alban's. Once in the fortress she is made the companion of Otho's daughter Ethelgida, who has never been outside the tower's walls and is entirely ignorant of her father's role as robber chieftain, and an object of scorn to the cursing grandame, Esther, whose thirst for revenge is deeper still than Otho's. She tells the traumatized Adeliza on her arrival in the fortress 'Thou shalt continue to possess thy functions yet awhile, until, proud damsel, on thy bended knee thou dost call on me to strike thee down a corpse on this chequered pavement.'[87] Later, when a gang rape by the banditti seems imminent, Adeliza does indeed beg from Esther a death blow, which the grandame nothing loath delivers, though Adeliza survives it. The horrific events of the last three volumes of the novel largely take place within the claustrophobic confines of Otho's besieged tower and its subterranean tunnels, as his Welsh foes try to rid themselves of the Banditti of the Black Forest and rescue Adeliza. Little is known of Nella Stephens, and it is difficult to make out from the text where her loyalties lay, but whether with the author's intention or not, the novel presents a haunting image of the Welsh as preyed upon by a marauding band of English robbers, operating from within their territories, who, while they struggle to resist, are undermining the ground on which they stand with an intricate network of concealed workings, and taking over for their own purposes the old mines and ancient remains of their national heritage.

Before the close of the novel, though, Otho's tower is betrayed from within and falls to the Welsh who are thus finally freed from the encroachments of his robber band. In her recent book *Female Gothic Histories*, Diana Wallace suggests that '[f]rom the late eighteenth century, women writers, aware of their exclusion from traditional historical narratives, have used Gothic historical fiction as a mode of historiography which can simultaneously reinsert them into history and symbolize their exclusion'.[88] Welsh Gothic historical fiction can be said to follow a similar pattern in terms of the power politics at work within the genre; in it the forgotten or repressed annals of Welsh history are reinserted into British history, and the past rewritten to highlight the exclusion of the Welsh and their concerns. It is unlikely that any Welshman was granted the opportunity to accuse Edward the conqueror to his face of what he did to Wales, but Earle's Welshman, in doing so, gave the release of expression to half-repressed sentiments. To what extent the Gothic genre in general, in its subsequent post-Romantic developments, aided Welsh writers in the endeavour imaginatively to embody their concerns, and to recognize and elucidate that repression, is one of the main questions explored in the second chapter of this book.

2

An Underworld of One's Own (1830s–1900s)

❧

In *A Geography of Victorian Gothic Fiction*, Robert Mighall suggests that locations and people 'perceived to harbour unreasonable, un-civilised and unprogressive customs or tendencies' become character-ized as Gothic by those who wish to distance their own supposedly more enlightened point of view.[1] In situations where one group has power over another, representing the more vulnerable group as Gothic also provides a quasi-humane rationale for their continuing domination. What interests Mighall is the way in which who and what is Gothicized changes according to the changing historical needs of the dominant culture. Before the Catholic Emancipation Act, when Roman Catholics still lived on sufferance in Protestant Britain without full civil rights or access to higher education, they were heavily Gothicized in the early Gothic novels as if to justify their subordination. As the nineteenth century advanced, an 'Imperial Gothic', as Patrick Brantlinger categorized it,[2] sought to label as Gothic the indigenous cultures of Britain's imperial colonies, thus justifying British intervention in their territories. Portraying might as right, the totalitarian tyrant as benevolent leader, exploitation as enlightenment, has in all epochs been the expected task of artists working within the status quo. The satirist Thomas Love Peacock mocks such manoeuvres in the opening pages of *The Misfortunes of Elphin* (1829) when describing the formation of Cantre'r Gwaelod, a mythic location in Cardigan Bay said to have been drowned by a tidal wave during the pre-Christian era. According to Peacock, its main port, the Port of Gwydion,

> had not been unknown to the Phoenicians and Carthaginians, when they visited the island for metal, accommodating the inhabitants, in return, with luxuries which they would not otherwise have dreamed of, and which they could very well have done without . . . imposing on their simplicity, and taking advantage of their ignorance, according to the approved practice of civilized nations; which they called imparting the blessings of Phoenician and Carthaginian light.[3]

Similarly, in the 'first-contact' fictions discussed in the last chapter, the English tourist visiting Wales participates in a process designed to encourage the Celt to shed his 'sinister' darkness and accept the blessings of anglicized light. It is one thing, however, to be Gothicized in fiction, particularly when one has the literacy tools with which to retaliate, as Welsh writers did; it is quite another to be Gothicized by official government report, a trauma to which the Welsh became subject in 1847, with long-lasting repercussions.

In the late 1830s and the first half of the 1840s, governing Wales was proving a problem for the English authorities; not only had there been a Chartist uprising in Newport in 1839, but from 1839 to 1843 'Rebecca' disturbances were widespread throughout southwest Wales.[4] The language of the Rebecca rioters was Welsh, and this factor had impeded the efforts of the English forces sent in to quell the riots;[5] a call for 'an Inquiry to be made into the state of Education in the Principality of Wales, especially into the means afforded to the labouring classes of acquiring a knowledge of the English language' provided the Government with an opportunity for intervention.[6] Monoglot English commissioners were duly sent into Wales to inquire into the levels of education attained by a largely Welsh-speaking population still in many parts monoglot. Not surprisingly, the *Report of the Commission of Inquiry into the State of Education in Wales* when it appeared in December 1847 found that standards of education in Wales were in general deplorably low. It then went way beyond its brief to connect this lack of educational access to the English language and English civilization with what it claimed to be the barbarity and immorality of the population, and

reported that 'petty thefts, lying, cozening, every species of chi-
canery, drunkenness . . . idleness' and 'want of chastity' were rife in
Wales. The English media took up this news with enthusiasm,
reporting of the Welsh that 'their habits are those of animals and
will not bear description'; according to the *Morning Chronicle*, 'Wales
is fast settling down into the most savage barbarism'.[7] The unwil-
lingness of the Welsh to dispense with a language and culture that
should have died with their loss of independence in the medieval
period left them trapped in the dark ages, according to this reason-
ing. The report insisted that

> The Welsh language is a vast drawback to Wales and a manifold
> barrier to the moral progress and commercial prosperity of the people
> . . . [The Welshman's] language keeps him under the hatches . . . He
> is left to live in an underworld of his own and the march of society
> goes completely over his head.[8]

The march of British society and the development of its widely
flung empire were of course proceeding apace during the mid-
nineteenth century; in contrast, Welsh culture, in so far as it sought
to stand apart from such developments, was seen as doomed to
attrition, buried alive by its loyalty to a zombie language that had
outlived its allotted span. It must have seemed all too appropriate
that in the 1840s, when these reports were being drawn up, the
south Wales coalfield was revealed to be the most extensive in
Britain; labouring underground, in 'an underworld' of their own,
was clearly the fate of the Welsh. On the surface, the coal the Welsh
produced was being used to empower the growth of an empire 'on
which the sun never set', but the British state in the 1847 reports
in effect relegates to its 'Ancient Britons', the Welsh, the burden of
embodying the dark side of its own past history, when colonized
Britain, under the Romans, was also, as Joseph Conrad's Marlow
put it, 'one of the dark places of the earth'.[9] Because they adhered
to the language of that barbaric past which England saw itself as
having long ago surmounted, the 'Ancient Britons' had opted to
remain in the zone of the repressed underworld. In his essay 'The
"Uncanny"', Freud speaks of the fantasy of being buried alive, 'the
most uncanny thing of all' to many people, as 'only a transformation

of another phantasy . . . the phantasy, I mean, of intra-uterine existence'.[10] The Welsh were entombed in the womb of Britain's past, according to the 1847 reports, and there they must perish down the dark shaft, 'under the hatches'.

But the enlightened British state would save them from such a fate, if it could. 'It must always be the desire of a Government to render its dominions, as far as possible, homogenous . . . Sooner or later, the difference of language between Wales and England will probably be effaced . . . an event which is socially and politically so desirable,' wrote Matthew Arnold in a further 1852 report on Welsh education.[11] As part of a systematic government attempt to bring about this effacement, the 'Welsh Not' regime was established in Welsh schools and children caught speaking Welsh within the school gates were punished. These measures took their toll on the numbers of Welsh speakers, which also declined as a result of the migration of a large number of incomers into the industrialized areas of south Wales during the second half of the nineteenth century. While about 70 per cent of the Welsh population spoke Welsh in the 1840s, with the more westerly counties such as Cardiganshire, Meirionethshire and Anglesey 100 per cent Welsh-speaking, only 49.9 per cent spoke the language by 1901.[12] Faced with such statistics, some observers from within Wales too viewed the demise of the language, and with it the end of the Welsh as a distinct ethnicity, as imminent and inevitable. It is not surprising in this context that much of the Welsh Gothic material published during the mid-Victorian years, whether by Welsh writers or others, incorporates portrayals of the Welsh as a doomed people and describes their obliteration from the annals of history; the first section of this chapter explores some such representations.

The doom of the Cymry

In 1836, Joseph Downes, a Londoner who had established himself as a surgeon in Builth Wells, Breconshire and adopted the Welsh patriot's cause as his own, was already protesting bitterly that the increasingly anglicized and, as he saw it, de-cultured Welsh gentry had as a group renounced any interest in their own literary inheritance and had distanced themselves from the rest of Wales, leaving the country without potential leaders. In his preface to *The Mountain Decameron* (1836), Downes complains that 'There is in fact, and literally, *no Reading Public in Wales*' apart from 'the better educated part of the more secluded Welsh peasantry':

> The gentry of Wales dispute this, but they had better *disprove* it. Let them do so by attaching some importance to so invaluable a resource, one so innocent, so exalting, so vital to good morals, as *reading* . . . Facts are stubborn things. *Seventeen* Welsh periodicals circulate well among the *humbler* classes! *One*, conducted with ability – and with great sacrifice by the spirited patrons of it, to the honour of their country – *one* acknowledged as worthy of support, by high critical authorities *not* Welsh – has at last *ceased to circulate for want of that support from the gentry*. Other orders, *seventeen* – the gentry *not one*: *verbum sat*.[13]

Given that the development of the Gothic genre generally in the early Victorian era has been seen as driven largely by the short stories (particularly the ghost story) published in the new literary magazines of the period,[14] the lack of many such outlets in Wales probably accounts in part for the relative paucity of Welsh Gothic publications during the mid-nineteenth century. The Welsh-language periodicals, numerous as they were, were largely sectarian, the mouthpieces of the Nonconformist religious sects, and they published little fiction of any kind; because of the sectarians' suspicion of fiction as 'untruth' and a waste of imaginative and intellectual energies the novel genre did not begin to establish itself in Welsh until the last decades of the century, after the heyday of Welsh Nonconformist chapel culture. Of course, some of Downes's despised gentry were no doubt reading English literary magazines; the anglicization of the Welsh upper classes – a process current throughout the eighteenth century[15] – was well established by the mid-1830s. The lack of support for Welsh journals in English is indicative of a general decline of interest in Welsh history and culture after the Romantic period, not only outside the country's borders, but also within them, amongst those classes increasingly educated in English only.

The antiquarian Celtic revival had at least succeeded, however, in reminding its audience of the past riches of Celtic cultures; consequently, their continuing decline was experienced by some as a loss, and that sense of doomed loss is reflected in the characteristic themes of mid-nineteenth-century Welsh Gothic writing. No longer so concerned with the Gothic experiences of visitors to Wales or with acts of Welsh/English union, it focuses rather on cursed Welsh families, doomed to obliteration by the sins or negligence of their forefathers, and on images of the Welsh as dragged back into the suffocating womb of their dark past. The English-language periodical to which Downes refers in the above quotation was probably the *Cambrian Quarterly Magazine and Celtic Repertory*, which appeared from 1829 to 1833, and to which Downes himself had contributed; this periodical regularly included in its pages tales with a strongly Gothic flavour.

In its first number, for example, the 'Legend of Iolo ap Hugh', by a contributor who calls himself 'Beuno', tells of a hillside cave 'on the northern border of Cambria' whose jagged mouth opens into underground caverns and tunnels of immense depth and reach, reputedly hollowed out by '[p]agans of old, when their rites were banished from "llygad y dydd" (the day's eye)'. As if the Druids still had the power to claim sacrifice for their gods, the cave possesses a malign magnetism: 'whoever approached within five paces of it would inevitably be lost', sucked inexorably deep into its maw.[16] On one occasion a passing shepherd to his horror saw that a local fiddler, Iolo ap Hugh, had for a wager, 'fiddled and capered him self within the fatal circle'. Suddenly, still fiddling, with 'his head dangled loose and unjointed on his shoulders', Iolo 'seemed as it were to skate into the cave, quite different from the step of a living and a willing man; he was dragged inwards, like the smoke up the chimney, or the mist at sunrise', never to reappear in the flesh.[17] Similarly, the 'Legend of Bala Lake', tells of the equally abrupt obliteration, under lake water this time, of an erring prince and his retinue, 'in the far-gone ages, when the Cymry were yet lords of this Beautiful Isle'. Because of his crimes against the peasants, the prince is cursed and told that vengeance will fall 'at the third generation'; as the palace rejoices at the birth of his grandson, the waters well up and cover the whole of the prince's domains.[18]

Such reworked legends suggest that the dark history of Wales will obliterate its people, sucking them back into a black hole; if they enter the gravitational pull of its circle they are cursed to oblivion.

The family curse narrative, as many critics have pointed out, was frequently deployed as a favoured theme within the Gothic fictions of England as well as Wales during this mid-nineteenth century period[19] but, according to one contemporary testimony at least, Welsh instances of the phenomenon had more impact. One of Downes's Welsh narrators in *The Mountain Decameron* tells his friends that no such tale of doomed English families has been recorded 'equally striking with what in this country has fallen under my own notice'.[20] *The Mountain Decameron* has a complex framing narrative, in which an English patient, who has been recommended by his doctor to take a Welsh tour for the sake of his health, is so delighted by the success of the medicine that to repay his physician he writes down for him the tales with which his fellow-travellers regaled him during the ten nights of his tour, those travelling companions being a retired Welsh army officer, a Welsh clergyman and an English doctor long established at Builth Wells who is revealed at the close to be Joseph Downes. It is the doctor who claims to know all about cursed Welsh families, but in fact a number of these travellers' tales are equally concerned with doom-laden families haunted by old curses. Like the 'legends' of the *Cambrian Quarterly*, the *Decameron*'s narratives are always presented as local folklore, but they are re-worked to such a degree, and have so little known precedence in folk annals, that they read more like fictions.

Take for example one of the most striking of the collection's family curse narratives, 'The tragical passion of Marmaduke Paull'. A Caernarfonshire man press-ganged into the army, Marmaduke Paull, after many years at war, returns, blinded, to find his wife dead and his only child, Ruth, grown up in his absence and disturb-ingly attractive to his starved senses. She reciprocates his feelings unequivocally, as she has been told by her mother on her death-bed that Paull is not in fact her blood-father. With rising hope that he may legally mate with Ruth, the blind man, led by a servant, sets out on a quest to find the midwife who tended his wife at the time of the child's arrival, as he has reason to believe that she can tell him more about Ruth's parentage. Margery Foulke, the midwife, is a reputed witch; according to the narrator,

> The suspicion of being in compact with the Enemy of man, as well as sometimes with fairies (or the Tylwyth Teg), in making proselytes in the one case, and changelings in the other, did formerly attach itself very seriously to the innocent and needful art and practitioners of midwifery, among the mountaineers of Wales.[21]

Paull finally tracks the midwife down, living in hiding underground within 'an ancient tumulus containing ashes of the dead', but the tale she has to tell him only spells out his doom.[22] Ruth is not his wife's child, but Margery's granddaughter, the illegitimate offspring of her daughter Elizabeth who was impregnated by none other than Paull himself just before the press gang took him. Paull's wife knew nothing of the fact that the infant she secretly took for adoption from the local midwife was fathered by her own erring husband. Margery herself never fully understands that Paull is the father of her grandchild, but she tells him how bitterly she cursed her daughter's seducer. 'Heaven! Heaven! why have you avenged the wrong of the mother, through such an instrument?' cries the distraught father, referring to his passion for Ruth: 'Oh I could *yet* have been blessed in it, yet have loved as a father, before this cursed sensual dream of these last few days – *now*, never more!'[23] At the close, father and daughter drown together, Paull deliberately allowing himself to be trapped by high tides off the rocky Caernarfonshire shore, and his daughter as deliberately joining him:

> The body of Marmaduke Paull and that of his ill-fated child . . . were found in close embrace in a hollow of a little reef rock, dry at low water, in whose wave-worn cleft no broader than a chest, they lay as in a single coffin formed for two bodies.[24]

The incestuous element in this tale is of a part with its death-wish ending as, according to Freud at least, repressed incestuous desires are the prime movers behind intra-uterine fantasies;[25] entombed in the cleft of the rock, drowned by the saline waters, Paull and his child return to the womb together.

A curse of longer standing haunts a Welsh family in Elizabeth Gaskell's story 'The doom of the Griffiths', first published in *Harper's New Monthly Magazine* in 1858. Gaskell often holidayed in Wales, at the home of her uncle Sam Holland in Tremadoc in Caernarfonshire, and set more than one of her stories and the central chapters of her novel *Ruth* (1853) in that locality. In 'The doom of the Griffiths', a fifteenth-century curse haunts a Tremadoc family: because Rhys ap Gruffydd had plotted to betray and bring about the death of the Welsh freedom-fighter Owain Glyndŵr, that 'great magician, damn'd Glendower' who, according to Shakespeare, could 'call spirits from the vasty deep'[26] had pronounced his family's doom. 'Thy race shall be accursed,' he had told Rhys:

> Each generation shall see their lands melt away like snow . . . And when nine generations have passed from the face of the earth, thy blood shall no longer flow in the veins of any human being. In those days the last male of thy race shall avenge me. The son shall slay the father.[27]

The curse is fulfilled in each generation, but when Owen Griffith, the son of the ninth generation, is born his father makes much of him, tending him with devotion after the death of his mother at his birth. He keeps the boy always at his side, and involves him in his own antiquarian interests, telling him 'half-jestingly' of the ancient curse. The telling of it becomes between them a repeated ritual of combined love and dread: the boy 'would crave, yet tremble, to hear it told over and over again, while the words were intermingled with caresses and questions as to his love'.[28] Then the son is sent away to school, where his classical education introduces him to 'the play of Oedipus Tyrannus, and Owen dwelt with the craving of disease upon the prophecy so nearly resembling that which concerned himself'.[29] In his absence the father marries again, and the jealous stepmother comes between father and son; Owen on his return to the ancestral home finds himself suddenly displaced in his father's affections and in his loneliness befriends and secretly marries a local girl by whom he has a son. The stepmother informs her husband that he has a grandchild by the local harlot; he in fury encounters the young couple, tears the child from his son's arms telling him it is not his own, and throws it to the mother: 'The furious action of the Squire had been almost without aim, and the infant fell against the sharp edge of the dresser down on to the stone floor . . . the lips yet warm with kisses, quivered into everlasting rest.'[30]

Owen, shocked and grief-stricken, is still mindful of the curse and realizes that he must do all he can to avoid any further encounter with the father whom he now deplores. He resolves to leave the district for ever with his wife, but first must collect his money and possessions from his parental home, Bodowen. With a terrible inevitability, father and son encounter one another again as Owen tries to escape his destiny; this time, as they struggle on a cliff-top overlooking the sea, it is the father who falls to his death, while Owen, falling with him, attempts till the last moment to save his life. Owen survives the fall, but knowing that he will be branded a murderer, he and his wife sail away at the close of the tale, 'wild, despairing, helpless, fate-pursued . . . into the tossing darkness and were never more seen of men. The house of Bodowen has sunk into damp, dark ruins; and a Saxon stranger holds the lands of the Griffiths.'[31] That final clause suggests that, just as Owain Glyndŵr prophesied, it was 'a race' rather than one family, or rather one family functioning as symbolic of a race, which was doomed to annihilation by its betrayal of its own freedom-fighters: the Cymry have sunk into ruin, cursed by their own dark history, and the Saxon has taken over their territories.

A similar atmosphere of predestined catastrophe pervades 'The doom of the Prynnes', a verse drama published posthumously in 1868 after the death of its author, the London-Welsh poet Sarah Williams (1841–68), or 'Sadie' as she called herself. The Prynnes are an extended family of Welsh exiles, living together in a London mansion 'that, like the fortunes of our family, / Had shrunk and withered to pathetic age.'[32] Their story is narrated by the youngest daughter of the family, Elin, who observes the developing attraction between her two cousins, Mark and Agnes. Her father, Cadwallader, is lost to the world in his antiquarian library, and her aunt, Mark's mother, is even further removed from everyday affairs by her growing insanity. In one scene, the aunt makes a dramatic appearance to pronounce 'the doom of the Prynnes':

A Prynne can only love a Prynne:
    Doom one.
The Prynne who weds a Prynne, weds Death:
    Doom two.
The Prynne who weds not Death goes mad, like me:
    Doom three.[33]

Doom two becomes the destiny of the two lovers, who are both killed by the literal fall of the house of the Prynnes. One stormy night, the winds uproot a mountain ash which the family's fore-fathers had brought from Wales and transplanted in their London garden 'to share / The changes in the family estate.'[34] The falling tree brings the whole house down with it, and kills Mark and Agnes, the family's hope for the future. But the Prynnes were a doomed race from the outset, particularly in comparison with the English. At one point Mark comments,

We have our special weaknesses, we Prynnes,
Our angers, fantasies, and ghostly fears,
No Saxon courage of tenacity;
We spring, and rush, and suddenly fall back:
Sometimes I almost hate to be a Prynne.[35]

As the Prynnes obviously represent the Welsh in this poem, it would appear that for Mark instability is of the essence of Welshness, and that the 'tenacity' of the Saxon has by now become stronger than they can withstand. The Welsh father-figures – Cadwallader in Sadie's poem and Owen Griffith senior in Gaskell's story – have both turned away from the modern world and obsessively immersed themselves in Celtic antiquities, but instead of animating their sense of identity their historical studies have but increased the gravitational pull which sucks them back into obliteration. These doomed incestuous families, the Paulls, the Griffiths and the Prynnes, appear to represent in microcosm the plight of their nation as described in the 1847 report – inward-looking, inward-loving and suffocating 'under the hatches' in an 'underworld of their own'.

    In such texts the Welsh are the living dead, doomed to extinction, and knowing it, while yet they live. In fact, however, the majority of the Welsh did not resign themselves to their cultural death after the publication of the 1847 report, but responded to it angrily as a 'betrayal' of their interests by Westminster and its appointed commissioners. The Nonconformist chapel culture had been singled out for particular admonition by the report, for encouraging through its 'night prayer-meetings, and the intercourse which ensues in returning home' the alleged propensity of Welsh women to indulge in sex before marriage.[36] Arguing that its findings were prejudiced by Anglican witnesses from whom the commissioners had gathered evidence, Nonconformist ministers now took the lead in denouncing the report; in so doing they found common cause with the remains of the Welsh antiquarian movement, along with the eisteddfod bardic culture it had established. During the second half of the century these defenders of Welsh culture gained considerable political power within a Liberal Party strengthened by the Liberal landslide of 1868 and the electoral reforms which followed it. A radical wing of Welsh Liberals established in 1886 the 'Cymru Fydd' or 'Young Wales' movement which campaigned for home rule and the disestablishment of the Church of England in Wales. A Welsh literary renaissance accompanied the birth of this new political movement and in fact outlasted it: 'Cymru Fydd' did not survive the 1896 refusal of the South Wales Liberal Foundation to merge with the home rule movement, but Welsh literature of the *fin de siècle* years continued to evoke the spirits of past freedom-fighters as inspirations to the living. In such writings, the notion of a Celtic 'underworld' is embraced as a source of pride and defiance rather than shame. However, in an epoch in which, as Jarlath Killeen puts it, 'no major ... thinker or writer ... was unconcerned about the occult',[37] this discourse of reanimated medieval freedom-fighters, Druids and bards attracted the interest of writers of occult fictions, with the result that these *fin de siècle* texts also often took on a Gothic edge.

Embracing the underworld

In the writings of the late nineteenth-century Welsh literary renaissance, the Goths are the historical, literal Goths, the Germanic Saxon forces which so effectively pushed back the Britons to wild Wales, and then, under Norman rule, completed their conquest in the thirteenth century. The indigenous culture features as a repressed force, potent with rebellion; Welsh heroes from the pre-conquest past and from later liberationist resurgences are called upon to participate in a new struggle to win home rule for Wales. In Ernest Rhys's *Welsh Ballads and Other Poems* (1895), for example, historical and mythical figures of Welsh resistance stir in their graves, come alive and walk the earth again to inspire the poet's contemporaries to fight for Wales's freedom. Ernest Rhys (1859–1946), born in London but reared for the most part in Carmarthenshire, was the son of a Welsh theological student and a Yorkshire woman; by 1906 he was to become editor of the Everyman series for Dent, and spend much of the rest of his life working on its list of 983 classic titles. But at this earlier stage in his career he presents himself as an adherent of the home rule movement, telling the reader in his 'Dedication' to *Welsh Ballads* that while exploring the ruins of pre-Norman Welsh castles he had learnt

> to know what life was to our last native Prince and his people, and how imperishable were the ideas which centuries have not destroyed. Nor shall they diminish, but grow more in the light of modern things, till we find the sword itself reviving in a song. In this plain faith these ballads were written.[38]

In the poems which follow heroes like Owain Glyndŵr arise and gather their armies about them once more. In 'The Ballad of the Buried Sword', even when the poet's vision of the 'dead Lord' risen 'with his soldiery' has faded, the image of Glyndŵr's sword remains, 'a silver flame, / Across the dark night of the Norman shame.'[39] Similarly, in 'The Ballad of the Last Prince', Llywelyn's 'severed head', perched as a trophy on the Tower of London, speaks one last 'mystic message' to his Welsh followers 'to fire our songs as we press on . . . – MOUNTAIN LIBERTY!'[40] And in 'The Death of Merlin', Merlin is 'regathered from his mother Earth' and stands forth with his Druids to proclaim 'to all the Cymraec fields – / Awake! Not long King Arthur's sleep / Shall be.'[41]

The figure of the 'once and future king' returning to reanimate and inspire a new generation of potential warriors in the cause of freedom is of course a familiar one. In Welsh-language culture it was at this time revitalized in one of the best-known poems of the literary Welsh Renaissance, 'Ymadawiad Arthur' (Arthur's Passing), which won for T. Gwynn Jones (1871–1949) his first National Eisteddfod chair in 1902. At the close of that poem, the dying Arthur sets sail to Avalon assuring his grieving companions that

> *i'm bro dof eto'n ôl*
> *Hi ddygaf yn fuddugol . . .*
> *A daw Y Dydd o'r diwedd,*
> *A chân fy nghloch, yn fy nghledd*
> *Gafaelaf, dygaf eilwaith*
> *Glod yn ôl i'n gwlad a'n iaith.*

> I'll come back to my land
> once more, bring her victorious . . .
> When the Day at last comes,
> and my bell sounds, I'll grip my sword,
> and a second time bring honour
> back to our nation and our tongue.[42]

The poem electrified its audience with its convictions that a 'wounded and sick' country, after 'captivity long and vicious' could still regain youth, health and independence if it willed itself to do so. The nineteenth-century traumas which beset Wales are often referred to in these *fin de siècle* texts, only to have their harmful effects reversed. In a prose parable by Gwyneth Vaughan (Annie Harriet Hughes, 1852–1910) 'Breuddwyd nos Nadolig' (A Christmas night's dream, 1905), for example, the Welsh language is represented as a wounded woman dying a lingering death on an exposed cliff top, scorned by the gentry and the clergy who pass her by saying, 'She is not fit company for me and my friends. She belongs to the lowly and servile. Let her be killed, and bury her from the sight of the world.' (*'Nid yw hi gymwys gwmni i mi a'm cyfeillion. Eiddo yr isel, a'r taeog, yw hi. Lladder hi yn farw, a chladder hi o olwg y byd.'*)[43] As a result of her 'betrayal' by these gentry and clergy, in particular through their damning false testimony to the commissioners of the 1847 report, the personified Welsh language is stretched out as if crucified on Gwyneth Vaughan's hilltop, and the death rattle is in her throat. But she is rejuvenated by one other passer-by, a good Samaritan who – though he also is an Anglican clergyman – gives her not a death blow but in effect a fresh blood transfusion. No warrior this time, but a sixteenth-century bishop, William Morgan, his reviving gift to the dying language is the Bible translated into his resonant Welsh prose.

Thus the heroes of the past are brought alive in the literature of the present in order to invigorate contemporary resistance, in a manner common to many embattled cultures at crisis points in their histories. According to the mid-twentieth-century Algerian analyst Frantz Fanon, whose work has proved seminal for later postcolonial theorists such as Homi K. Bhabha, for a colonized people to lay claim to their own myths and heroes, and then to imbed them in a literature labelled 'national', constitutes a vital step towards their freedom. Literature of this type is

> a literature of combat, because it moulds the national consciousness, giving it form and contours and flinging open before it new and boundless horizons; it is a literature of combat because it assumes responsibility, and because it is the will to liberty expressed in terms of time and space.[44]

Amongst Anglophone writers, one of the most active combatants in the struggle to mould the Welsh national consciousness anew in the 1880s was, like Downes, an Englishman by birth. Charles Wilkins (1831–1913) was born in Gloucester, the son of a bookseller who moved to Merthyr Tydfil and had become postmaster of the town by 1851. His son became the librarian of Merthyr's subscription library, a historian of some note – he published *The History of Merthyr Tydfil* (1867) and *The History of the Literature of Wales from 1300 to 1650* (1884) – and a journalist. In 1882, he launched his journal *The Red Dragon: The National Magazine of Wales* with the manifest intention of awakening Welshmen to the riches of their inheritance, and the need to fight for it. *The Red Dragon* featured articles pleading for the restoration of the Welsh language in areas, such as Cardiff and the towns of Gwent, where it was rapidly disappearing, and patriotic poems inciting the Welsh to join the struggle for Celtic home rule.[45]

Wilkins also published one novel, *Kilsanos: A Tale of the Welsh Mountains* (1894); the tale's narrator is a Londoner who has retreated from the city to lodge in an idyllic hill farm above Merthyr, only to be appalled when he first visits the town itself: 'what struck me most was the noise of the works. Sullen, deep sounds, as of a mighty hammer, and the whirl of the wheels, with a harsh, grating noise like that of an immense saw cutting iron in twain.' Accompanying this clamour he also hears 'wails, as of human voices', and comments '[i]f I had heard that it was a place of torture and that what I heard were groans and cries of agony, it would have seemed only too true and natural'.[46] Yet, it is not so much these industrial scenes which provide the Gothic element in *Kilsanos* as the narrator's interest in quite another aspect of his age, the occult movement: he succeeds in drawing about him a 'little circle . . . to get into communion with the other world'. Thomas, the village grocer and herbalist, William, the vicar's son, and the narrator, with Gwen, the farmer's daughter, as their medium, sit at 'a circular table' and call on the spirits to answer their questions with some success: 'the intelligence given forth is distinct from the circle, replies being made which were not in the power of any in the circle to give'.[47] The narrator has very deliberately chosen a Welsh farmhouse as his retreat because 'a finer place for exile, and solitude, cannot be imagined' and because in their 'vigorous innocence' his Welsh companions in this rural idyll are receptive to the spirits: '*Only the innocent in heart shall see God*', he reminds his readers.[48] Eventually he discloses to Thomas his long-held resolve to will himself to die and subsequently to return in order 'clearly, unmistakably' to prove the existence of 'a life beyond' and thus nerve humanity 'to endure, to be patient, in the living out of a good life, even though "Dharma tarry long."'[49] Soon afterwards his narrative ends, and Thomas continues the story, informing the reader that his friend has indeed died, of an illness rather than suicide (that is, of a willed 'natural' death, rather than some crude act of self-harm), and that he has subsequently reappeared, twice to Thomas alone, and once to the little seance circle, as they can all testify: 'What was that light, faint at first, then gradually taking human form? We all saw it . . . then near us, distinctly clear, stood the lost one.'[50]

Of course Wilkins was not the only Welshman – or woman – of his generation to be interested in the occult movement; another fervent supporter of the *fin de siècle* Welsh renaissance, the art patron and collector Winifred Coombe Tenant, was 'regarded as the most important psychic medium of her period, and the chief subject of study by members of the Society for Psychical Research', to whom she offered her services as a medium under the pseudonym Mrs Willett.[51] Nor was the editor of *The Red Dragon* the first writer to draw on the teachings of the occult movement in fiction located in Wales; in 1883 Kegan Paul published a novella entitled *Across the Hills* in which lives are forever changed and the spirit world manifests itself for healing purposes after a train breaks down 'at an out-of-the-way station in Wales'. According to this book's preface, its author, whose name is given as Frances Mary Owen, 'herself saw "Whatever is it that death has to reveal"' shortly after she had completed the manuscript.[52] The tale's narrator is a well-known (but unnamed) 'public man' who sets off to walk across the hills to the village of Llanfurdy in the company of a stranger also stranded by the train breakdown. Before the walk ends, he is a changed man: 'It seemed to me as though a veil had fallen . . . I had never truly lived before. I had crept along the highway; now, for the first time, the evolution of my life had brought me to walking erect.'[53] The stranger who has wrought this transformation is an unnamed young Welsh woman who, during the course of their walk, demonstrates her talents as philosopher, spiritual guide and water diviner, before sacrificing herself in order to save the life of a blackberry-picking child who happens to slip off a cliff edge as they pass. She dies in the narrator's arms, but subsequently twice reappears, continuing after death in her role as spiritual guide. Herself fulfilled by her act of disinterested love in saving the child – dying, 'she looked up into my face for one moment with the supreme joy of the saviour' says the narrator[54] – she returns to lead the living towards their fulfilment. 'She seemed with every sentence she drew from me to be revealing me to myself, and as if she created thought in me too, of which I had not known myself capable,' says the narrator of their conversation: 'I was revealed to myself, a complex marvel of sympathies and affinities united to all other living creatures by the strongest bonds.'[55]

Both the philosophy and the skills of the young heroine of *Across the Hills* accord interestingly with some contemporary ideas as to the nature of an older religion increasingly associated during this period with aspects of the occult, that is, druidism. Amongst druidic circles, the Ovates (one of the three grades of Druidry) were said to be skilled in water-divining;[56] in the novella, the two walkers come across a tramp lamed by a wound to his foot which needs bathing but 'there seemed little prospect of finding any [water] on that parched road between the hills'. Then, 'I saw the lady smile a little, and break off a small bough from a bush nearby'; with its divining help she finds 'a tiny trickling stream' in no time.[57] Both her tree-knowledge, and her calm certainty that nature will work with her suggest her affinities with a religion 'devoted to the appreciation of life . . . life as a whole, the great system of life', or so druidism is described in an 1890s article entitled 'Druidism and popular Welsh occultism' serialized in the journal *The Platonist*.[58] The resurrection of the 'lady' after death also parallels druidism, as described in the article: Druids apparently believed 'that the departed have the power to return at times to this world, and appear to their kindred and friends'.[59] And her joyful act of sacrifice, in saving the child's life while losing her own, is in accord with the article's account of the druidic belief that 'love losing and finding itself for its life in another was the eternal archetype of the microcosm of the universe, humanity'.[60] The way in which her conversation brings the 'public man' many stages on up an evolutionary ladder also echoes the 'old religion' too, as it is described in *The Platonist*. The Druids apparently held it that 'life was . . . evolutional; not automatically so, but by virtue of the primordial uncreated spirit-life who dwells in super-kosmic Light', and that 'the great work of every man, through many successive incarnations, was to develop his sense of reality', so that he (or she) became aware 'that the phenomenal universe is only the outwardness of the real universe – the spiritual, – which those can discern or cognize whose inner senses have been trained for the purpose, which faculties are latent in all men but evolved into exercise only in the few'.[61]

According to the *Platonist*'s essayist, 'This system came originally from Asia'. Druidism is thus presented as an amalgam of the wisdom of the East, combined with the Christian lore of self-sacrificing love and a Darwinian understanding of evolution – to which the Welsh hold the key. This 'high civilization obtained in Britain at the landing of the Saxons, dating back to times immemorial', claims the essayist, and it is evident still in 'the strange survivals of clairvoyance and kindred psychic faculties and powers among the Welsh even of to-day'.[62] The essay closes with a plea to the modern Welsh to share their great civilizing wisdom with that notable catalyst of the *fin de siècle* occult movement, Madame Helena Petrovna Blavatsky, who founded the Theosophical Society in New York in 1875:

> There could be no fitter task for those who have preserved through so many centuries their traditions of the East and of the wisdom-religion than to strike hands with its modern expositors and give their aid to the great-hearted Mde. Blavatsky and her co-workers in upholding 'the truth against the world'.[63]

As that last quotation indicates, *The Platonist*'s version of druidism owes much to the fabrications of the late eighteenth-century antiquarian and forger Iolo Morganwg who, in his zeal to impress upon his Romantic colleagues the wisdom of the old Welsh bards, added substantially from his own fertile brain to the medieval manuscripts that he collected and published. The Welsh National Eisteddfod with its Gorsedd and its motto '*y gwir yn erbyn y byd*' (the truth against the world), though presented by Iolo as authentic tradition, is now known to be largely his invention.[64] But however unreliable its sources, the argument of the essay succeeded in effectively reversing the stereotypical nineteenth-century representation of the Welsh as a barbaric race, lower down on the evolutionary ladder of their species than the more civilized English. The darkest, furthest recesses of that 'underworld' to which according to the 1847 report they adhere, far from holding them back from progress, now becomes the ground from which the Welsh can disperse true enlightenment to their benighted brethren on more than one continent.

In that spirit occultism also featured in the writings of Anne Adaliza Beynon Puddicombe, née Evans (1836–1908), who gained international fame as the novelist Allen Raine. The daughter of a Castellnewydd Emlyn solicitor, Allen Raine married an English banker and lived for much of her life near Croydon. She retained close connections with her native land, however, and chose rural west Wales as the setting for the majority of her eleven novels and numerous short stories. Although she did not begin her authorial career until relatively late in life, by 1906 her publishers, Hutchinson, were announcing with pride that 1,713,500 copies of her novels had been sold, and 'this', they added 'did not include American sales': five years later, by 1911, her British sales figures alone had risen to well over two million.[65] According to her biographer, Sally Roberts Jones, 'Allen Raine herself had some experiences of séances',[66] an interest apparent in her fiction from its outset. She started her authorial career through winning a National Eisteddfod competition in 1894 with *Ynysoer*, which was serialized at the time in the *North Wales Gazette*, and later posthumously published as a novel under the title *Where Billows Roll* (1909). The novel's two central protagonists are the strange twins Iolo and Iola Lloyd whose very appearance suggests an otherworldliness: 'their lithe, straight forms, their light clothing, and their silence, distinguished them at once from other people, and a sort of swaying or swinging in their gait, which suggested the fluttering of a bird or butterfly, could not be mistaken'.[67] They are feared by some of their neighbours in the small seaside town of Aberseithin; the vicar 'would have them brought before the justices and tried for witchcraft'. His neighbour, Mrs Morgan, agrees, complaining that, 'I have seen Iolo look at some people exactly as if he could see a ghost behind them.' But Nesta, her daughter, has befriended the twins and defends them, saying of Iolo, 'It is only evil people who need fear him. Iolo says that he sometimes sees something – "shadows of evil" he calls them – standing behind or beside people.'[68]

In fact, Iolo is a clairvoyant, prone to trances in which hidden truths are disclosed to him; his sister Iola knows that there is 'a peculiar depth in his character, which no earthly knowledge would outweigh'.[69] The twins have a mission, to heal and help the inhabitants of the nearby offshore island Ynysoer (Cold Island) who have been soundly Gothicized by their Aberseithin neighbours. Seen as backward and primitive, with very little English, the indigenous population of the island are 'generally looked upon with suspicion and roughly repulsed' and have lived and died on Ynysoer, 'almost as much isolated from the rest of the world as Robinson Crusoe on his desert island'.[70] The townspeople appear to have projected on to the islanders their own acquired sense of inferiority and made them the scapegoat for their own subordinated lives. But the so-called 'witch twins' are 'to these poor buffeted, down-trodden people like creatures of another world, who, though they could not keep death away, yet lightened the path to it'.[71] Their help is much needed when Dai, one of the islanders, is accused and convicted of killing a man from the mainland; Iolo, in a trance, sees the true culprit, a mad woman, but Dai, fortified by what he has learnt from the twins, refuses to allow them to appeal for a stay of execution. He tells Iolo, 'if you love me, do not betray that miserable old woman. I could never accept my life at the price of hers . . . her life of suffering has made her what she is.' He sacrifices himself for her sake and for the sake of the islanders as a whole, having realized that the townspeople in their animosity towards their chosen scapegoats 'will never rest until one life has been sacrificed at Ynysoer, and then they will repent. I am willing to be that one.'[72] After Dai has duly been hanged, so involved have the twins become in his struggle that neither of them long survive him. His – and their – sacrifice is not in vain, however. The Ynysoer inhabitants insist on visiting the twins' grave on the mainland 'without the shrinking fear which used hitherto to keep them imprisoned on the island', the towns-people on closer acquaintance begin to accept them, and eventually within both groups the twins are exalted as the equivalent of local saints: 'For many a long year, even to the second and third gener-ation, the names of Iolo and Iola Lloyd were held sacred, and their memory was blest.'[73]

In Raine's novel, then, as in Owen's and Wilkins' novellas, that 'underworld' to which the Welsh were doomed becomes not only their own salvation but a beaconing light of true progress to a dark-ening world. It is the breakdown of the century of progress, as represented by the faulty railway train, which leads to the public man's enlightening experience in *Across the Hills*; in *Kilsanos* the hellish conditions of the Merthyr workers inspires the protagonist's quest to establish the evidence of their salvation; in *Ynysoer* an extreme case of Gothicization leads to its healing reversal. Enlight-enment is not won without death in each case, but it is an exalted death, of supreme aid to the rest of mankind, and connected in all three cases with the supposed particular qualities of the Welsh as possessed of an unusual spiritual depth precisely because they clung to their old underworld in the face of society's onward march. With the infusion of occultism into the representation of the Welsh, the 'betrayal' of the 1847 report has been reversed: what was seen as primitive is now seen as enlightened, what was backward is now the most progressive. Other fictions expressing a similar ethos and also informed by their author's involvement in the occult movement include the later works of Arthur Machen (1863–1947), particularly *The Secret Glory* (1922), in which not druidism this time but the history, mythology and continuing mystical influence of the early Celtic Christian saints inspire the protagonist's spiritual quest.[74] At the turn of the century Machen had joined the Hermetic Order of the Golden Dawn, founded in 1888; though he could subsequently be dismissive of the society, which in his autobiography *Things Near and Far* (1923) he satirizes as the Order of the Twilight Star, the occult movement undoubtedly influenced his work.[75] However, Machen's fame today – as the only generally acknowledged Welsh Gothic writer – rests largely on the fictions he published before 1900, *The Great God Pan* (1894) and *The Three Impostors* (1895), the tone of which is very different from that of his later works. For the ghost story writer M. R. James they left 'a nasty after-taste'; Machen's was 'rather a foul mind', as far as James was concerned, though 'as clever as they make 'em'.[76] Recently, in Ireland and Wales, Machen has also been accused of another kind of nastiness: his critics see him as a Welsh writer who 'wants to be "English" (the superior race) but fears he is contaminated by (undesirable) Welshness', and as a betrayer of his people who wrote a 'unionist narrative of doomed native races'.[77] Yet, while it is certainly the case that the characteristic Machen tale pits Saxon rationality and material progress against primitive forces preserved by the 'little people' of the underworld 'in the west', it is not always clear where his allegiances lie. The next section of this chapter investigates in greater detail the complexity of his representation of Wales in the works he wrote before 1900, which include 'A fragment of life' and *The Hill of Dreams* as well as *The Great God Pan* and *The Three Impostors*, though the two former novellas were not published until the twentieth century.

Arthur Machen's underworld in the west

Machen was born Arthur Llywelyn Jones, his given name patriotic-
ally emphasizing a Welshness which his place of birth – Caerleon
in Monmouthshire – from the outset problematized. Because
Monmouthshire was omitted from the second Act of Union between
Wales and England, for legal administrative purposes the county
was from 1543 to 1974 designated 'English', and appeared as such
on many British Isles maps, including Ordnance Survey maps,
though its native inhabitants for the most part continued to identify
themselves as Welsh throughout that period. In his autobiographical
writing Machen consistently refers to his birthplace as being 'in the
heart of Gwent',[78] the name of the old Welsh kingdom in the area,
thus declaring its Welshness, but in his fictions his English narrators
often speak of Caermaen (his fictional Caerleon) as being in 'the
west of England'.[79] The discrepancy illustrates Machen's habit of
representing Wales in his writings from two differing points of view
– he sees the country through English eyes as well as through his
own. Of the fictions he wrote before 1900 only in two cases do the
narrators identify themselves as Welsh, in *The Hill of Dreams* and in
'A fragment of life'; in both of these the representation of Caermaen
and its history differs significantly from its portrayal in *The Great
God Pan* and *The Three Imposters*.

Mark Valentine suggests that *The Hill of Dreams* is 'a study in
potential autobiography', in that it depicts a life and death that could
well have been Machen's own;[80] certainly, the history of its hero
Lucian Taylor closely resembles his author's early years. Machen's
mother, born Janet Machen, the daughter of a Scottish naval captain,
became a chronic invalid while he was yet a child; his father, John
Edward Jones, a Welsh clergyman, failed in his attempts to rise
within church hierarchies and in 1880 was forced to declare himself
a bankrupt. Consequently, though his education at a Hereford boarding school was intended to prepare Arthur, their only child, for the
university, he found himself at seventeen impoverished and under
the necessity of earning his livelihood as best he could. In 1883 he
left Wales for London, to try to forge for himself a career as a writer
and translator, sustained at first 'mostly by dry bread, green tea and
quantities of shag tobacco', according to his biographer.[81] Yet, in

his autobiographical writing, his sense of his good fortune in the details of his birth is frequently emphasized. 'I shall always esteem it as the greatest piece of fortune that has fallen to me that I was born in that noble, fallen Caerleon-on-Usk, in the heart of Gwent,' he says in *Far Off Things* (1922):

> the older I grow the more firmly am I convinced that anything which I may have accomplished in literature is due to the fact that when my eyes were first opened in earliest childhood they had before them the vision of an enchanted land. As soon as I saw anything I saw Twyn Barlwm, that mystic tumulus, the memorials of peoples that dwelt in that region before the Celts left the Land of the Summer.[82]

In *The Hill of Dreams*, which was originally published under the title *The Garden of Avallaunius*, that is, the garden of the man of Avalon, Lucian's career follows a similar trajectory in the same locations, with the focus on his intense adolescent inner life. At his boarding school in England, he yearns for his Caermaen home, imagining it as it was after the Romans had left but before the invasions of the Saxons and Normans: '[H]e loved to meditate on a land laid waste, Britain deserted by the legions . . . Celtic magic still brooding on the wild hills and in the black depths of the forest.' But his 'masters did not encourage these researches'; as far as they were concerned 'healthy English boys should have nothing to do with decadent periods'.[83] Lucian was not a 'healthy English boy', however, and the '*twyn*' near his home, his 'hill of dreams' with its old tumulus, continued to lure him 'with stronger fascination'. At last, one holiday evening, obeying a strong compulsion, he climbed down into the old fortifications on the *twyn* and took off his clothes. As he lay naked in the hollow of the enclosure, 'beautiful with his olive skin, dark haired, dark eyed, the gleaming bodily vision of a strayed faun', 'quick flames' seemed to quiver 'in the substance of his nerves, hints of mysteries, secrets of life passed trembling through his brain, unknown desires stung him'.[84] The ecstasy of this semi-erotic experience stays with him, and when later, after his father's bankruptcy, he hears on the hill above Caermaen 'a clear and piercing music . . . ending with one long high fierce shrill note with which the steep hills rang', he becomes assailed by delusions that he has indeed crossed a time boundary: 'Perhaps a boy in the school band was practising on his bugle, but for Lucian it was magic. For him it was the note of the Roman trumpet . . . In his imagination he saw the earthen gates of the tombs broken open, and the serried legion swarming to the eagles.' He has heard the Romans sounding the retreat and leaving Wales in haste, leaving it to its indigenous population and to him:

> he himself was in truth the realisation of the vision of Caermaen that night, a city with mouldering walls beset by the ghostly legion. Life and the world and the laws of the sunlight had passed away, and the resurrection and kingdom of the dead began. The Celt assailed him, becoming from the weird wood he called the world, and his far-off ancestors, the 'little people' crept out of their caves, muttering charms and incantations in hissing inhuman speech; he was beleaguered by desires that had slept in his race for ages.[85]

Still enwrapped in these visions, he encounters Annie Morgan, the daughter of a local farmer, and initiates a sexual liaison with her, during which she starts 'whispering beautiful, wonderful words, that soothed him as a song. He did not know what they meant.'[86] Since Annie was presumably speaking Welsh, which evidently did not strike Lucien's ears as 'hissing inhuman speech', then the 'little people' of the hill are not Celts but those earlier more primeval Gwent inhabitants whom he also hails as his 'ancestors'.[87]

This new world into which Lucian has been plunged is his 'garden' of Avalon, that is, Afallon, the 'place of apples' to which the dying King Arthur was taken for healing and from which he will return when needed, according to the myth. Annie becomes his goddess whom he worships with secret masochistic rituals: 'he would softly and tenderly repeat the praises of his dear, dear Annie' while pressing gorse thorns into his flesh, 'offering his pain with his praise'.[88] But the pathological element in the relationship is not in Annie herself but in the heated imagination of her suitor, whose disturbance increases after he has to leave Caermaen for London, to make his fortune as a writer. There he is caught up in such a misery of loneliness that he obsessively projects his self-disgust onto the Londoners passing him in the busy city streets and begins to fear that they are all repelled by him: he sees in their faces as their gaze falls upon him 'an evident horror and disgust, and something of the repugnance that one feels at the sight of a venomous snake, half-killed, trailing its bleeding vileness out of sight'.[89] His recollections of his previous intense experiences in Caermaen darken, until at last he becomes 'oppressed by the grim conceit that he himself still slept within the matted thicket, imprisoned by the green bastions of the Roman fort. He had never come out, but a changeling had gone down the hill, and now stirred about the earth.'[90] Avalon has stolen him away, and an alien walks in his body about the London streets. Caught up in these paranoid delusions, Lucian dies a suicide or, as his landlady thinks, a drug addict who took an accidental overdose.

The Hill of Dreams is a striking psychological study of a disturbed adolescent experiencing his life in the Gothic mode rather than a Gothic novel as such, but every key aspect of Lucian's story – his fascination with the Roman town in Gwent and its pre-Roman history; his sense of connection with its past inhabitants, the 'little people'; his sexual initiation and masochism; his experience of himself as a repulsive outsider in the eyes of Londoners – also feature in his Gothic fictions. *The Great God Pan*, *The Three Imposters* and the story 'The shining pyramid' all, like *The Hill of Dreams*, contrast Caermaen scenes with London ones, but in them Caermaen is perceived and presented to the reader from the point of view of the Londoners whose gaze rests disparagingly on wild Wales. From the perspective of the upper-class dilettante English men of letters or dabblers in science who act as the narrators of these tales, Lucian's Avalon is indeed vile and poisonous.

In *The Great God Pan* Caermaen is the setting of its anti-heroine Helen Vaughan's childhood; she plays in its great woods with a 'strange naked man', like a 'faun or satyr' in appearance, a figure referred to with appalled horror here but similar, of course, to the 'gleaming vision' Lucian had of himself in the old fort.[91] Helen is the product of Dr Raymond's experimental brain operation upon his lover Mary, in which he 'lifts the veil' between the natural and supernatural worlds, providing Mary with one glimpse of 'a great wonder' before the onset of incurable madness. In his depiction of Mary's willingness to undergo the operation in order to please her lover, Machen switches gender roles, giving to Mary the masochism which characterized Lucian's adoration of Annie in *The Hill of Dreams*. According to Dr Raymond, in that moment of wonder after the cutting of 'the veil' Mary saw 'the great god Pan', and the birth of her child Helen some months later marks the fruition of the experience. Grown adult, Helen causes havoc amongst the male population of London's West End as she, in effect, seeks to show them Pan; one gentleman after another becomes her prey, caught in a web of horror from which they can only escape through suicide. Charles Herbert, one of her victims, to whom she was briefly married, tries to convey the nature of his experience to one of the tale's multiple London narrators:

> Villiers, that woman, if I can call her woman, corrupted my soul. The night of the wedding I found myself sitting in her bedroom in the hotel, listening to her talk. She was sitting up in bed, and I listened to her as she spoke in her beautiful voice, spoke of things which even now I would not dare to whisper in blackest night, though I stood in the midst of a wilderness . . . In a year, Villiers, I was a ruined man, in body and soul – in body and soul.[92]

Fred Botting suggests that what Helen reveals here are 'secret forces at the heart of things, forces that should, the narrator moralizes, remain buried, no doubt because their sexual nature is linked to female desire'.[93] This in effect is the world of delight which his passion for Annie revealed to Lucian in *The Hill of Dreams*. But in nineteenth-century upper-class London society it cannot be tolerated; it constitutes such a destabilizing threat to a gentleman's view of the feminine, of himself and of his civilization that it is unendurable. '[H]ealthy English boys' cannot bear such 'decaden[ce]'.

Finally the group of London gentlemen who are witnesses to Helen's activities corner her and give her the option of exposure or suicide; she chooses the latter. Robert Matheson, the doctor who attends her deathbed, reports on her dissolution which is supernaturally rapid: as she lies on her bed 'the firm structure of the human body that I had thought to be unchangeable, and permanent as adamant, began to melt and dissolve'. He watches as the disintegrating corpse moves backwards with fantastic speed through the cycles of evolution as described by Darwin, seeing 'the body descend to the beast . . . and that which was on the heights go down to the depths, even to the abyss of all being . . . at last I saw nothing but a substance like to jelly'.[94] The primeval slime reasserts itself; what the doctor is describing is a known natural process but when the evidence of it is speeded up and forced upon the senses, as in this deathbed scene, the effect is horrific, particularly to one who insists against all evidence on retaining the belief that 'the firm structure of the human body' is 'unchangeable, and permanent as adamant'. In life Helen similarly forced upon her gentlemen victims a recognition of natural female desire which to them was equally horrific: Machen is playing with his characters' and his readers' pruderies. As Robert Mighall suggests,

> to attempt to uncover a sexual meaning that the text cannot express is to be taken in by Machen's rhetoric . . . Ultimately there is no sexual secret at the heart of Machen's text . . . There is no secret at all, for all (Pan) is the secret.[95]

But when one of the narrators later visits Caermaen and sees the house in which Helen was reared he verges close to understanding her energy as but a force of nature. As he looks at the house, the prototype of which was apparently Bertholly House under Went-wood, near Caerleon,[96]

> the faint sweet scent of wild roses came to me on the wind and mixed with the heavy perfume of the elder, whose mingled odour is like the odour of the room of the dead, a vapour of incense and corruption . . . I stood at the edges of the wood, gazing at all the pomp and procession of the foxgloves . . . and beyond them deep thickets of undergrowth where springs boil up from the rock and nourish the waterweeds, dark and evil.[97]

This is the scenery which is described as paradisiacal in *The Hill of Dreams*; neither evil or corrupt in that fiction, it is rather the source of all spiritual as well as physical nourishment, and a fit setting for the 'man of Avalon'.

But in Machen's horror fictions, as opposed to his more autobiographical writings, men of letters and scientists, Londoners to a

man, enter this hallowed territory of Gwent and attempt to pene-
trate what they see as its dark secrets. In 'The novel of the black
seal' from *The Three Impostors*, for example, the ethnologist Professor
William Gregg visits Gwent (which he refers to as 'the west of
England'[98]) because he has reason to believe that the secrets of the
strange seal he has discovered will be revealed to him there. Having
become convinced 'that much of the folk-lore of the world is but
an exaggerated account of events that really happened', he has a
particular interest in Celtic fairies, and hopes to discover that 'the
obscure and horrible race of the hills still survived, still remained
haunting wild places and barren hills, and now and then repeating
the evil of Gothic legend, unchanged and unchangeable'.[99] Primeval
slime is of the essence of these little people's secret too: the professor succeeds in deciphering the strange hieroglyphics on the black
seal which 'tell how a man can be reduced to the slime from which
he came, and be forced to put on the flesh of the reptile and the
snake'.[100] But the only person in the tale who is depicted actually
using this secret knowledge is the professor himself, who reduces
to slime a local Caermaen boy born after his mother apparently had
a close encounter with the 'little people'. The tale closes with Professor Gregg recording his decision to go to 'the final trial and
encounter', on the Grey Hills above Caermaen, there to 'meet the
"Little People" face to face'.[101] As Gregg is seen no more, but his
watch and ring are found on one particular spot on the hillside
'dotted over with grey limestone boulders', the encounter would
appear to have led to his abduction and probably to his own dissolution into slime. This likely end can, however, be seen as an act
of revenge on the part of the 'little people' for the loss of their boy,
and not as one which Gregg's author necessarily deplored.

Furthermore, 'The novel of the black seal', like the other 'novels'
included in *The Three Impostors*, is set within a framing narrative
which exposes them all as mischievous deluding fictions, told only
to deceive their immediate hearers within the tale. They are narrated by 'three impostors' in order to draw from their dupes, two
Londoners, Dyson and Phillipps, information as to the whereabouts
of 'a young man in spectacles' sought by Professor Lipsius, the
impostors' employer. Neither Lipsius nor the young man have any
connection with Caermaen, or Wales for that matter; the only

context in which we see them is London, yet their story incorporates acts of far greater unequivocal evil than those of the Welsh
'little people'. The chain of events which constitutes the narrative
proper commences when the innocent 'young man in spectacles',
Joseph Walters, is lured into Lipsius's circle only to discover that
his mentor is no better than a vicious criminal, ready to murder
in order to steal a prize, in this case the golden Tiberius, a rare
Roman coin. Once the murder is revealed to him Walters flees
from Lipsius's house, taking the coin with him and, in his horror
of the crime, throwing it away in the street. By chance Dyson sees
him do so; he picks up the coin and tells his friend Phillipps of his
curious find. Consequently, both of them become sought after by
Lipsius who sets his impostors on them to befriend them under
various disguises and catch their interest by spinning their tall tales.
Before the close Walters is caught by the impostors and suffers at
their hands a more horrific death, by slow burning, than any hinted
at elsewhere in Machen's fiction. And the deed has evidently been
carried out with extreme sadistic enjoyment by at least two of the
impostors, who laugh and banter over it, regretting that Lipsius has
unfortunately had to miss the treat. London, then, in this text is
much more of a hell on earth, populated by torturing demons, than
Caermaen and its past and present inhabitants.

Dyson, who is represented as something of a gullible fool, sus-
ceptible to flattery, in *The Three Impostors*, where neither he nor
Phillipps fully realize the extent to which they have been duped,
reappears in the short story 'The shining pyramid', first published
in 1895. A farmer's daughter, called Annie, has disappeared from her
home 'in the west', above 'Castletown' and not far from 'Croes-
yceiliog' but described by Dyson as a 'quiet corner of England', and
Dyson is called in by his friend Vaughan to investigate the mystery,
in Sherlock Holmes style.[102] Through decoding a series of curious
hieroglyphic signs that appear in the neighbourhood, he eventually
deduces that she has become the sacrificial victim of a tribe of
'little people', 'four feet in height, accustomed to live in darkness,
possessing stone instruments, and familiar with the Mongolian cast
of features', who inhabited the area 'before the Celt set foot in
Britain' and who flourish in it still.[103] One night, he and Vaughan
witness her probable end, which takes place on a local hilltop in 'a

circular depression'. As they watch in hiding, the hollow stirs and seethes

> like an infernal cauldron. The whole of the sides and bottom tossed and writhed with vague and restless forms that passed to and fro without the sound of feet, and gathered thick here and there and seemed to speak to one another in tones of horrible sibilance, like the hissing of snakes . . . It was as if the sweet turf and the cleanly earth had suddenly become quickened with some foul writhing growth.[104]

Then, the whole hollow bursts into flame, a 'shining pyramid' of fire in which the watchers momentarily hear a woman's scream through the 'venomous' hissing, and glimpse 'the tossing of human arms' amidst a myriad bestial figures 'hideously deformed', 'their almond eyes burning with evil and unspeakable lusts'.[105] The scene is a rendering in satanic mode of Lucian's fiery experience in the hollow of the old fort above Caermaen in *The Hill of Dreams*.

In *Far Off Things*, Machen describes how, in the second half of the 1890s, 'it suddenly dawned' upon him that his writings to date 'had all been the expression of one formula, one endeavour . . . I had been inventing tales in which and by which I had tried to realize my boyish impressions of that wonderful magic Gwent'.[106] In those first tales, however, he realized that he had 'translated awe, at worse awfulness, into evil'; 'one dreams in fire and works in clay', he says of his craft.[107] *The Hill of Dreams*, started in 1895, just after the completion of these tales of horror, constituted a conscious attempt to 'amend my ways' and cast off the influence of Robert Louis Stevenson, whose *Dr Jekyll and Mr Hyde* (1886), he recognized, had affected his work: 'I was to abandon the manner in which "The Three Impostors" had been written, which was not my manner but Stevenson's and to get a style, or something like a style, of my own.'[108] The more authentic Gwent experience he depicted in *The Hill of Dreams* is still one of 'awfulness' as much as 'wonder', however, leading as it does to Lucian's haunted torment in London and his probable suicide. The pre-1900 text which more closely represented Machen's mature style was 'A fragment of life', written in 1899 though not published until 1906. At the opening of the tale, its protagonist Edward Darnell is 'sincerely of the opinion' that he is an 'English City clerk', living a humdrum suburban life in Shepherd's Bush, but by its close he has regained 'the far-shining glories of the kingdom which was his by legitimate inheritance'.[109] Though 'Darnell had received what is called a sound, commercial education, and would therefore have found very great difficulty in putting into articulate speech any thought that was worth thinking', he manages to shed this ideological 'rubbish heap' after he has discovered his true lineage in 'old family papers', documents with 'a string of uncouth Welsh names linked together by the word "ap" in a chain that looked endless'.[110] At the opening of the tale, he and his wife talk only about whether or not they can afford to furnish a spare room; at its close he is telling his wife of 'the old grey house in the west' and

> the records of the old race from which he came . . . The family went back and back, he said, far into the dim past, beyond the Normans, beyond the Saxons, far into the Roman days, and for many years they had been petty kings, with a strong fortress high up on the hill . . . one of them, the most remote of all, was called a saint, and was supposed to possess certain mysterious secrets often alluded to in the papers as the 'Hidden Songs of Iolo Sant'.[111]

This is in effect a sanctification and romanticization, as opposed to Gothicization, of the Twyn Barlwm ancestors, represented as satanic 'little people' in the earlier tales.

Why it takes so long for Darnell to claim his Welsh ancestry is indicated by one scene in 'A fragment of life', which initially seems incidental to the story. Mrs Darnell has an aunt who seeks sanctuary in her niece's home, telling her that her husband is unfaithful to her. The husband then appears, to inform the Darnells that their aunt is in fact 'stark, staring mad', and he has 'had to put her away'. According to him she has been driven mad not by any peccadillo on his part but by 'a little Welsh skunk named Richards', who is himself 'not mad, he's bad'. 'He's been running some sort of chapel over at New Barnet for the last few years,' says Mr Nixon, 'and my poor wife – she never could find the parish church good enough for her – had been going to his damned schism for the last twelve-month. It was all that finished her off.'[112] Nixon has 'thrashed' Richards 'black and blue', but too late, the mischief has been done. Where the truth lies in this affair is never clearly established, but the incident as it stands helps to explain why Darnell's ancestors changed their name from 'Iolo ap Taliesin ap Iowerth' in the six-teenth century, at the time of the Acts of Union of Wales and England, and why their descendant ignores his family history for so long. From the point of view of his suburban London acquaintance, the 'Welsh' are deceiving, dangerous 'skunks', who take advantage of the vulnerable and work on their credulity, and who can be thrashed with impunity; it would clearly not promote the career of an English city clerk to be associated with such low life.

Once Darnell has turned his back on his secretarial identity and embraced his Welshness, such considerations fall from him, how-ever, and he – and his wife with him – enter into a far more securely transcendent state than that enjoyed by Lucian in *The Hill of Dreams*. Through immersion in the worlds of the old Welsh bards and early Celtic saints, his ancestors, he grows to realize that 'the soul is made wise by contemplation of mystic ceremonies and elaborate and curious rites'; 'the whole world is but a great ceremony or sacra-ment, which teaches under visible forms a hidden and transcendent doctrine'.[113] The veil of mundanity is lifted naturally, without the need of a brain operation. Darnell's story opens with the protagonist awakening from a dream of 'an ancient wood, and of a clear well' to his suburban existence; at its close that dream has become his new reality. 'So I awoke from a dream of a London suburb, of daily labour, of weary, useless little things,' he tells the reader,

> and as my eyes were opened I saw that I was in an ancient wood, where a clear well rose into grey film and vapour beneath a misty, glimmering heat. And a form came towards me from the hidden places of the wood, and my love and I were united by the well.[114]

This tone of mystic transcendence, inspired by the Welsh land-scape and by what is represented as the persistent influence of the early Celtic Christian church, remains dominant throughout Machen's later works, such as the Grail quest fictions *The Secret Glory* and *The Great Return* (1915).[115] In them, as in the occult novels discussed earlier in this chapter, immersion in the Welsh underworld becomes the way to sanctification; in so far as they adhere to their cultural difference, and maintain age-old rites and rituals, the tribe of the Cymry are seen as forerunners in humanity's progress towards its full spiritual evolution. As the twentieth century advanced, however, the importance Machen attached to high religious ritual as a necessary component of human advance positioned him at odds with political movements intent on establishing more material, social and egalitarian progress. In 1937 when the *Left Review* published a pamphlet entitled *Authors Take Sides on the Spanish War* Machen was amongst the very few contributors who declared for Franco, as a defender of Christianity against its Communist detractors,[116] thus positioning himself starkly at odds with the mass of his fellow south Walians during the interwar years, many of whom fought in Spain on the Republican side. But although the occult movement, by the 1930s at any rate, had become tinctured with fascist associations, the Gothic was by no means thus limited, or not at any rate in Wales where the first half of the twentieth century saw the publication of Gothic fictions in which the destructive influences, leeching the life out of humanity and endangering its progress, become not Communism but its opponents, capitalism and the hierarchies of the church (or rather, in this case, the chapel) and state. The next chapter of this volume examines some representative examples of anti-capitalist and anti-hierarchical Welsh Gothic.

3

Haunted Communities
(1900s–1940s)

In *Ghostly Matters: Haunting and the Sociological Imagination*, Avery F. Gordon argues that a haunting experience is one in which 'a repressed or unresolved social violence is making itself known'. '[H]aunting', she says, 'is one way in which abusive systems of power make themselves known and their impacts felt in everyday life, especially when they are supposedly over and done with (slavery, for instance), or when the oppressive nature is denied.' The awareness of injustice abides in the subject's unconscious and flares into consciousness at the haunting moment 'when the people who are meant to be invisible show up without any sign of leaving, when disturbed feelings cannot be put away, when something else, something different from before, seems like it must be done'.[1] In terms of social development towards the eradication of injustices, the experience of being haunted is thus presented by Gordon as potentially progressive, in that it raises into consciousness past wrongs and creates a restlessness to learn from them and amend them. In a gender context, it is a process akin to that which in feminist terms used to be known as 'consciousness raising', when the personal is recognized as the political. In a class context, it could also be compared to the moment in Brechtian epic theatre when the ordinary day-to-day conditions of habituated life are suddenly interrupted, and thus 'uncovered' and exposed to the audience's gaze as strange and alienating; 'instead of identifying itself with the hero', the audience of epic theatre, as Walter Benjamin explained, 'is called upon to learn to be astonished at the circumstances within which he has his being'.[2] The haunting moment similarly exposes previously accepted conditions to the individual as unjust, inhumane and benighted – in a word, as Gothic.

Much of this book argues that the conquest of Wales, its ethnic subjugation and subsequent attempts to subordinate or eradicate its cultural difference haunt the Welsh imagination, and find expression in Welsh Gothic literature. But other instances of social injustice have also, of course, affected Welsh communities and been represented in their literature. In this chapter the focus is on two such instances, both in a sense related to Wales's colonial experience in that it is unlikely that they would have taken the extreme forms they did had the country enjoyed more autonomy and had a greater control of its own resources, but both also endured by similarly afflicted communities in Britain and elsewhere.

The 1870s and 1880s were years of acute agricultural depression in Wales, which left the communities of the rural counties much impoverished; in Cardiganshire, for example, the average income per head was so low that whereas the mean tax collected for income per head in England in 1875–6 stood at £15.7, in Cardiganshire it was nearly half that, at £8.4 per head, compared with £12 in Wales generally.[3] Many agricultural workers emigrated, many more moved down to the south-east counties of the country to find employment in iron, steel and tin works, and in the Welsh coalfields which were at this time becoming amongst the most productive globally. While the population of Wales was distributed more or less evenly throughout its counties at the beginning of the nineteenth century, by its close the south-easterly valleys were densely inhabited while much of the rest of Wales had become what the poet Harri Webb referred to as an under-populated 'green desert'.[4] In the 1881 Census, industrial Glamorganshire's population was recorded as 518,383; by 1911 its numbers had more than doubled, to 1,130,668, nearly half of the total population of Wales, but in Cardiganshire the figures fell from 95,137 to 80,769 during the same period. Towns like Pontypridd at the mouth of the Rhondda more than trebled in size, from 93,493 in 1881 to 288,564 in 1911, while small rural centres like Tregaron in Cardiganshire shrank to two-thirds of their former size.[5] Within the industrial townships and pit villages there were, however, very few opportunities for employment, for men or women, other than in the production of raw materials; the sociologist Graham Day points out that 'while Wales was virtually the only producer of tinplate and sheet steel in Britain, only 11% of the former and 4% of the latter were processed for finished products within Wales'. Consequently, 'no self-sustaining industrial base' was developed in a country in which the mines and furnaces were usually controlled by external investment, with the profits 'creamed off and realized elsewhere'.[6] For those who left the land to cram into the packed terraces which mushroomed under the shadow of the pits, there were therefore few prospects of escape for themselves or their children from dependence on underground labour, with its concomitant threat of sudden death from rock fall, explosion, coal-gas or flooding, or of slower death from silicosis. 'We were more or less living with death every day,' testified a Llwynypia inhabitant, remembering her childhood in that coal-mining village in the 1900s: 'Because there wasn't a week passing by, there wasn't someone being injured, someone being killed. There was always that tragedy hanging over . . . I felt that as a child. That there was something hanging over us all the time.'[7] These are the communities which haunt the imaginations of such writers as Rhys Davies (1901–78), Glyn Jones (1905–95), Gwyn Jones (1907–99) and Gwyn Thomas (1913–81), all born and brought up in the south Wales valleys. Industrial fiction tends to be categorized as realist in terms of genre but in many instances, as the second half of this chapter aims to illustrate, the work of these writers borrows darker tones from the Gothic mode in calling upon readers to recognize what was alien and unjust about the ordinary, everyday conditions of life in the coalfield townships.

At least two of the above authors acknowledged as their immediate forefather within the field of anglophone Welsh writing another author not of the valleys himself, Caradoc Evans (1878–1945). In *The Dragon Has Two Tongues: Essays on Anglo-Welsh Writers and Writing* (1968), Glyn Jones refers to him as 'the man who Professor Gwyn Jones has taught us to regard as the first of the modern Anglo-Welsh',[8] and describes his and Dylan Thomas's pilgrimage to visit Caradoc, as he calls him, in 1934 in search of inspiration at the outset of their careers as writers. Brought up in Cardiganshire, Caradoc Evans made his name on the strength of his series of linked short stories about the rural communities in which he spent an impoverished childhood in the 1880s, *My People* (1915) and its sequel *Capel Sion* (1917). His widowed mother had been disinherited by her Nonconformist farming family for marrying an Anglican, and according to her son was consequently barred from membership of her local Calvinist Methodist chapel because she could not contribute to its funds: 'lacking the money and having a heavy burden of young children, she would not pay, and was, according to the custom, treated as an outcast'.[9] In his fictions her son wreaks vengeance on the ministers and deacons who thus further darkened lives stunted by rural poverty; the rulers of his Welsh chapels are monsters to a man. *My People* was greeted with horror in Wales, where an attempt was made to ban it.[10] But its reception in England was much more favourable and its 'exuberant grotesqueries', in Tony Conran's words, also 'set the tone' for a new rebellious generation of Welsh writers in English who relished its 'anti-puritan, anti-pedagogue, anti-ruling class' stance.[11] Arthur Machen, for one, certainly appreciated a book that he categorized as unquestionably Gothic, saying of it,

> Never have I come into so wild and dark a country as that shown in *My People*. Black savagery, black magic, black superstition, all pretending to be Methodism: Witch Doctors and Medicine Men more dread and powerful than any such to be discovered in Africa; and these calling themselves Respected Religious Teachers! . . . I had to shut up *My People* and take down the ABC Railway Guide: to assure myself that the Great Western would take one into the heart of the Black Desert in seven or eight hours.[12]

But *My People* was by no means the first or last text to Gothicize Welsh chapel culture. As well as assessing some of the darker aspects in Caradoc Evans's writings, the first section of this chapter also explores the manner in which Gothic tropes were employed to darken satirical attacks on what was seen as the Nonconformist sects' excesses both before and after the publication of *My People*. The chapter as a whole explores the fictional representation of fears specific to the changing communities of Wales during the period when coal became king.

The Devil in Zion

In order to appreciate why Caradoc Evans's writings had the effect they did, it is important to bear in mind the history of the representation of Welsh Nonconformity in literature, a history recently chronicled by M. Wynn Thomas in his *In the Shadow of the Pulpit: Literature and Nonconformist Wales*.[13] Welsh Calvinist Methodism, the sect which came into being in the 1730s with its leader Howel Harris's conversion and which adopted Calvinism in 1743, was from the outset subject to attack. The mock sermons of the anti-quarian and poet Lewis Morris of Anglesey (1701–65) castigated the Methodists as hypocritical and lascivious: in 'Young Mends the clothier's sermon' (*c.*1743) a Methodist preacher advocates his flock to 'Dance and Skip about, for I will absolve you from your Sins. But whatever you do, Do in the dark, that our enemies may not triumph over us for the eyes of the wicked Peep into every corner.'[14] Similarly, in William Roberts from Llŷn's *Ffrewyll y Methodistiaid* (The Scourge of the Methodists, *c.*1747), an interlude intended for popular fair-day entertainment, the argument that because they are already saved through predestination all they do must be pure is used by Methodist leaders intent on seducing the fairer ewes of their flock. Siencyn Morgan, in real life a Bala schoolteacher and advocate of Methodism, overcomes Ynfydog (i.e. Foolish Woman)'s resistance to his designs on her person by telling her that:

> *Nyni sy'n llawn o bob duwiolfryd*
> *Ac yn bucheddu'n ddifrycheulyd,*
> *Nid yw carwriaeth rhyngom ni*
> *Ond cynnwrf asbri'r Ysbryd.*[15]

We are full of sanctity
And live spotlessly,
Love-making between us
Is but the agitation of the [Holy] Spirit's vivacity.

Later, Ynfydog, deserted by her Methodist lover and pregnant, returns on stage as a raving lunatic, undone by the same antinomian persuasions, that the elect can do no wrong, as those which led to Wringhim's deed of murder and his insanity in James Hogg's Gothic novel *The Private Memoirs and Confessions of a Justified Sinner* (1824).

Before the close of the eighteenth century some of the early anglophone Welsh novelists had also started similarly to castigate Methodists for their hypocrisies, though their attacks were probably influenced not so much by the Welsh-language interlude as by a spate of popular anti-Dissent plays directed largely against English Methodists. In *Everywhere Spoken Against: Dissent in the Victorian Novel*, Valentine Cunningham argues that the continued popularity of plays like Isaac Bickerstaffe's *The Hypocrite* (1769) and Samuel Foote's *The Minor* (1760) and its sequel *The Methodist* influenced the representation of Methodism in the work of the English Victorian novelists, and encouraged the development of stereotypical portrayals of hypocritical, avaricious and lascivious preachers and deacons in the work of Frances Trollope, Charles Dickens and others.[16] But figures similar to Dickens's hypocrite Stiggins in *Pickwick Papers* (1836–7) also flourished earlier in such texts as Anna Maria Bennett's *Anna, or, Memoirs of a Welch Heiress* (1785) in which the Reverend John Dalton, 'the son of a journeyman carpenter, in a large town in South Wales' and one of the book's worst villains, exploits the orphan Anna in a manner which the text represents as characteristic of Methodist preachers. After an encounter in his youth with 'a late celebrated methodist teacher', Dalton had 'pleaded a call of the spirit': 'To strong voice, a primitive look, a lank thin person, and a large wig, he added the cunning and cant of an itinerant preacher.'[17] Avarice is his major vice; he steals Anna's inheritance when she is left as a child in his care. Avarice in conjunction with sanctimoniousness also characterizes the Methodists featured in *Walsingham, or, The Pupil of Nature* (1797) by Mary Robinson (1756–1800), who claimed Welsh descent on her mother's side.[18] In the novel, a Methodist landlord, 'inordinately addicted' to alcohol, bullies his tenants including a penurious poet who pleads, 'Consider my infants; if you drive them into the street they must perish!'[19] His 'sanctified persecutor' assures him that 'The Lord will protect *them* . . . But *I* must be *paid!*'[20] Robinson married the illegitimate son of Howel Harris's brother, Thomas Harris; she derides her Welsh Methodist father-in-law in her *Memoirs* as one who 'would frequently fine the rustics (for he was a justice of the peace, and had been Sheriff of the county) when he heard them swear, though every third sentence he uttered was attended by an oath that made his hearers shudder'.[21] An avaricious Methodist hypocrite also features in Robert Evans's *The Stranger; or, Llewellyn Family* (1798): the hero Marmaduke while trying to earn a living in London is cheated of the rewards of his literary labours by the 'enthusiast' Mr Holiword. Mr Fairpage, an honest editor, later informs him that Holiword is 'one of the greatest villains in all Westminster; a man who makes use of religion for no other purpose than to deceive the ignorant and well-meaning'.[22]

A more sustained exposition of the evils of Methodism is central to *Fitzmaurice* (1800) by William Frederick Williams, the author of *The Witcheries of Craig Isaf* (1805) discussed in the fifth chapter of this book. Edward Fitzmaurice, the novel's hero, is disinherited when his rich aunt Deborah takes as her second husband the Reverend Mr Tone, 'who had a call by the spirit from selling herrings'.[23] Methodism drives Deborah to near madness: 'her piety now grew outrageous, and some of her friends actually thought her a proper object of confinement; an idea her husband was not willing to discourage'.[24] Eventually, Edward receives a pathetic letter from his aunt telling him that 'I am locked up in a garret; my wicked husband will kill me . . . do pray come and let me out.' When Edward hurries to the rescue, the Reverend Tone, inebriated in the parlour in the company of his mother and grandmother, tries to persuade him that his aunt is in the country. '"'Tis false," cried Edward . . . "hypocrite! I insist on seeing her." "Here's language to the elect!" muttered the women as well as they could articulate.' Mrs Tone is eventually discovered, locked up and bound in the garret; penitent after her release she confesses to her nephew that she had suppressed her first husband's will in his favour: 'as I was told the elect could do no wickedness I thought myself very justifiable'.[25] The notion that antinomianism was a Gothic creed was thus well established in popular fiction and drama long before the publication of Hogg's novel.

The religious revivals which swept Wales periodically throughout the nineteenth century, culminating in the 1904–5 revival, incited further literary critiques. In 1863–6, after the 1859 revival, the Welsh-language periodical of the Anglican church *Yr Haul* (The Sun) serialized the mock memoir *Wil Brydydd y Coed* by Brutus, the pen-name of the periodical's editor David Owen (1795–1866), an ex-Baptist preacher from Llŷn, excommunicated for attempting to gain money through false pretences. From his new home with the Anglicans, Brutus penned a number of satires deriding his former Nonconformist brethren and their itinerant preachers and rogue deacons; *Wil* features a preacher who incites his audiences to such impassioned worship that women are regularly carried out from his services in hysterics. The preacher takes advantage of their vulnerability, but when he is accused of fathering a child by one of his flock, and of trying to persuade her to abort it, his deacons succeed in whitewashing his name. Nevertheless, to some of his clearer-headed neighbours his crimes are evident enough: 'The fiend is certainly in Wil,' says Siencyn to Dai Luke, who agrees 'Yes, the devil himself, and not one of his agents, is in him.' (*'Mae'r cythraul yn sicr yn Wil'* . . . *'Ydyw, y mae'r diawl ei hun, ac nid un o'i agents, ynddo.'*)[26]

Revivalism also leads to sexual licentiousness and insanity in Allen Raine's novel of the 1904–5 revival, *Queen of the Rushes* (1906), in which Nance Rees's reason gives way under the heady influences of the revival along with the less elevated pressures of her tumultuous emotional life. When a body recovered from the sea is thought to be Nance's, her friend Gwenifer, at the inquest called to investigate the death, testifies as to Nance's derangement, telling the Coroner that 'the Diwygiad [revival] had touched her heart so deep her mind was not strong enough to bear it'.[27] The 1847 reports' accusation against the chapels, that their 'night prayer-meetings, and the intercourse which ensues in returning home' resulted in illicit sexual liaisons,[28] is endorsed in this text in which Nance is roused to adulterous love for a member of her congregation and tries unsuccessfully to woo him on the walk home from heated revival meetings which her husband, the novel's hero, disdains to attend. In another novel of the 1904–5 revival *A Prophet of Wales* (1905) by Max Baring, the pseudonym of Charles Messent (1857–

1929), it is, however, the sincerely intentioned revivalist himself, rather than one of his flock, who is reduced to madness by the clash between sexual and spiritual enthrallment. Believing that he has inadvertently killed his married temptress by thrusting her from him over a cliff edge, the Reverend David Llewellyn leaves his 'severe-looking' pulpit in Rheobath Chapel, 'in itself a menace to sin, and a fit tower from which to hurl denunciation on the sinner', and takes 'the penitents' pew' publically to confess that he has 'sold myself to the devil! . . . Can't you see the brand of Cain on my forehead?', before rushing out to commit suicide in the lake in which he supposed his victim had drowned.[29]

The Devil is in Zion with a vengeance in these texts; together they construct a stereotype of the Nonconformist – in particular, the Calvinist Methodist – preacher and chapel deacon as at best incapable of resisting impulses which according to their teachings are satanic, and at worst as criminally hypocritical, lascivious and avaricious. Cloaking all vices under the whitewash of antinomian-ism, they present themselves as of the elect, and hence incapable of wrong-doing. Members of their flock are either hounded to madness by the contradictions in their leaders' behaviour or adopt similarly hypocritical positions themselves. But the writers who con-structed this stereotype were in the main Anglican participants in that bitter clash between church and chapel which was a ubiquitous aspect of nineteenth-century Welsh life; from the Nonconformists' point of view, misrepresentation was but to be expected of an Anglican portraying chapel people. Caradoc Evans follows in the tradition of the chapel-blackening novelists and playwrights, but his fictions roused more horror than theirs in Wales because his were from the first presented as written by no outsider to the Welsh chapel congregations, but by 'one of themselves'. *My People* was introduced by its London publisher Andrew Melrose on the dust-jacket of its first edition as a 'realistic' picture of the Welsh peasantry by one who 'knows it' because he is of it, and whose sincere aim is 'to portray that he may make ashamed'.[30] In the many letters he published in the *Western Mail* defending his position, Caradoc Evans claimed for himself the role of social reformer, stating that 'I write because I believe that the cesspools of West Wales should be stirred up, because I want to see my people freed from religious tyranny, because I love my country so much that I would exhibit her sores that they may be healed.'[31] 'His people', however, found it difficult to accept his claim at face value, in part because his publications were proving popular with English audiences who saw them as validations of long-held racial and class stereotypes. It cannot be said of the nineteenth-century chapel-blackeners that their universal aim was the correction of social injustice; on the contrary, in many cases their critique of chapel culture arose from middle-class prejudice, evident in the many scornful references to the lowly social status of the Nonconformist preacher and his congregation. The question as to whether Caradoc Evans was but a betrayer of 'his people', a 'renegade' as Lloyd George called him,[32] or whether he was indeed haunted by a profound sense of social injustice impressed upon him in childhood which he later sought to protest against in his fictions was one which from the first divided his readers.

My People (1915) and *Capel Sion* (Zion Chapel, 1917), which focus narrowly on the supposedly typical west Wales rural village of Manteg, depict everyday Welsh life as a veritable hell on earth. There is no escape from the chapel in self-enclosed Manteg, just as there is no escape from the pit in the industrial villages. Zion's leaders proclaim themselves the messengers of a sadistic and avaricious God and feed on the superstitious worship of its impoverished congregation, bullying it into submission with the threat of hellfire. In 'A father in Sion', the deacon Sadrach Danyrefail announces that his wife Achsah is mad, and must be confined in the hayloft, and introduces his mistress into the household in her place. Achsah eventually escapes only to discover that during the period of her imprisonment six of her children have died without her knowing; her resulting bewilderment and grief make her mad indeed. Because he has been punctilious in his contributions to the chapel Sadrach's reputation is unsullied, however, and his wrongdoing goes unpunished. Similarly, in 'Lamentations', Evan Rhiw commits incest with his daughter Matilda, but manages to escape retribution even though his crime is common knowledge because, according to his chapel minister, the Reverend Davydd Bern-Davydd, God has judged that 'The man has a clean heart and an adder in his house.'[33] The 'adder' is the unfortunate Matilda, declared to have seduced her father, whose alleged 'clean heart' was demonstrated by his abundant contributions to the church funds. Women and girls are powerless in Manteg against the corrupt chapel controllers, whose care is for funds not souls. When Hannah Harelip in 'Redemption', one of the *Capel Sion* stories, realizes that her master, by whom she is pregnant, intends to marry another she threatens to denounce him in chapel but is told that 'it is against God's will for a servant to charge her master, that God does not permit them who sit in the loft of Sion to murmur against them who sit on the floor and in the high places'.[34] The God of Manteg has been constructed by his preachers and deacons in their own image as severely patriarchal and insatiate in his appetite for financial 'sacrifice'; without independent means of their own Caradoc Evans's female characters have no safe place amongst the elect, and either succumb to madness or are killed off if they dare to protest. After Siloh Penlon, 'a doltish virgin' according to the deacons of Zion chapel,[35] has been abused and left pregnant by deacon Amos, she saws through the four pillars of the chapel before a deacons' meeting, but when the loft falls Amos is uninjured: the God of Zion looks after his own.

The vitality and originality of these tales lie largely in their singular style, based, according to Caradoc Evans's own account, on a combination of the narrative mode of the Old Testament, with its magisterial brevity, and the suggestive allusiveness of the popular music hall artistes of his day.[36] Tragedies occur with shocking abruptness and very little or no emotional affect on their witnesses and perpetrators, leaving the reader half horrified, half cruelly amused. So extreme is the behaviour of the chapel leaders that it is difficult not to see them as caricatures, more comical in their exaggeration than frightening in their power: Caradoc Evans's devils in Zion approach too closely the burlesque to evoke hauntings of social injustice, for all his protests to the contrary. Yet, underlying each tale is another pervasive horror which partly accounts for the inability of Manteg's inhabitants to respond humanely to the recurring disasters which befall them. Most of them are struggling to survive, their material deprivations rendered more devastating by their universal belief that poverty is God's punishment upon them for their sins or those of their families; the fruitlessness of their incessant labour on unyielding soil is the expression of His righteous wrath. In 'The way of the earth', an aged couple, Simon, now paralysed, and Becca, now blind, have toiled throughout their lives to scrape together enough pennies from their meagre acres to win back for themselves a place in Zion, after having been excommunicated from chapel membership when their only child was born before their marriage. Having lost their savings in the attempt to save their pregnant daughter from similar disgrace, they are now 'waiting for Death' in penury, with 'no further use for life' and no prospect before them but 'sterile moorland', now growing 'wilder and weedier', out of which their 'great toil' had once made a 'fruitful garden'.[37] But at least they are spared the fate of Nanni in 'Be this her memorial' and Griffi in 'A sacrifice unto Sion' who are both reduced by the combined effects of poverty and the struggle to prove themselves worthy of Zion not simply to the status of animals and vermin, but to being the food of animals and vermin. Nanni saves from her weekly poor relief pittance of 3s. 9d. enough to buy a farewell gift of a Bible for the departing Respected Josiah Bryn-Bevan as he leaves Manteg for a pulpit elsewhere, but in so doing she reduces her own sustenance to starvation point, which she unsuccessfully attempts to stave off by eating rats. Bryn-Bevan, who cares so little for her gift that he has already passed it on to a deacon, discovers her body:

> Mishtir Bryn-Bevan went on his knees and peered at her. Her hands were clasped tightly together, as though guarding some great treasure. The minister raised himself and prised them apart with the ferrule of his walking-stick. A roasted rat revealed itself. Mishtir Bryn-Bevan stood for several moments spellbound and silent; and in the stillness the rats crept boldly out of their hiding places and resumed their attack on Nanni's face. The minister, startled and horrified, fled from the house of sacrifice.[38]

The minister's inability to respond humanely is encapsulated in his use of the stick to poke at the body of his abject worshipper, as if it were untouchable.[39] Similarly, in *Capel Sion*'s 'Sacrifice' story, Griffi, once a respected deacon at Zion, 'offended awfully in his death'. Spending all his time and energies on chapel affairs, Griffi left the farming of his land to his wife, 'who laboured until the members of her body were without feeling'.[40] After her death his avaricious son cast him out as useless; finding that he is discredited as a result in Zion, Griffi steals one of his son's pigs and feeds it with all the nourishment he can scrape together in the attempt to fatten it into a fit reconciliation offering to the chapel. But when his starved corpse is found to have been gnawed by the pig, the villagers interpret the tooth-marks as the mark of the Devil, eating his own. Poverty is literally of the Devil in these texts, yet though the reforms Caradoc Evans's dark stories most obviously ask for are religious, the injustice which they speak out against more persuasively, perhaps, is the material impoverishment and human degradation of lives left to wither in the 'green deserts' – or rather, to use Machen's phrase, 'Black Desert' – of late nineteenth-century rural Wales.

Their contemporary audiences, however, focused, with horror or delight, on Caradoc's chapel representations; during the 1920s and 1930s the notoriety of *My People* encouraged the publication of more Welsh anti-chapel fictions, many of them further fuelled by now by a psychoanalytically informed persuasion of the harmfully repressive effects of such dogmatic creeds. In the story 'Llwyd' from *A Moment of Time* (1926) by Richard Hughes (1900–76), author of *A High Wind in Jamaica* (1929) and a follower of Freud, a boy born with 'a clouded brain' is intellectually awakened by the intense delight he takes in his visions of '*ellyllon*' (goblins), which seem to him to inhabit the wild landscape about his mountain home in north Wales. Eager to know more, knocking 'with both hands on the doors of Knowledge, yelling for admittance', he speaks of his visions to his father. But the father is a chapel-goer, and 'the chapels do not hold with fairies'. Instead, he fills the boy's mind with the 'Terrors of hell', until the 'fairies, fleeing before them, vanished', and the boy regresses: 'the thunderclouds from Sinai grew solid as rock . . . blocking him in from his imaginations with their eternal adamant'.[41] Another young Welsh man ultimately blighted by his chapel creed is the collier Reuben Daniels, hero of *The Withered Root* (1927) by Rhys Davies. Daniels's career as an evangelical revivalist ends in disillusionment, sexual disgrace and early death, but he had earlier been warned by a more sophisticated friend, versed in Freudian analysis, that his religion kills the spirit of his country rather than nourishing it: 'You Welsh!' Philip Vaughan proclaims,

To me there seems to be a darkness over your land and futility in your struggles to assert your ancient nationality. Your brilliant children leave you because of the hopeless stagnation of your miserable Nonconformist towns; the religion of your chapels is a blight on the flowering souls of your young.[42]

The blight of Calvinism is also the predominant theme in *The Deacon* (1934) by Alun Llywellyn (1903–88), in which a self-tortured pillar of the chapel is eventually forced by his family's suffering to recognize the dehumanizing nature of his creed. The novel closes with a dramatic chapel scene in which the deacon Idwal Probert, with his long-suffering wife dead and the son whom he had excommunicated (for loving an illegitimate girl) a helpless invalid, confesses in public to the error of his ways before rushing out to commit suicide. He admits to his congregation that, 'I set up my will, my own will, and sought no other thing. I put the Lord's name to it and called it His commanding . . . I made him false sacrifice. It was sacrifice of those I loved.'[43] Similarly, in *Creed* (1936) by Margiad Evans, the pseudonym of Peggy Whistler (1909–58), the dark intensity of the text owes much to its use of Calvinistic imagery and vocabulary as its hero wrestles with his inhumanely exacting God, finally overcoming him in a burst of extreme feeling. Francis Dollbright shouts out wildly, 'like a man clean mad, possessed by freedom': 'Oh God, I have taken separate existence from you, and you cannot pour my one soul back into your self! . . . From your millions you have lost me, and all your aeons will never bring me back.'[44]

Creed dramatizes a general withdrawal from that intense religious involvement that had characterized nineteenth-century Wales; by the 1930s not only fictional characters but the mass of the Welsh population were freeing themselves from the grip of a Calvinist God. The chapels were emptying and it was socialism and the trade union movement which now provided the motivating drive of a distinctive Welsh culture. But that coal culture which gave birth to the militancy of the trade union movement in Wales was itself haunted; such were the everyday conditions of the miners' working lives that in the attempt to embody them the south Wales authors of the 1930s and 1940s at times abandoned their more characteristic realist mode, and explored the world of the collier and his environment using a darker and more haunted colouring than that of naturalism. The second section of this chapter discusses the use of the Gothic mode in some of these industrial fictions.

Coalfield Gothic

The everyday working conditions of those employed in the coal industry, at its productive peak in south Wales in 1911, readily evoked horror. A Blaenavon collier, William Henry Taylor, who himself published a novel (*The Cheated Death*, 1925), described in matter-of-fact but chilling detail the dangers of coal extraction:

> if you had a pretty active roof . . . the coal would crush and it would be easy to mine, and your chief worry would be control of the roof. But other times you would have to hole or undercut it. You would lie on your side and hack away and hole under it as much as a yard. And then there were various methods of getting it down, sometimes you would have to sprag it . . . and then you would withdraw these sprags . . . you would hear groans and cracklings and it would fall. Otherwise you would have to drill a hole and put gunpowder in or use clamps and wedge . . . and that would exert pressure on the coal and eventually bring it down.[45]

Deep underground under an 'active roof' with nothing but 'sprags' (i.e. wooden pit props) to keep it up, and under necessity to bring that roof down periodically as part of the process of coal extraction, the colliers worked daily under threat of death or burial alive, knowledge of which would of necessity have been repressed by their communities under 'normal' conditions, only to flare out at the next disaster. As we saw in the last chapter, the fear of being 'buried alive' is, according to Freud, to many 'the most uncanny thing of all';[46] unsurprisingly, therefore, the fact that their fathers and friends were compelled by economic necessity to live under such a threat haunted the imaginations of a generation of Welsh writers. In fictions usually penned decades after the heyday of coal production in Wales, when the mining industry was already in decline, the colliers' children recorded a haunted remembrance of 'the price of coal'. In his short story 'The pit' (1945), Gwyn Jones, for example, portrays a man trapped underground in an old pit who becomes traumatized by his awareness of the unnatural sacrifice the mine would have demanded during its working days:

> With frightful vividness he thought of the piled-up hillside above him. Four hundred feet of unbroken rock under which to creep and creep till your lantern gave out and you were part of the dark for ever . . . [H]e had . . . the feeling . . . that some blacker shape in the darkness stretched out hands after him. 'Don't!' he cried: 'Don't!' . . . But he had given the darkness life and a power of listening – listening to his footsteps, listening to his words, listening to the horrors that tightened around his heart.[47]

A native of New Tredegar, Gwyn Jones (1907–99) was the son of a miner; through education he escaped the darkness of the pit himself, but the strangeness of the way in which his father and his colleagues earned their living clearly haunted him.

Glyn Jones (1905–95) from Merthyr was the son of a postman, not a collier, but his experience of the Depression in south Wales, which he described as 'a more agonizing experience even than the Second World War',[48] and his recollection of the maimed lives of many of those around him during his childhood who worked underground, resonates in his surreal symbolist fantasy 'The kiss' (1937). The story begins with a dead miner, lying 'deep in the coalfield . . . feeling close over his face the pressure of the imminent black rock, and the water, and the light fingering of the tall earth roofing his grave', who 'stirred out of his first death wanting faintly with two broken hands to push the pitch night back into the stones'.[49] Though 'there was no voice to call him Lazarus out of the rock, to bring his feet rotting with death out on to the grass again', he succeeds in reaching the surface, and delights in the simple realities of life and light:

> Inched against his opening eyelids was a stem growing from the green tangle of grasses. It was a daisy . . . The workman, smiling and detached, forgetting in his pleasure his death and his burial, sat up to look at it twisting towards the morning sun.[50]

He longs 'to see the bodies of men and women once again with passionate and even commonplace movements as the restless urgency used them'.[51] But the first person he encounters is his brother whose hand has been mangled and shattered into pulp, presumably also through a pit accident. He helps his brother home; their mother who 'recognized the dead voice of her son' is agitated when he asks to see his brother's wound. '"No, no," she cried, almost hysterically, "don't undo those bandages again. You mustn't do it. It is terrible. It is terrible."' She cannot bear to see their wounded lives uncovered. But 'don't be afraid of an action for healing' her son tells her, as he reverently unwinds the bloodied cloth: exposure is necessary if the healing of the wrong is to begin.[52] When the hand is finally exposed, however, it is so terribly damaged, 'a shapeless black mass of stinking flesh like some bad inward part cut from an animal', that the mother faints at the sight. But her son '[v]ery tenderly, with tears running down his face . . . bent forward and kissed the putrid flesh of his brother's hand'.[53] It is an act of compassion, born out of the darkness which the collier has endured, but what it exposes as the everyday conditions of labour in the coalfield is a ghastly spectacle of horror.

For those who, like Glyn Jones and his family, lived above the pits and alongside colliers but had no experience of mining at first hand, the thought of how their neighbours earned their living in the dangerous tunnels branching underneath their streets may well have pressed upon their imaginations more hauntingly than it did on the miners themselves, precisely because they had no actual experience of pit work. The strangeness of the colliers' daily disappearance down the mine shaft was not for them demystified and rendered 'normal' by the day-to-day routine and camaraderie of the workplace. In his autobiography *Print of a Hare's Foot* (1969), Rhys Davies, similarly positioned as the son of a Blaenclydach grocer with a shop just above Tonypandy in the Rhondda, records that he thought of the colliers 'as a race apart':

> The race dwelt in the perpetual night of down-under and, day-shift or night-shift, sat less in the sun than other men. Ghosts summoned from the underworld by Odysseus came to my mind when, one dawn, I saw night-shift men going home from the Clydach pits . . .

Coming nearer the black-faced cavalcade brought subterranean tangs
into the new air.[54]

Rhys Davies's stories and novels characteristically feature the surface
world of the pit villages; his characters rarely go underground themselves and yet all their lives are shadowed by the pit. In 'The last
struggle' (1946), Megan Pugh, a collier's wife who is out of love
with her husband Sam Two Fingers (his hand too was maimed in
a pit accident), believes she has escaped from the pit's grasp when
Sam is trapped underground and all hope of his rescue is abandoned.
She leaves the village immediately and takes a holiday spending
some of the insurance money, but is appalled on her return to
discover that Sam has unexpectedly survived. When she sees at their
door, 'the ghost of Sam, grey and silent', 'for her it was a dead man
looking at her. He was still grey from his burial, and thinner, and
in his eyes lurked that stagnant glow of one not fully back in the
world.' The terror of his resurrection renders him more demonically
inescapable to her than ever: 'That night she went down to the last
depths of the world.'[55]

In effect, in Rhys Davies's stories, all the inhabitants of the pit
villages live in the 'depths' underground, not only the colliers. In
a story tellingly entitled 'The pits are on the top' (1942), a young
couple on a bus journey overhear their fellow passengers, one of
whom carries a funeral wreath, discussing a recent death from silicosis and referring to the ubiquity of the disease in the neighbourhood: 'There's two men got it in our street," says one: 'You can
hear them coughing across the road.' At this, 'the young man with
the girl covered his mouth and coughed hard. His girl had sat still
as a rabbit.'[56] She is haunted by her foreboding that her lover has
not escaped the collier's disease either; the 'pits are on the top' and
they too are its victims. As they leave the bus, the other female
passengers nod to each other 'knowingly, with a little grimace of the
mouth and lowering of the eyelids'. The girl sees the look, recognizes its relation to 'the fear knotted deep in her', and is angered:
'It's . . . it's their *way*,' she tries to explain to her collier; '"Sitting
there and . . . And looking at me when we came out, looking at
me like as if I'd soon be one of them . . . even," she added, the
hysteria getting a hold, "carrying a wreath in my lap!"'[57] The terrible

acceptance on the part of her fellow passengers of early death as inevitable, as part of the price of coal, embitters her more at that moment than the likely death itself. The women's passivity in the face of such injustice and their assumption that she too will have to resign herself to such a widowed fate as theirs is too much for her to bear. But she too quickly represses and covers up her recognition, telling herself instead that once they're married she will look after her collier.

The same doomed atmosphere of incipient and inevitable early death also envelops the pit villagers in another of Rhys Davies's tales 'The dark world' (1942), though here the key death is that of a young wife, not her collier husband. In fact, the lives of the miners' wives were also all too frequently cut short. Life expectancy was lower for women than men, for all the health hazards of the men's employment; women died earlier, worn to the bone by childbirth and the incessant effort to maintain standards of hygiene before the establishment of pit baths or domestic water supply. In *Our Mothers' Land*, Dot Jones provided statistical evidence demonstrating that the death rates for valleys' women of child-bearing age were from 1890 to 1910 'significantly higher than for men', in contrast with the figures for England and Wales as a whole where the mortality rates for women were lower than for men in every age group. 'Such a "traditional" mortality pattern is characteristic of pre-industrial communities,' she comments: 'Like living in an undeveloped economy, early marriage to miners was not good for a woman's health.'[58] In 'The dark world', Rhys Davies captures a young boy's dawning recognition of this characteristic coalfield mortality pattern, and what it means for the community as a whole. Two bored Rhondda boys, Thomas and Jim, indulge their macabre taste for visiting the homes of the newly dead, on the pretext of 'paying their respects'; 'they would search through the endless rows of houses for windows covered with white sheets, the sign that death was within', and find them readily enough.[59] But one evening, unexpectedly, they view the corpse of a young woman, with her dead baby at her side, who had in life been known to Thomas, and the scene changes his outlook, bringing home to him the reality of the grief and loss death entails, and the manner in which his community is peculiarly blighted. He feels terror, a sense of 'nightmare menace coming nearer'.[60] As he emerges afterwards out onto the terraced street, it seems to him that

> all the night was weeping. The dark alley was an avenue of the dead, the close-shuttered houses were tombs . . . There was something horrible in the dark world. . . . At the top of the hill leading to his home he paused in anguish. The bare high place was open to the hostile heavens, a lump of earth open like a helpless face to the blows of the wind and the rain.[61]

It is the helplessness of these communities – trapped in suffering and dread – that emerges most strongly from these stories and gives them the power to evoke that haunting sense of profound social injustice, which the characters glimpse fleetingly, perhaps, but devastatingly before they resume everyday life again. For the most part they are habituated to the conditions of their labour: 'The cross of custom held us', says Ken Etheridge (1911–81) of the pit village communities in his 1940 poem 'Blades in the Slag'.[62] It was during the early decades of the twentieth century, however, the period in which these stories are set, that the south Wales workers and their union leaders developed their understanding of the root cause of these injustices to such effect that they transformed the political face of Wales. In the 1900 general election, Keir Hardie in Merthyr won the first Westminster seat for what was then the Independent Labour Party; by the 1945 general election, twenty-seven of Wales's thirty-five parliamentary seats were held by Labour candidates. The analytic tool they relied upon to cut through the confounding sense of doomed helplessness was, of course, Marxism, which explained to them the economic and psychological ways by means of which capitalism prevailed, and the manner in which the apparently helpless masses

> grow attached to their masters, like a herd of slaves or horses. The hereditary masters are the purpose of this whole society. This world belongs to them . . . and they stand where their feet have grown, on the necks of those political animals that know of no other destination than to be attached to the masters and subject to them, to be at their disposal.[63]

The south Wales author who most effectively fictionalized Marx's Gothic metaphors, illustrating the manner in which the 'tradition of all the dead generations weighs like a nightmare on the brain of the living' while capital still functions as 'dead labour which, vampire-like, lives only by sucking living labour',[64] was, arguably, Gwyn Thomas, from Cymmer, near Porth in the Rhondda, the youngest of twelve children of an unemployed miner and exhausted mother, who died shortly after his birth. An oppressed community, suffering but unable to break free of its hereditary masters, is central to his 1946 novella 'Oscar', set in the industrial villages of south Wales during the Depression years. Oscar, like his father before him, is the local capitalist exploiter and landowner, the landlord of the village's lines of terraced houses, and also the owner of the mountain above them and the coal tip on which his tenants scramble for fuel. As unemployed miners they sustain themselves and pay his rents by picking coal off his tip for five pence a bag, which he sells on for one and seven pence; Oscar patrols the tip with his gun and shoots to kill if he finds any tenant absconding with a lump of coal for his own use. The whole community, according to Oscar's servant Lewis, the story's first-person narrator, is bitterly conscious of its subordination and dehumanization; like Lewis, it has 'become a kind of shadow to this Oscar',[65] and yet cannot will itself to take the ample opportunities Oscar's heavy drinking and womanizing habits afford to free itself of this monstrous and literally murderous incubus. Lewis's mother, who lives in one of Oscar's terraces, is widowed, her collier husband dead of lung disease; although she despises her son for accepting the post of the capitalist's personal servant, he can find no other paying occupation with which to support the two of them. Like the rest of the villagers, he knows of 'no other destination' than to be at Oscar's disposal. 'The poor hug to their heart all the yesterdays they know have not been lived and the burden is a heavy one,' says Lewis; 'only those whose poverty seems to have existed from the earth's beginning have to put up with being dragged below the surface by the dead chains of past years, past days. But Oscar was free.'[66]

Lewis's friend Danny thinks similarly; though he knows 'somebody'd be doing the world a kindness to put [Oscar] out of the way' he also is paralysed by 'the tradition of all the dead generations'.

'You can't be afraid for years and years and then say: "To hell with fear,"' he tells Lewis. 'It's not as simple, boy. It stays, like blood and bone, part of what makes you live.'[67] All the villagers are 'going around with a rope on their necks jerking them to a halt every time they tried moving forward'.[68] At one point in the tale, however, Danny is suddenly provided with an opportunity to rid the village of its incubus. When Oscar attacks him with a whip for attempting to take coal from his tip, Danny succeeds in pulling Oscar from his horse to the ground, and stands above him with a stone. 'If I had any sense,' he said, 'I'd bring this down over your head and if I did that, I'd have the feeling I'd done one useful thing on earth. But I don't like giving pain. People of my sort don't as a rule. We just get it . . . and we pass over the feeling how the hell we stood it for so long.'[69] So he lets the moment pass, and Oscar promptly shoots at him and brings about his death. His distraught widow, Hannah, swears that she is 'going to kill that bastard of an Oscar . . . I'll do it just to get clean again',[70] but once more when the opportunity, engineered by Lewis, arrives she cannot bring herself to do so. Lewis realizes that

> people who have lived in places like those Terraces and who have been kicked around for the sole benefit of others, have been afraid of things for so many years and for such good cause that they get into the habit of being afraid even when their brains are screaming at them that there is no sense in their fear.[71]

Finally, Oscar is destroyed, not in the end by any act of violence but simply by the withdrawal of labour, a one-man strike; Lewis is with him as, drunk and obese, he clambers home from the village across his mountain top and the alienated servant allows him, unassisted for once, to proceed on his own momentum and topple over the mountain edge into a deep quarry. But even this passive aggression, for all its success, is enough to fill the servant's mind with a profound negativity: all he desires after Oscar's fall is

> to talk in the dark with that quiet, distant woman who was my mother, and who was no doubt wise about why there was so little

peace in the strange tormented area that separated me from Oscar and Danny, the shrinking ditch between the stirring and the resting.[72]

It feels like death to rid his world of Oscar, so much has servicing Oscar become his identity.

In 'Simeon' (1946), Gwyn Thomas creates another Oscar: Simeon is also a landowner, inhabiting a large house on the higher slopes of a mountain overlooking the pit village from which he draws his servants. One of those servants, Ben, is also the narrator of this tale and he too experiences himself as bound by the labour of generations to the role. 'There had been so many slaves in my family we got more pliable from father to son,' he says:[73]

> My father always said patience dampened the ground at your feet so that your foot trod on it without a sound, and people never heard you as you passed on your way to the grave, and you weren't bothered as much by people then as you would be if you went stamping on the hard ground like a self-important horse, drawing attention to yourself.[74]

But even this taught patience is eroded when the narrator learns the dark secrets of Simeon's household: two of his cowed daughters, trapped in the house, have been raped by their father and have had a child each by him, living dead children who looked 'terribly like Simeon, and although they were kids their faces looked old . . . they sat, as silent as if they were dead nearly'.[75] So hungry for complete ownership is Simeon that he has drained the blood even of his own kith and kin, making them his dark shadow. Finally, when Eleanor, Simeon's third daughter who as yet knows nothing of her father's crimes, returns to the house from which her older sister had sent her away for safety, and Ben realizes that she too is now endangered, he determines to kill Simeon, but once again finds that he cannot do it: 'my limbs were frozen . . . I shouted to myself that now was the time and I couldn't wait any longer, but my voice just laughed at itself . . . and I still couldn't move'.[76] It is Eleanor herself, not as indoctrinated in the ways of subservience as the other members of the household, who in the end succeeds in killing her father, simply by holding in front of herself a knife onto which the momentum of his incestuous passion dashes him.

What Gwyn Thomas fictionalizes in these Gothic tales is the difficulty of acting in the light of a perceived social injustice to which a community has adapted itself to such an extent that deprivation has become its 'natural' habitat. Following Marx again, he suggests with some optimism at the close of both 'Oscar' and 'Simeon' that should the haunted community but withdraw its collaboration and stand firm, the oppressive system would be toppled by the momentum of its own deregulated greed. In 1946, however, such optimism must have seemed warranted: the Labour landslide of the 1945 general election had produced a government which promised to fulfil the demands of Welsh socialism and which did indeed bring about the nationalization of the coal industry in 1947 and the development, under Aneurin Bevan, of the National Health Service. A decade later, though, in 1959, when the village of Capel Celyn in the Tryweryn valley was drowned by Liverpool Corporation, haunting associations with other long-term injustices were aroused, as the next chapter illustrates.

4

Land of the Living Dead (1940s–1997)

୬

In 'The Zombie-makers', written in 1969–70 by Abergwesyn's poet Ruth Bidgood (1922–) but not published until 2012, the building of reservoirs by English city corporations in mid Wales and the forestation of its hillsides which, she says, have together 'cut the heart out' of the area are compared with the killing of Llywelyn, the last indigenous prince of Wales:

> Seventh hell is for the zombie-makers
> who cut the heart out while it faintly beats,
> and clamp whole valleys to a heart-and-lung machine
> of reservoir and forestry – work now, die later –
> then switch off. As the blood congeals,
> here come the corpse cosmeticians, bland embalmers,
> to prettify the violated body
> with labelled forest trail and picnic area,
> and fake a ghoulish animation
> that is not life, and mocks at death.
>
> If you must kill a land,
> let it die, then.
> Llewelyn's head, a death-in-life on Cheapside once,
> rotted at last to the dignity
> of dust, like the sundered body
> under the altar in remote Cwmhir.[1]

The reference to Llywelyn's head, displayed in London as a conqueror's trophy, underlines the political thrust of the poem: the lifeblood of Wales is still being drained in accordance with decisions made elsewhere and outside its control. This is not a land of the living but a land of the living dead, with its animated corpse prettified and offered up for tourist consumption. 'The Zombie-makers' bears comparison with 'Reservoirs' (1968) by R. S. Thomas (1913–2000) in which the poet asks 'Where can I go, then, from the smell / Of decay, from the putrefying of a dead / Nation?' But in Thomas's poem blame for the nation's decay is attributed as much, if not more, to the Welsh themselves than to their rulers. The reservoirs of Wales, with their Welsh-speaking villages far down below the bland surface of the water, constitute the troubled subconscious of the nation itself in this poem: 'the English' have but elbowed 'our language / Into the grave that we have dug for it.'[2] Wales and her language are dying, and the Welsh themselves, repelled and turning away from their decaying heritage, are complicit in their demise.

Concern as to the fate of the language haunted many Welsh writers in the middle decades of the twentieth century, with good reason. From 1900 to 1970, the percentage of Welsh-language speakers had continued to decline precipitously with each census figure, losing an average 4 to 5 per cent in each decade, from 49.9 per cent of Wales's population in 1901 to 20.9 per cent in 1971. To be Welsh-speaking increasingly came to be represented, particularly in Welsh-language literature, as a nightmarish condition. In 1935, the poet Gwenallt (David James Jones, 1899–1968), for example, asked his country,

> *Paham y rhoddaist inni'r tristwch hwn,*
> *A'r boen fel pwysau plwm ar gnawd a gwaed?*
> *Dy iaith ar ein hysgwyddau megis pwn,*
> *A'th draddodiadau'r hual am ein traed? . . .*
> *Nid wyt ond hunllef yn dy wlad dy hun,*
> *A'th einioes yn y tir ond breuddwyd gwrach.*

> Why have you given us this misery,
> The pain like leaden weights on flesh and blood?
> Your language on our shoulders like a load,
> And your traditions shackles round our feet? . . .

You are merely a nightmare in your own land,
And your survival but a witch's dream.[3]

Similarly, in 1949, T. H. Parry-Williams (1887–1975) in his poem 'Hon' (This [female] one, i.e. Wales) refers to Wales as a kind of succubus which survives only through feeding off her own children. Simply to dwell in the homeland is to be haunted: the poet sees 'between earth and heaven, / apparitions and voices all about the place' (*'wele, rhwng llawr a ne / Mae lleisiau a drychiolaethau ar hyd y lle'*.). He tries to shrug off the grasp of his country but that only makes her dig in her nails deeper: 'I feel the claws of Wales tearing at my breast,' he says, 'God save me, I can't escape from this one.' (*Ac mi glywaf grafangau Cymru'n dirdynnu fy mron / Duw a'm gwaredo, ni allaf ddianc rhag hon.*)[4] Wales is a witch's dream that refuses to die; the Welsh might, indeed, have dug a grave for their culture, but the corpse keeps clawing its way to the surface, to excruciate the living with the sight of its decay. In the middle years of the century, these dark preoccupations found expression in Gothic fictions in which the protagonists are represented as haunted by Welsh history: the princes and warriors of pre-conquest Wales rise from the dead not so much to encourage the modern Welsh as to castigate them for their heedlessness and neglect of their language and culture. The first two sections of this chapter explore representative examples of such material, focusing primarily on Welsh-language fictions. By the 1980s, however, when resistance to Margaret Thatcher's government found expression in the Meibion Glyndŵr second-home house-burning campaign, this apparent Welsh reawakening seems itself to have caused some unease amongst English-language readers, for whom Wales is represented once again in Gothic fictions as a dark vampiric country, ready to suck the blood out of any unwary stranger who crosses its borders. The last section of this chapter examines a few anglophone texts located on the border between Wales and England which exemplify this tendency.

The return of the repressed

A volume that established a precedent for many which followed it was *Chwedlau'r Meini* (Legends of the Stones, 1946) by Meuryn (Robert John Rowlands, 1880–1967), a poet and journalist from Caernarfon; in it the narrator records the strange influences ascribed to some of the old stones in his neighbourhood. He had been warned to stay away from the *Carreg Saethau* (Stone of Arrows) on which prehistoric hunters sharpened their arrow-heads: a shepherd told him that he had once encountered the ghosts of his forefathers near its site, and heard them wail with grief at the plight of the fatherland. 'The cry I heard rose from the great ravine below me, as if the lid of Annwn [the Celtic Underworld] had been lifted, and it contained in itself all the pain and despair of pre-history,' said the shepherd (*Yr oedd y waedd a glywais i yn codi o'r ceunant mawr otanaf, fel petai caead Annwn wedi ei godi ac yn cynnwys ynddi ei hun holl wae ac anobaith y cyn-oesoedd*).[5] But the narrator's curiosity is aroused by such a claim, and he often loiters in the neighbourhood of the stone, until he himself one day has a similarly supernatural encounter:

> '*Yn y cwmwd hwn,*' *meddwn wrthyf fy hun, 'y bu fy nghyndadau yn byw erioed . . . a thystia pob diferyn o waed sydd yn fy ngwythiennau y byddai pob copa walltog ohonynt hwy ar y blaen ym mhob gornest – ym mhob ymgyrch i amddiffyn eu treftadaeth rhag y gelyn.' Yna digwyddodd peth rhyfedd iawn . . . Gwelais ddyn mawr tal, mewn gwisg . . . o'r cynfyd, yn dyfod ar letraws y foel yn unionsyth tuag at y Garreg Saethau . . . Yr oedd ei lygaid mawr yn fflamio yn ei ben . . . ac yr oedd yn amlwg i mi mai myfi oedd achos ei gynddaredd . . . [Y]n yr awr gyfyng honno y clywais innau'r Waedd.*[6]

'In this neighbourhood,' I said to myself, 'my forefathers have always lived . . . and every drop of blood in my being testifies to the fact that they would have been to the forefront in any battle – in any attempt to defend their inheritance from the enemy.' Then a very strange thing happened . . . I saw a large tall man, in prehistoric costume, coming across the ridge immediately towards the Stone of Arrows. His great eyes flared in his head . . . and it was clear that I was the object of his wrath . . . In that tense hour I too heard the Cry.

The spectre's appearance is very familiar to the narrator; it closely resembles an old photograph of one of his ancestors of whom he has often been told 'you are exactly like that old man' (*Yr wyt ti'r un ffunud â'r hen ddyn yna*),[7] but now the family features are ablaze with a wrath directed against him because he has not defended his inheritance as he should.

A sense of profound shame at not having adequately defended the foundations of one's identity against threat also dominates an iconic novel of the early 1960s, *Un Nos Ola Leuad* (One Moonlit Night, 1961) by Caradog Prichard (1904–80). When this novel was published, the experience of political impotence was troubling Wales in relation to the drowning of Cwm Tryweryn and its Welsh-speaking village Capel Celyn to provide a reservoir for Liverpool. For once, all Welsh MPs had supported the popular campaign to prevent the flooding of the valley, but to no avail: the dam-building went ahead, but the spectre of Cwm Tryweryn as a national disgrace which should never have been allowed to happen remained to haunt and fuel later independence campaigns. Dark lakes with shameful secrets lying below their desolate waters play an important role in Prichard's novel, in which a young boy growing into adolescence becomes obsessed by his failure to halt his mother's slide into madness. Set in a slate-quarrying village in north Wales just after the First World War, the tale is told from the child's point of view; he knows his mother is lonely, poverty-stricken and despairing, and that the community about them can offer little succour, shattered as it is by both the demise of the slate-quarrying industry and the losses suffered in the war. His sense of impotence becomes a repressed agony, intensified by the experience of having to commit his mother to mental hospital, and finally vents itself when a local girl, who has herself been much abused, offers him intimacy. Gently, he kills the girl as if to put her out of her misery, is sentenced and imprisoned, but returns to the village as soon as he is released, to the nearby Black Lake, which haunts him throughout the text and seems to speak to him with the voice of a deposed and despairing queen, yearning for an avenger of her wrongs. 'My kingdom is the grievous waters that lie beyond the ultimate sorrow,' he hears the queen of the Black Lake say: 'To fight and to lose and to win and to be vanquished was my lot; to battle and to conquer and to squirm beneath the boot of the oppressor.' (*Fy nheyrnas yw'r dyfroedd gofidus a orffwys y tu hwnt i'r gofid eithaf . . . Ymladd a cholli ac ennill a cholli fu fy rhan; brwydro a gorchfygu ac ymgordeddu dan sathr y treisiwr.*') The conquered queen appears to express the woes of his mother, of the girl he killed, of his community and his country, and his own sense of a separate identity is swallowed by her excess of despair. 'I swallowed the sun,' says the queen at last, 'and took the moon for a pillow to my resting place' (*Minnau a lyncais yr haul; a'r lloer a gymerais yn obennydd i'm gorweddfan*).[8] Night, death and the abandonment of hope pervade the novel.

A year after *One Moonlit Night* was published the death of the language in which it was written was predicted in a 1962 radio broadcast by Saunders Lewis, the leader of Plaid Cymru, the Welsh National Party which he had founded in 1925. Informed by census evidence showing the continuing rapid decline in the numbers of Welsh speakers, he saw it as inevitable that

> Welsh will end as living language, should the present trend continue, about the beginning of the twenty-first century . . . Thus the policy laid down as the aim of the English Government in Wales in the measure called the Act of Union of England and Wales in 1536 will at last have succeeded.

He concludes the talk by asserting that it will need 'nothing less than a revolution to restore the Welsh language in Wales. Success is only possible through revolutionary methods.'[9] One immediate result of this warning was the formation of Cymdeithas yr Iaith Gymraeg, the Welsh Language Society, and the beginning of its activist programme of non-violent law-breaking protests. The struggle of the Welsh language and culture to survive and to retain its place in the modern world was also reflected in the novels of Islwyn Ffowc Elis (1924–), who had stood unsuccessfully as a Plaid Cymru candidate in a 1962 by-election. In his *Y Gromlech yn yr Haidd* (The Cromlech in the Barley, 1970), Bill Henderson, an Englishman farming in Wales, is angered by the presence on his land of three large standing stones, the remains of a Celtic burial site, and he determines to get rid of them. But from the great holes left after the stones have been pulled down, primeval forces arise which take

inexorable vengeful hold of the farmer. 'They're everywhere!' he
cries. "Hairy, knotted, satanic things, rising and still rising from the
holes I made' (*'Maen nhw ym mhobman!* . . . *'Pethau blewog, cymalog,
satanaidd, yn codi ac yn dal i godi o'r tyllau wnes i'*). Then, he addresses
the released forces directly:

> *O'r gorau. Mi'ch codais chi o'ch bedd. Ond fe gawsoch ddigon o amser i farw.*
> *Tair mil a hanner o flynyddoedd. Ydy hynny ddim yn ddigon ichi?* . . . *Sut*
> *roeddwn i i wybod ych bod chi yma o hyd?* . . . *'Dydych chi ddim i fod yma.*
> *Mae'ch amser chi wedi hen fynd heibio. Does dim lle ichi yn y byd 'ma*
> *heddiw. Dydyn ni ddim yn credu mewn pethau fel chi* . . . *Na, peidiwch .*
> *. . peidiwch â dod i mewn imi* . . . *gadewch lonydd i 'mhen i, beth bynnag!*
> *F'ymennydd i, Henderson, ydy hwn!*[10]

All right, I disturbed you in your graves. But you had plenty of time
to die. Three and a half thousand years. Is that not enough for you?
How was I to know you were here still? You're not supposed to be
here. Your time has long gone by. There's no place for you in this
world today. We don't believe in things like you . . . No, don't, don't
come inside me, leave me alone, my head, at least. This is my brain,
Henderson's!

The disturbed dead represent the continuing vitality of a Celtic
language that has had thousands of years in which to die but which
remains 'here still' to appal Henderson. Soon, its released powers
have indeed possessed the brain of the English farmer, and taken
over his identity. He can no longer recognize his wife, and says to
her 'Who are you? Why don't you leave me in peace in my grave
– I, Kia, and my children and the children of my children. What
did we do to you? What harm did we do?' (*'Pwy ydych chi? Pam na
adewch chi lonydd imi yn 'y medd?* . . . *Y fi, Kia, a 'mhlant, a phlant 'y
mhlant? Beth wnaethon ni i chi? Pa ddrwg wnaethon ni?'*) According to
his wife, even his physical appearance has changed: 'It's as if his skin
is getting darker every minute,' she says. 'He looks different . . . he
looks like a primitive savage. *This is not Bill!*' (*'Mae fel petai'i groen
yn mynd yn dywyllach bob munud . . . Mae'i olwg o'n wahanol . . . yn
debyg i . . . anwariad cyntefig . . . Nid Bil ydy hwn!'*).[11] Her husband
has become entirely possessed, body and soul, by the spirit of a
long-dead Ancient British chieftain who now castigates her for

troubling his rest. In tales like these the repressed powers of an old culture conquered 700 years before and told there was 'no place' for it in the modern world return to haunt the inmates of present-day Wales.

In anglophone texts of the post-war period, it is, however, the modern-day Welsh rather than their undead ancestors who shake off their subordination and reclaim their land from English incomers. Class and ethnic animosities surface in violent guise in *Tales of the Squirearchy* (1946) by Nigel Heseltine (1916–95); just as Caradoc Evans's Gothicized the world of the Welsh chapels in which he had been reared, so Heseltine renders as a Gothic nightmare a world with which he was intimately familiar. He was brought up by his paternal grandmother Edith Buckley-Jones and her second husband Walter in Cefnbryntalch Hall near Llandyssil, Montgomeryshire, his parents having virtually abandoned him; his father, Philip Heseltine, who was later to win fame as a composer under the name Peter Warlock and who was himself a student of the occult, died probably by his own hand when his son was fourteen.[12] From the final decades of the nineteenth century, with the establishment of the county and local councils, the gentry of Wales had been slowly been forced to relinquish much of their former influence and prestige; as M. Wynn Thomas puts it, in an essay on *Tales of the Squirearchy*, 'an interloping English class, a colonial relic, not only surviving but still enjoying social privileges and exercising social authority' was 'shorn by an erstwhile Welsh peasantry of the political and economic power on which it had depended for so many centuries'.[13] *Tales of the Squirearchy* fictionalizes this demise; in it the gentry's attempt to continue with the rituals of ruling-class leisure as if their world was not in fact falling into ghost-riddled absurdity is exposed as darkly comic.

In 'Cam-Vaughan's shoot', for example, Cam-Vaughan, the local landowner, has invited his friends, including a retired army general, to a 'shoot'; the story opens as their host greets his guests in front of his manor, Parc Gw0eledigaethau-Sais (the Park of the Englishman's Visions), 'a rolling kingdom of oaks and deer; the walls around it were forty feet high'. Cam-Vaughan and his friends are 'long men together among Welshmen', that is, among the servants, their 'beaters', whose role it is to beat the covers and frighten out the pheasants to be shot. The English, it would appear, are still in easy, long-established ascendancy over the subordinated locals: as they leave for the shoot, roaring down the four-mile drive of Parc Gweledigaethau-Sais, they scatter before them 'the stones and the mud and the few villagers who were not among the beaters, and who stood in gaping crowds at the gates of the park'. But all the while Owen, the head keeper, of whom the text pointedly says 'he's Welsh', 'grinned like an evil ghost at his masters', anticipating the reversal to come.[14] During the shoot, as the beaters beat up the birds and the gentry aim and fire, suddenly 'out among the crowded pheasants floated little balloons. The General shot and one exploded.' The beaters laugh, and follow up their mockery of the shoot by an open challenge: they stop beating the cover, and line up facing the gentry. 'Then the General raised his gun and fired; there was nothing else to do.'[15] Faced with mutiny, he can do nothing but follow his training and fire what for him and his cohorts constitutes a fatal first shot. In response to it, the loaders, who had been servicing the gentry's guns, 'ran into the wood and joined the beaters', who are also armed; together of course they easily outnumber the squire's party. 'There could be but one result. The beaters came out and beat the wounded with their sticks till they died . . . Owen slit Cam-Vaughan's throat.' Then, the servants progress in triumph back to their late master's house:

> At the brass gates of Parc Gweledigaethau-Sais Owen saluted the few villagers and they acknowledged his salute. Along the drive of the rolling park they drove singing *Swspan* [*sic*] *fach* . . . the butler took Owen's victorious arm to lead him through the leaden entrance-doors. The beaters stood around the brake stamping their cold feet on the gravel and on the brick stairway; then they followed Owen in and shut the door.[16]

The Welsh have replaced their English 'betters' with remarkable ease, as if to the manor born. The abrupt plunge from satire into horror – from balloons to bullets, as it were – exemplified in the telling of this tale is typical of Heseltine's abbreviated style, which he apparently developed under the influence of Caradoc Evans whose work he admired.[17]

The Welsh worker also achieves ascendancy over the remains of the squirearchy in *The Proud Walkers* (1955) by C. E. Vulliamy (1886–1971), this time more or less non-violently though not without supernatural aid. Colwyn Edward Vulliamy, whose ancestors came from Italy to Wales in the seventeenth century, was born to a landed family from Glasbury in Radnorshire, and published fiction under the pseudonyms Anthony Rolls and Twm Teg as well as under his given name. In *The Proud Walkers*, a devil and an angel are sent as disguised agents by their respective bosses to compete for the souls of the villagers of Llaneinioes [Soul's Parish], some of whose English residents are apparently unaware that they are not in England. When a man is killed in a bare-knuckle boxing fight Mr Sparrett, one of the local gentry, announces 'that he considered the whole affair to have been . . . a violation of all decency; by no means what you would expect in a country like England'. 'Very true,' replies the vicar, 'with a subtle indication of reproach, . . . "very true, but I'm afraid it's not as unexpected in a country like Wales"'.[18] The winner of the fight is Dafi Tyno, an unemployed collier visiting his mother in the village, who sees and falls in love with Aithra, the daughter of the local squire Percy Malworth d'Arqueville. Both devil and angel fight for Dafi's soul but as the devil can offer him riches he wins the struggle with relative ease, and in a few years Dafi has become Sir Davey Tyno, owner of a vast estate and a Cardiff office, with Aithra as his wife. *The Proud Walkers* includes an array of mock Gothic characters such as the village witch, Sibli, the only soul in Llaneinioes who suspects Sir Davey at the close, saying of him, 'There's no man has rose like young Dafi without he sold himself to the Devil.'[19]

Both of these texts would appear to suggest, however, that though Welsh land may change hands and revert to the Welsh the anglicization of Wales is too firmly established for any significant change to take place in terms of language or class relations; there is no suggestion in either that the Welsh language is restored with the land's new owners, and though the new landowners may be more at ease with their tenants than the former gentry, there is no indication that they contemplate initiating any co-operative political changes. Within mid-twentieth-century Welsh-language fictions, fears as to the loss of traditional Welsh culture, with its religion as well as its language, still loomed, as depopulation continued to erode the rural areas and the census figures each year recorded the decline in the numbers of those speaking Welsh and attending Welsh chapels. Burdened with the consciousness of this decline, the Welsh in many of these fictions are represented as threatened with a living death.

A zombie culture

The zombie, whose appearance in Western culture was largely a product of film media rather than the printed book, was introduced relatively early into Welsh-language fiction, in the 1960s. Due to their origins in Haitian Voodoo culture, zombies were from the first associated with the subjugation and revolt of the colonized: in such films as *White Zombie* (1932), for example, they featured as undead slaves rebelling and revenging themselves on their colonial masters. The first Welsh zombies were, unexpectedly perhaps, the brainchild of a Presbyterian minister, the Reverend David Griffith Jones (1922–88) from the village of Tremain near Cardigan, who at the time he wrote his novels *Ofnadwy Ddydd* (Day of Horror, 1966) and *Y Clychau* (The Bells, 1972) was serving as the Welsh secretary of the Mission to the Lepers. In his first novel, the dead are roused in defence of the Reverend Jones's religion rather than his language or culture. The sensational events of *Ofnadwy Ddydd* begin when Sam Tomos, the local gravedigger of the village of Bryngrug near Wrecsam, sees a frightful apparition in front of him as he walks home over the Moelfan, his local mountain, one night:

> *Cafodd [Sami] ysgytiad hyd at ei sodlau pan wawriodd yr ofnadwy ffaith arno mai un o'r pentrefwyr a gladdwyd ganddo ym mynwent Moelfan y diwrnod cynt oedd yn awr yn dirwyn ei ffordd 'farwol' ar draws hen fynydd y Moelfan.*
>
>   *'Tom! Tom Williams, Hafan, myn diain i! . . . Mi dorras i fedd y gwalch dydd Mawrth 'ma, ac mi 'roeddwn . . . yn i roi o'n saff yn y twll prynhawn ddoe . . . [Rh]oddais i ddigon o bridd ar i ben o i'w gadw yno hyd Ddydd y Codi! Be' fflam ma'r diawl yn 'i wneud ar y mynydd 'ma rŵan?'*[20]

Sami was shocked to the marrow when the dreadful fact dawned on him that it was one of the villagers who had been buried by him in Moelfan cemetery the day before who was now taking his funeral walk back across the old Moelfan mountain.

'Tom! Tom Williams, Hafan, my God! . . . I cut the rogue's grave this last Tuesday, and I put him safe in the hole yesterday afternoon . . . I put enough earth on his head to keep him there till Judgement Day. What the hell is the bastard doing on this mountain now?'

Slowly, he realizes that not only Tom Williams but all the village dead have risen, and that it is not Moelfan's graves alone which are empty but all the graves of the Isle of Britain.

Eventually, Sami and the alerted local police force discover that the dead walk in response to the ardent prayers of one of the village's Nonconformist ministers, Isaac Charles. The minister had become incensed by the arguments of the atheists of his day against the existence of God. 'How dare Simpson [that is, the Richard Dawkins of the age] and the rest suggest that the Age of Belief is over, Isaac asked himself. What right have they to say that religion is nothing but a relic attached to mankind since the pagan darkness, and that man is growing out of it?' (*'Sut y meiddiai Simpson a'r lleill awgrymu fod cyfnod Cred ar ben, gofynnai Isaac iddo'i hun. Pa hawl oedd ganddynt i ddweud nad oedd crefydd yn ddim ond rhywbeth wedi glynu wrth ddynoliaeth o'r tywyllwch cyntefig, a bod dyn yn tyfu allan ohono?'*)[21] In his anger Isaac had sunk to his knees in the cemetery the night before Sami saw the apparition on the mountain side, and asked the last man to be buried there to rise in order to prove for once and for all that God lives and reigns:

Tomos Williams! Yn enw'r Hollalluog Dduw, erfyniaf arnat i adael y pridd a dyfod allan . . . i gynorthwyo'r Arglwydd i unioni'r cam a wnaeth dynion drwg i'w Erbyn . . . Tyrd allan . . . ac os yr Arglwydd â'i myn, tyrd â'r eneidiau eraill yn rhydd o garchar y tir llygredig hwn![22]

Tomos Williams! In the name of Almighty God, I beseech you to leave the earth and come out . . . to assist the Lord to right the wrong made by evil men against Him . . . Come out . . . and if the Lord wills it, bring with you all the other souls free from the prison of this degraded land!

At these words, all the dead of mainland Britain rise forthwith, along with Tomos Williams, but unfortunately for the minister's cause they prove nothing but a liability, for they not only terrify the living but also kill and eat them in characteristic zombie fashion (their cannibalism is attributed in *Ofnadwy Ddydd* to the fact that the prehistoric dead, for whom such feeding habits may, it is suggested, have been normal, have risen alongside their more civilized descendants). Government representatives arrive at Bryngrug from Westminster to persuade Isaac Charles to revoke his prayer and return Tomos Williams and his followers to their graves, and reluctantly he agrees to do so. Once that feat is accomplished, however, the Welsh minister is abruptly murdered with the secret compliance of Westminster, as too potentially dangerous to be allowed to live. But in the novel's last scene the sudden appearance within his library of the risen Christ literally shocks to death the atheist Simpson, who had plotted with the government to murder Charles. Christianity, and in particular Christianity as practised by the Welsh, is thus avenged, though so luridly that one cannot but feel some sympathy with the National Eisteddfod judges who in 1964 refused this novel a prize on the grounds that it was blasphemous.[23]

Undeterred, the Reverend Jones went on to write a second zombie novel located this time on Cors Fochno, a vast peat bog bordering the seaside village of Borth in Cardiganshire. A diverse group of three men and a woman have been brought together as a scientific research party by an Englishman, George, to investigate the components of the mysterious bog in which 2,000-year-old plants still flourish. Camping in tents on Cors Fochno, the researchers are often awoken by the eerie sound of bells wafted towards them across the bog. They take succour from these disturbed nights in a Borth café, ominously called The Bells, where the strange appearance of one of the regular customers but further alarms the narrator: 'Shem sat like a goblin at one of the further tables . . . He was entirely bald and without eyebrows. As I looked at him I felt some indistinct fear, the same unease as that which had come over me when I first saw the marsh' (*'Eisteddai [Shem] fel corrach wrth un o'r byrddau pellaf . . . Roedd yn hollol benfoel, a heb eiliau. Ymdeimlwn â rhyw fraw anelwig wrth sbio arno, yr un anesthmwythyd a ddaeth i mi pan welais y gors gyntaf.'*)[24] Subsequently, Morgan, a hanger-on of the group who is in fact an escaped convict, discovers the secret of a strange mound in the centre of the bog: 'There are hundreds of bodies in there,' he tells the researchers, 'It's some kind of burial chamber.' (*'Ma 'na gannoedd o gyrff fanco . . . rhyw fath o siamber gladdu.'*) One evening at dusk Morgan leads the group over the boggy terrain to the chamber, and the narrator sees the ranks of well-preserved corpses for himself, 'lying on shelves rising in circles of lines up to the dark roof, their naked feet towards the altar'. (*'Gwelwn y cyrff yn gorwedd ar silffoedd yn esgyn yn gylchoedd o resi i'r to tywyll, eu traed noeth tua'r allor.'*) To his surprise he finds his café acquaintance amongst them: 'Shem was there for sure . . . The old tramp was as dead as a door-nail.' (*'Shem oedd yno'n sicr . . . Roedd 'r hen drempyn cyn farwed â hoelen.'*) Then, suddenly, startlingly, the strange marsh bells start to ring out, with ghastly results: '"The bells!" Morgan screamed, "The infernal bells! . . . Look! The dead are rising!" . . . "Run!" shouted George.' (*'"Y clyche!" sgrechiai Morgan . . . "Y clyche uffernol! . . . Drychwch! Ma'r cyrff i gyd yn symud!" . . . "Rhedwch!" gwaeddai George.'*)[25]

But one of the corpses, a figure whom they had previously espied from afar on the Borth skyline, standing as if guarding the bog, is now moving towards them: 'It stretched its arms and hands out straight in front of it. It came closer and closer, threateningly, ghastly in appearance' (*'Estynnai'r peth ei ddwy fraich a'i ddwylo'n syth o'i flaen. Deuai'n nes bob eiliad, yn bygwth, yn erchyll yr olwg'*).[26] Griffith Jones does not use the term 'zombie' to describe the inhabitants of the Cors Fochno death chamber; he refers to them only as 'figures'. The above quotation indicates clearly, however, that he sees them as zombies, in accordance with the familiar image already well established by 1972 in a succession of horror films from *White Zombie* to *Night of the Living Dead* (1968); any member of the risen dead who does not speak but approaches the protagonist threateningly with arms outstretched must surely be a zombie.

In the event, the four researchers manage to escape, but Morgan is caught by the zombies and dragged down by them to his death in the black bog. Back at the camp, George, the scientist, tries to solve the mystery of these 'figures'; like the prehistorical plants on Cors Fochno they have survived by drinking the marsh's waters, he suggests: 'The secret is in the water, in the black fluid. The strange beings . . . have lived on it.' ('*Mae'r gyfrinach yn y dŵr, yn yr hylif brwnt. Ma'r bodau rhyfedd . . . wedi byw arno.*') According to Dai, another of the researchers and a south Walian who speaks in dialect, the history of the funeral chamber could be connected with the local myth of Cantre'r Gwaelod, which tells of a local Celtic princedom wiped out in prehistoric times when a flood tide crashed through an inadequately guarded sea barrier at Borth bay and drowned the area and its dwellers, leaving only the sound of their devotional bells to be heard across the water on still nights. Dai suggests that the zombies could be the original inhabitants of Cantre'r Gwaelod:

> *Ma'r hen stori'n gweud fod y môr fanco wedi torri miwn dros y Borth ac Aberdyfi. Wel, be wna'r dynion bach ond rhedeg am 'u bywyd, ontefe? . . . Fe ddeuthon nhw yma, yn barod i farw. Fe godon nhw'r twmpath 'na, rhyw fath o siamber gladdu, ontefe? Falle'u bod nhw wedi gorwedd lawr yn y twmpath, yn barod i farw . . . Fe stopodd y dŵr. Odd syched arnyn nhw a ishe bwyd. Aethon nhw mas . . . ac yfed y dwr brwnt. Yn rhyfedd iawn fe gadwon nhw'n fyw felna.*[27]

The old story says that the sea by there broke in over Borth and Aberdyfi. Well, what could the little chaps have done but run for their lives, isn't it? They came here, ready to die. They built that mound, some sort of burial chamber, isn't it? Perhaps they lay down in the mound, ready to die. The water stopped. They were thirsty and hungry. They went out . . . and drank the dirty fluid. Strangely enough they stayed alive that way.

But at this point the risen dead of the marsh attack the camp, and the researchers flee to the Borth café only to find awaiting them there another very different enemy. Word of their experiments on Cors Fochno and of the disturbances in the area that they have provoked has reached Whitehall, and a Home Office official, Godfrey Snooks, has been sent to Borth to restore order. He announces that 'Mochno will be drained of all the dirty and dangerous fluid which characterizes it.' ('*Bydd Mochno'n cael ei sychu o'r holl hylif budr a pheryglus sydd yn ei nodweddi.*') But George, an impassioned advocate of the extraordinarily extended life-giving properties of the marsh water, vehemently protests against this decree: 'The fluid is essential,' he says, 'it's priceless! That fluid is everything!' ('*Mae'r hylif na'n hanfodol . . . yn amhrisiadwy! . . . Mae'r hylif 'na'n bopeth!'*) Protest is useless, however; nothing can shake the Whitehall decision or its disregard for the unique qualities of this ancient preservative. 'The decision has been made,' Snooks says, 'There can be no reconsideration' (*'Mae'r dewis wedi'i wneud. Ni ellir ei ailystyried.'*) The process of draining the marsh begins forthwith, but before Snooks can leave, the old Celtic inhabitants of the marsh appear, dragging their rapidly disintegrating corpses, already showing the effects of the draining away of the marsh water, along the streets of Borth towards the café, thirsting for revenge. Though they are too much weakened to do corporal damage, their appearance is enough for Snooks, who dies of a heart attack at the mere sight of the living dead of Cors Fochno. Yet, his decision to drain the marsh has already signed their death warrant also, and the researchers mourn their demise. Whitehall wanted a homogenous, easily controllable state, without alien presences, but through their interventions they brought to an end an old unique world which had survived against the odds for centuries. The intensity of the characters' anger against Snooks suggests that a connection between the longevity of the Cors Fochno living dead and that of the linguistic culture in which this novel participated. Both are seen as threatened by the historical insistence of the centralized state on maintaining close control of its territories and eradicating as 'sinister' any element that cannot be conscripted into one homogenous whole, but speaks a different language and belongs to a different world. For all its mocking disparagement of the centralized state as represented by Snooks, *Y Clychau* is very pointedly not anti-English, however: of all its characters it is George, the Englishman, who is most appreciative of the unique qualities of the marsh water, and most devastated at its loss. As in Griffith Jones's first novel, it is not the English per se but the centralized state that is the enemy of both the zombies and the modern-day Welsh, whose religion and Celticity the zombies represent. To most of the inhabitants of Borth and Bryngrug, the risen dead are, however, as unappealing and threatening as they are to the Whitehall officials.

According to Christopher Lockett, zombies are the ultimate embodiment of what the French theorist Julia Kristeva has conceptualized as the 'abject', that is, that which is rejected with horror as alien though it is in fact part of the self. 'The corpse', writes Kristeva,

> is the utmost of abjection. It is death infecting life. Abject. It is some-thing rejected from which one does not part, from which one does not protect oneself as from an object. Imaginary uncanniness and real threat, it beckons to us and ends up engulfing us.[28]

Given that 'the more obviously dead (i.e. mutilated or decayed)' the corpse, 'the greater our fear and revulsion', zombies, as Lockett points out, are abject indeed.[29] Abjection is of the essence of Griffith Jones's zombies; though they represent the undead powers of the Welsh past yet they repel many of the present-day inhabitants of Wales, as well as proving a danger and irritant to the centralized state. The living Welsh fear being dragged down into the dark bogs of their past by these undead spectres. Kristeva draws from her consideration of the corpse as abject the conclusion that 'it is thus not lack of cleanliness or health that causes abjection, but what disturbs identity, system, order'.[30] The corpse is outside the system of the living; its destiny is decomposition and dematerialization. Should it resist obliteration, and try to claw its way back into life again, the effect would indeed be disturbing. In 1536, the Act of Union had assigned to Wales its place in the prevailing system as 'annexed to and with this realm of England'; Henry VIII, 'of a singular zeal, love and favour that he beareth his subjects of . . . Wales minding and intending to reduce them to perfect order, notice and knowledge of his laws . . . and utterly to extirpate all the singular sinister uses and customs differing from the same', had lain down the conditions of the union, leaving Welsh difference as for dead, outside the new order.[31] As a reanimated Welsh culture struggled back into life in the 1960s, even while the census figures indicated that the clock was ticking away the decades towards its lin-guistic death, its literature constantly evoked a sense of impotence, self-loathing and abjection.

At the close of the 1960s the experience of political impotence was further exacerbated by an event that strongly divided popular opinion in Wales, the investiture in Caernarfon in 1969 of a prince of Wales not recognized as such by some of his Welsh subjects.

Many cheered him on his way, but others saw the investiture as a humiliating desecration of the country's true history and a celebration of its conquest; in particular, the military groups the Free Wales Army and *Mudiad Amddiffyn Cymru* (the Welsh Defence Movement), born out of the frustration felt when the drowning of Tryweryn, appeared to provide proof that Wales could not adequately be defended by constitutional means, were strongly opposed to it. The poet Gerallt Lloyd Owen, in his collection *Cerddi'r Cywilydd* (Songs of Shame, 1972) which deplores the investiture, saw his nation at this time as passively proceeding on course to its obliteration:

> *Awn heb yr hoen i barhau*
> *I'r nos na ŵyr ein heisiau,*
> *Awn i gyd yn fodlon gaeth*
> *Efo'r hil i'r Farwolaeth.*

> We go on without will to survive
> To a night that won't need us alive.
> We go willingly, all, every breath,
> In a race to the death.[32]

A decade later such fears seemed realized in the failure of the first Welsh devolution referendum in 1979; Wales, it would seem, was still wary of its new reanimated image and preferred what seemed to be the greater economic security of the established order. The result heightened internal differences and frustration, and resulted in an increase in the number of Welsh-language Gothic texts, in which it was no longer English government officers or farmers who were haunted for destroying Welsh relics but the Welsh themselves.

'O'r ddaear hen' ('From the old earth') by Gwyn Thomas (1936–) first appeared as a television drama in 1981 (the script was later remodelled into a short story). As in Meuryn's and Islwyn Ffowc Elis's fictions, interfering with old stones is an act that leads to terror in this tale also: set in the 1960s it opens with William Jones's discovery of an old stone head in the garden of his council estate house, which has been built on land in bygone times consecrated to the Druids. According to the archaeologist Miriam Vaughan, to whom the head is taken, it is Celtic and of great antiquity. But a supernatural and fearful presence appears to accompany it; the apparition is seen by William Jones's wife, by Miriam and lastly in greater detail by Miriam's daughter, Anna, who recognizes it as Cernunnos, the Celtic 'God of the animals, the Other World, and the darkness' (*'Duw'r anifeiliaid, y Byd Arall, a'r tywyllwch'*).[33] Anna's father, Arthur, refuses to give credence to this talk of apparitions, but it is he who is finally punished for the interference with the stone. As he drives off with the head in the back seat, intending to get rid of it as rubbish before it disturbs his household further, he suffers a fatal accident: passing the council estate he begins to feel 'a presence' behind him in the car, and turns his head. 'For a second he saw a large animalistic head, with horns. In that second he lost control of the vehicle', which overturns (*'Am eiliad gwelodd ben mawr, anifeil-aidd, a chyrn. Yn yr eiliad honno collodd reolaeth ar y car'*).[34] The details as to the exact way in which Arthur Vaughan dies, pierced by the steering wheel and engulfed in flames, echo an earlier description of the rites of the Druids as they offered human sacrifice to their gods. Those who refuse to give credence to the power of old gods but try to abject them as refuse are themselves doomed, the tale suggests.

Roy Lewis's story 'Y bwystfil' (The beast), published in his collection *Dawns Angau* (The Dance of Death, 1981), follows a similar pattern, but here it is a Doberman dog that is possessed by the spirits of the old world, and attacks and kills his owner. Owain and Rebecca Huws along with their dog Rolo have settled in Cwm Nant Eigr, a house built across an old pathway called Sarn which leads from an iron-age settlement, Caer Arthur, on the hill above the house, down to the stream below it. One night a shadow comes down the old path and Rolo attacks it as it passes the house trying to reach the stream; much is his master's surprise to find the dog killed as a result of this encounter. But Rolo is not dead for long; he reappears, much changed. 'Something had happened to his mind', says the narrator: 'Looking into his eyes I was ready to believe that he was dead. Rolo had been a loyal and loveable dog. The creature in Cwm Nant Eigr was a – a devilish parody' (*'Yr oedd rhywbeth wedi digwydd i'w feddwl . . . [O] edrych i'w lygaid roeddwn i'n barod i gredu ei fod e yn farw. Yr oedd Rolo yn gi annwyl a ffyddlon. Yr oedd y creadur yng Nghwm Nant Eigr yn – yn barodi cythreulig').*[35] Rolo has become a zombie dog, possessed by the ancient powers of Caer Arthur, who subsequently kills his owners, because they have thoughtlessly broken the connection between the old fort and the stream though building their home on the Sarn. The message of this story, too, then is that the cloud of witnesses from the old world who observe the activities of the modern Welsh will not forgive them for ignoring or discounting their responsibilities towards their heritage.

In Angharad Tomos's influential prison novel *Yma o Hyd* (Here Still, 1985) not their dogs but the Welsh themselves are described by the narrator as a nation of zombies. Fearing that she is about to succumb to passivity in the face of cultural imperialism, the novel's narrator Blodeuwedd says,

> *Dwi 'di troi yn sombi. Dwi run fath ag oen bach yn disgwyl tu allan i'r lladd-dy. Dyna sut betha ydan ni'r Cymry bellach . . . Gwnewch rywbeth i mi cyn bellad a bod ddim rhaid i mi sefyll ar fy nhraed fy hun ac ymladd. Hen genedl fasocistaidd ydan ni bellach. Wedi cael ein llyncu'n llwyr.*[36]

> I've turned into a zombie. I'm like a little lamb waiting outside the slaughter-house. That's the sort of thing we Welsh are by now . . . Do anything to me as long as I don't have to stand on my own two feet and fight. We're a masochist nation by now. Been completely swallowed.

Blodeuwedd is possessed by the fear that the language and culture of Wales are dying and that the passive Welsh have like zombies reconciled themselves to their own death.

The same fear weighs heavily on the narrator of an earlier novel by Angharad Tomos, *Hen Fyd Hurt* (Mad Old World, 1982). In her dreams Llywelyn the last prince of Wales appears to Heulwen, a member of Thatcher's army of the young unemployed, and calls upon her to fight for her culture before it is too late, and to awaken her fellow countrymen and women to fight with her: 'He speaks to me,' she says, 'and his voice fills the heavens. *Child of the sun, keep the dream . . . Time is short. They must be woken. The Welsh must once again be brought to battle.*' (*'Mae'n siarad â mi ac y mae ei lais yn llenwi'r ffurfafen. Blentyn yr haul, cadw'r freuddwyd . . . Mae'r amser* yn brin. Mae'n rhaid eu deffro. Mae'n rhaid cael y Cymry eto i'r Gad.')[37] When Prince Charles visits Caernarfon to display his new bride – that is, in 1982 – Heulwen feels some protest must be made, and expects some guidance from Llywelyn as to what action to take, but receives none. No protest occurs, and afterwards she finds it difficult to live with her sense of guilt and shame: 'Llywelyn's pretender had gone by, and I had done nothing to stop him . . . I could not rid myself of the terrible guilt that I had disappointed Llywelyn' (*'Yr oedd ymhonnwr Llywelyn wedi mynd heibio, ac nid oeddwn wedi gwneud dim i geisio ei rwystro . . . ni allwn gael gwared o'r euogrwydd dychrynllyd fy mod wedi siomi Llywelyn'*).[38] Still out of work and with no hope for the future, she hears over the radio Saunders Lewis's voice delivering his 'Fate of the language' lecture, a repeat to mark the twentieth anniversary of the original broadcast. His voice prophesying doom sounds in her ears 'like a plaintive cry struggling to emerge from a coffin' in order to 'toll the bell and sound the last trump' for the death of her language (*'Yr oedd fel llais cwynfanus yn ceisio dod allan o arch . . . Yr oedd yn canu'r gloch, yn seinio'r utgorn olaf'*).[39] In utter despair Heulwen throws herself through a plate glass window and ends up in the local mental asylum, where she feels at last as one with the other self-confessed zombies of her 'mad old world'.

In 1982 when this novel was published Angharad Tomos was serving as chair of Cymdeithas yr Iaith Gymraeg, the Welsh Language Society. A character who shares her commitment to language politics, but not the non-violent stance of the Welsh Language Society, is the hero of an English-language novel published in 1985, Mary Jones's *Resistance*. Its narrator, Ann, a middle-aged woman who has recently been diagnosed with cancer, visits a remote Welsh hotel in the hope of acquiring some peace of mind. Initially, she desires nothing but escape; it is tedium to her as she walks in the mid-Wales countryside to be reminded at every turn of past losses, in the form of graffiti admonishing passers-by never to forget the shame of their conquered princes and drowned villages:

> I crossed a bridge and I read 'Cofia Dryweryn' on its parapet, and 'Cofia Abergele' I was urged further on, by the crenellated wall of a tumbledown farm. 'Cofia, cofia' everywhere, exhorting me to

remember, remember . . . Just when you thought you were safe, choosing the middle of nowhere to lose your identity in, the struggles inherited from defeated ancestors leapt out at you from country waysides. [40]

But she is befriended by another resident in the hotel, Aled, a Welsh freedom-fighter who, it is later disclosed, is using the remote hotel to plot a resurgence; as a young man who simply wants to live out his life in Welsh and have some hope that future generations will also be able to do so, Aled does draw on her sympathies. However, before the close of the novel he is killed – the only victim of his own prematurely exploded bomb – in a manner prefigured in an earlier scene in which he and Ann, out walking, come across a dolmen. Aled lies across it, still trying to explain his cause:

> 'Killing a language is like killing an octopus, you know. Not simple, like killing a man.' He was sprawled now against the massive slab – his outflung arms grasping its sides as though he steeled himself for the sacrifice, or challenged the gods. I turned away, hating all that smooth stone slabs have ever meant to things of flesh. [41]

Old stones, old struggles, prove nothing but destructive in this text too, but Aled's passion has elicited some response from the narrator. The sentence with which the novel closes - 'It is a base instinct, the will to survive'[42] – appears to refer to the life of the Welsh language as well as to human life in general and Ann's own life in particular. The survival instinct may be 'base' in more than one sense – crude and primitive as well as primary – but it is vital, and Ann's own closeness to death has led her to appreciate the intensity of the will to live. Though she has herself been disinherited of it, the Welsh language has become no zombie language but a living reality to her through her experiences in the hotel.

In the texts discussed above in this chapter the return of the past in the form of spectral apparitions of old leaders, and powers embedded in old stones, works in the present to reanimate living truths, repressed by the status quo. Their resurgence may be destructive and experienced by the living as guilt-inducing and burdensome yet many of these fictions see them as necessary for cultural survival: to be thus haunted is what it means to be Welsh. Wales, however, has, in relation to its size, a long and porous border country which, since at least the Norman Conquest and its establishment of Marcher lordships, has been inhabited by a mixed population of Welsh and English. The history of the border as a site of perpetual tension and uncertainty has dominated its representation in many fictions located on or close to Offa's Dyke, the long earth barrier between Wales and England built by an Anglo-Saxon king in the second half of the eighth century to keep the Welsh out of England. In the final pages of her novel *Country Dance* (1932), for example, Margiad Evans comments on the manner in which the story of her heroine, Ann Goodman, a border dweller of mixed Welsh and English ancestry, 'represented the entire history of the Border . . . that history which belongs to all border lands and tells of incessant warfare', though Ann herself 'was never conscious of the two nations at war' within her.[43] The potentiality of violence in the border territory pervades Evans's text, and accounts for its shadowed ominous tone. By the 1990s, after the bombing and house-burning campaigns of the 1970s and 1980s, that tension had by no means decreased, and in anglophone texts it was frequently represented to the reader by means of familiar Gothic tropes, as the final section of this chapter indicates.

Border vampires

In *The Knighton Vampires* (1993) by Shropshire-based Guy N. Smith (1939–) the small Welsh border town of Knighton in Radnorshire is a profoundly troubled zone. It is receiving more than its historically likely share of attention from activists participating in the arson campaigns, which had indeed been a feature of 1980s Wales, but the activity was largely limited to Welsh-speaking areas in north and west Wales. The aim of Meibion Glyndŵr, the arsonist group, was to provide a disincentive for the purchasing as holiday homes of scarce housing in National Trust areas, which priced out of the market local people who could otherwise have stayed in the area and raised a new generation of Welsh speakers within it. Few border towns suffered from the arsonists' attacks, but when Smith's novel opens, his fictional Knighton is in the grip of fear, a cottage having

just been burned down by arsonists in the vicinity. The townspeople
are angered by this threat to their livelihood which appears to be
largely dependent on servicing English tourists to the area. As the
town's oldest inhabitant, Sid Knowles, explains to the novel's hero,
John Mayo, a visitor to the town, '"these Welsh loonies are trying to
drive out the English. I'm Welsh," he added, almost apologetically.
"But Knighton's multi-racial. Welsh and English. We mix, no
bother. It's these activators, or whatever you call them, as is stirring
it all up."'[44] The town is up against not only human but supernatural
foes, though; a coven of female vampires appear to be aiding and
abetting the arsonists in driving out the English through a series of
strategic hits. Before he too is killed by the vampires Knowles draws
on Arthurian myth in an attempt to explain to Mayo the meaning
of these events. Though long since conquered,

> the Welsh dead won't accept defeat, they're lying there in their graves
> awaiting the call. And when the time comes they'll rise up like that
> there Dracula chap and drive the English back over the border. Well
> we've got the vampires, haven't we, and these anarchists are settin'
> fire to English-owned buildings. It's like the dead 'ave got up out of
> their graves and are takin' their revenge hundreds of years after they
> was killed.[45]

Mayo soon discovers, however, that the Knighton vampires are no
supernatural threat, but the employees of Glyn Idle, a local Plaid
Cymru candidate who is hiring women to act as vampires in order
to frighten away potential English second-home buyers and lower
the cost of housing in the area, thus making home-buying more
affordable to the local Welsh and increasing his likely share of the
vote.

The Knighton Vampires' representation of the Welsh threat in the
border towns may be exaggerated, but its depiction of the border
country as a zone which is neither Welsh nor English yet haunted
by the two countries' warring past is familiar. 'There was a curious
sense in which we could speak of both Welsh and English as foreigners as "not us",' writes Raymond Williams of the inhabitants
of the Welsh border village Pandy where he was reared: 'historically
it reflects the fact that this was a frontier zone which had been the

location of fighting for centuries'.[46] Living perpetually between
contending pressures, with neither of which one can entirely affili-
ate oneself, creates a hybrid border consciousness, seen at times from
the outside as a vacuum into which it is easy to project notions of
slippage between natural and supernatural worlds, as well as between
two material cultures. As Darryl Jones suggests in a recent essay on
borderlands and the occult, from the outsider's point of view 'these
borderlands, these interstices . . . in their violation of seemingly clear
category distinctions, are the sites of revulsion and therefore of
horror'.[47] The border is abject in Kristeva's sense of the term; it
'disturbs identity, system, order'.[48] At any rate in the early 1990s,
as the struggle for differentiation which finally culminated in the
second successful 1997 referendum on Welsh devolution gained
momentum, the border became the location of a number of Gothic
fictions, in which forces whose powers are from the past attempt
to prey upon the present-day inhabitants.

The Lancashire-born Phil Rickman first came to Wales in the
1980s as a reporter for the BBC, investigating the Meibion Glyndŵr
campaign; he settled near Hay-on-Wye, on the Herefordshire/
Monmouthshire border, and has located many of his subsequent
fictions in that area. In his novel *Crybbe* (1993), the inhabitants of
the Anglo-Welsh border town of that name strike visitors 'from
Off' as curiously repressed: 'They're not real these people,' says one,
'They're bloody zombies.'[49] The speaker, a 'New Ager', has been
brought into the town by the Australian, Max Goff, a ley-line
enthusiast who intends to reanimate Crybbe by restoring the stones
marking its old ley lines, pulled up by the townspeople in the sixteenth century. All he succeeds in doing, however, is getting himself
and others murdered through releasing the dark energies of its
vampiric sixteenth-century mayor, Michael Wort, whose baleful
influence had hitherto been kept at bay by the curfew tolled in the
town church at ten each night and by the stoic passivity of the
townspeople, who have been taught by their forefathers to repress
their natural responses:

> They kept their heads down, that was all you could say about them
> . . . that was how towns and villages on the border always used to be.
> If there was any cross-border conflict between the English and the

Welsh, they never took sides openly until it was clear which was going to win . . . So keeping their heads down had got to be a way of life.[50]

Accordingly, they never speak to one another of the apparition of a black beast, Black Michael's dog, which ravages through the town at nightfall just before the curfew bell rings out; though 'they all know about it . . . they won't admit it'.[51] Wort had succeeded in making the whole town his prey because of the inherent fragility of sites on borders; according to Jean Wendle, the town's spiritual healer, or white witch, 'When we make a frontier . . . when we split something physically asunder in the landscape, especially when we build something like Offa's Dyke to emphasize it, we create an area of psychic disturbance that doesn't go away.'[52] By means of their ingrained stoicism, the Crybbe townspeople survive the re-awakening of their local devil more effectively than their New Age visitors, however, and succeed in restoring order, though not without continuing cost to their psychological vitality.

In yet another 1993 novel located on the Anglo-Welsh border, Regan Forest's *Bridge across Forever*, Ellen Cole, a young American visitor to Wales, stands on 'the medieval bridge in Wrenn's Oak that connected Wales to England . . . with one foot in England and the other in Wales', and finds herself immobilized by an 'overwhelming dark sorrow'.[53] Prevented by this supernatural force from stepping into England she has to return to Wales, where she not only discovers that she has Welsh blood but is wooed by a local who turns out to be the ghost of her own seventeenth-century ancestor, Brennig Cole, long cursed by the witch who inhabits the troubled water under the bridge. Ellen is only saved from the grip of the Welsh demonic by the sudden appearance of her American boyfriend, come in search of her, and standing on the English side of the bridge. 'Don't cross the bridge into Wales! I'll come over there!' she calls out to him, and both manage to make their escape because 'the witch's strength was hate-powered. It weakened against the force of love.'[54] In such texts as these, Offa's Dyke is a liminal zone between the natural and the supernatural, as well as between two countries; along its path the powers of the underworld are released. Such portrayals reflect the view of the Welsh as exotically 'other', as 'strangers'; to cross the border and enter the Welsh 'Reservation' is to enter alien territory, and encounter exotic 'others', who harbour a repressed but perpetual resentment against their dispossessors, likely to manifest itself in a demonic manner particularly at the crucial barrier point of the borderlands.

However, the 'foreigners' native zone may well have an alluring and seductive quality to travellers who are themselves at odds with elements in their own culture experienced as repressive and over-controlled. Nostalgia for an older, freer way of life can lend appeal to the notion of crossing the border and 'going native'. That nostalgia is what induces a young English couple to settle in an unnamed Welsh village close to the border in *Fairy Tale* (1996) by Alice Thomas Ellis (Anna Margaret Duckworth, 1932–2005), only to find themselves becoming the puppets of an older age's malevolent fairy men, all-powerful in the area. Because their own womenfolk were eradicated in the nineteenth century by the powers of Welsh Nonconformity, the fairies require the services of human females for reproduction purposes; they sacrifice human males as a useless irritation. Inspired by her 'New Age' guru Moonbird, Eloise has 'come to an ancient Celtic land to rediscover her spiritual roots, to grow close to the earth'; she duly gives birth to a fairy changeling, only to find it fleeing from her at the first opportunity, leaving her bereft: 'She was fighting to hold on to something that did not love her, something that sprang from her arms with a great howl of triumph.'[55] Her partner Simon unwittingly evades the end destined for him by the fairies, however; when they come to exterminate him, he happens to be wearing Eloise's nightgown, and the fairies, clearly unaccustomed to cross-dressing, are confused as to his sex. So both return to England in one piece but with their New Age illusions shattered; the land and its true natives, the fairies, have used and discarded them, wishing them and their kind nothing but death: 'If, as Moonbird held, the Earth was our mother, then all mankind was an abortion, unwanted.'[56]

Though Wales is as much a fey country steeped in death in *Fairy Tale* as it is in other earlier 1990s fictions, one year after the publication of Alice Thomas Ellis's novel it had started on a new life, with its 'yes' vote to the second Welsh devolution referendum in September 1997. With the dawning of this new era, a perceptible change occurs in the nature of Welsh Gothic, a change to be discussed in this volume's epilogue. But the plethora of witches and fairy demons associated with Wales in the above texts is a reminder of the fact that in following the development of the Gothic genre in Wales as a historical phenomenon, the focus on history has tended to overlook the importance within the genre of certain recurring Gothic motifs and figures which extend across the complete span of Welsh Gothic writing, from the 1780s to the present day. To make up for this lack, the second part of this book examines in greater detail some representative figures exemplifying those ubiquitous supernatural presences that lend local colour to the bulk of Welsh Gothic materials.

PART II
'Things that go bump in the Celtic Twilight'[1]

5

Witches, Druids and the Hounds of Annwn

ം

Welsh folklore is stocked with an array of phenomena of dark omen which have since been purloined by its fiction writers and poets. It is particularly abundant in death portents: the *toili* (phantom funeral), *cannwyll corff* (corpse candle, a flickering flame haunting the paths of those about to die) and *aderyn y drycin* (storm bird, knocking on the window panes of those about to die) offer rich resources to writers of terror and serve to presage doom in many literary texts. Essentially, though, these harbingers of death remain figures of folklore and appear as such unchanged in literature; that is, no attempt has been made, as yet at any rate, to develop them imaginatively in works of creative writing, so as to enhance or change their significance. The same cannot be said of the four figures on which the second part of this book focuses: the witch, the Druid, the hound of Annwn and the sin-eater.

The witch is a global phenomenon in folklore, of course, but there are unexpected and distinguishing aspects to the history of Celtic witches. The latest research suggests that during the sixteenth and seventeenth centuries about fifty thousand Europeans were condemned in the law courts and executed as witches, and that about 80 per cent of that number were women. The bulk of the cases occurred in Germany, but about two thousand were executed in Britain, hanged in England and burned at the stake in the Lowlands of Scotland. Only three were condemned and executed in

Wales, however, none in the Scottish Highlands and only four in the whole of Ireland. These figures suggest that in Celtic Britain attitudes towards people suspected of witchcraft differed from those in other parts of the Isles: the Celtic communities showed greater reluctance than elsewhere to hand their witches over to the authorities. The cause of this discrepancy cannot have been differences in law, for though Scottish law differed from English law, with the laws against witchcraft harsher in Scotland than in England until 1604 when James I took the English throne, the laws governing the Scottish Lowlands and Highlands were the same, and there was only one legal system for England and Wales. Religious differences no doubt accounted for some of the disparity: Scottish Presbyterianism, then already a force to be reckoned with in Lowland Scotland, was harsh in its condemnation of witchcraft, harsher than the Church of England, at the time the dominant church in Wales as in England. And yet the religious differences are not so significant as to explain why when thousands of witches were executed throughout Protestant and Catholic Europe, only three died in Wales.

It was by no means because of a lack of potential candidates for the appellation 'witch' that the Welsh numbers were so low. On the contrary, from folkloric evidence at least, it would appear that throughout this period and well on into the eighteenth and nineteenth centuries, every other Welsh village had its local witch. About seventy people, only eight of them men, are named as known witches in Eirlys Gruffydd's study of witchcraft in Wales, but though their fame was such that their names have come down to us, very few of these were taken to court. In 1588, Cardiff bailiffs were formally reprimanded for not being assiduous enough in bringing witches before the bar, but still no cases were recorded.[2] And on the few later Welsh occasions when they were, the local communities of the so-called witches often spoke up in their defence. In 1656, thirty-one of her neighbours testified in defence of the virtuous character of Dorothy Griffith from Llanasa in Flintshire when she was tried as a witch, and as a result her judge, who earlier that year had condemned to death three so-called witches from Chester, just over the border, had to release her as innocent.[3] In 1657, some of her neighbours helped Ann Ellis, also from Flintshire, to escape from the prison in which she was held, awaiting trial as a witch.[4]

The case of the three Welsh people who were hanged as witches is unusual in that members of the higher social ranks participated in the persecution. In 1622 on the Llŷn peninsula, Sir John Bodfael wrote to his father-in-law, Sir John Wynn of Gwydir, complaining that his tenants were much disturbed by a dispute in which one family accused another of witchcraft; as a result of his complaint three of his tenants, a brother and two sisters, Rhydderch ap Ifan and his sisters Lowrie and Agnes, were brought to court and executed as witches.[5] But as the feud had been raging for some years before Sir John's letter, it is a question whether the case would ever have got to court without the noblemen's intervention. Left to their own devices, the Welsh peasantry did not usually take their witches to court, nor did the Irish or the Gaelic-speaking Scots. In the light of this history, the first section of this chapter assesses the representation of witches in the literary culture of Wales, that area which adhered most strongly to the Celtic linguistic heritage.

The witch as wise woman and avenger

Before the development of the novel genre, there are scattered references to witches in Welsh writing: Peredur kills the seven sorceresses of Gloucester in the early medieval prose tales of the Grail;[6] witches feature in a thirteenth-century poem by Tudur Penllyn;[7] Twm o'r Nant in one of his eighteenth-century interludes *Tri Chryfion Byd* refers to witches; and they also inhabit a disreputable sphere of hell in Ellis Wynne of Lasynys's *Gweledigaethau y Bardd Cwsg* (Visions of the Sleeping Bard, 1703).[8] But from the early days of the novel genre, in both of Wales's languages, witches feature significantly. In 1805, William Frederick Williams published *The Witcheries of Craig Isaf*, a Gothic history set in the Welsh Marches in the years following the death of William the Conqueror. A Norman lord sent his motherless twin daughters, Alice and Fryswith de Beaulieu, over the border to England to be cared for by their aunt while he enlisted in support of the disinherited Robert, Duke of Normandy, imprisoned in Cardiff Castle by the usurper Henry. The novel is much concerned with the rights of inheritance; when the twins arrive at their aunt's castle her first care is to establish which one of them was firstborn. Following the strict Norman laws of primogeniture, which would not at this pre-conquest time have prevailed in Wales, she proclaims that the firstborn Fryswith will inherit her property, and proceeds to make great distinction between the twins, treating Alice very much as a second-class subject, dependent upon the patronage of her sister. Enraged by her aunt and alienated from her twin, Alice vows vengeance and her oath is overheard by a local witch who, promising aid, leads her out of her aunt's lands and back across the border into Wales, telling her:

> South of this place . . . stands a mountain, called by the wandering shepherds, Craig Isaf. – The place is lonely, and as the benighted traveller approaches . . . awful yet indistinct forms flit before his eyes, and the secret terrors of his soul inform him that he is treading on forbidden ground. No wolf seeks, on that hill, a den for her young – no bird rests upon it – it is shunned by man and beast, and the Cambrian peasant often relates to a trembling circle the various instances of power evinced by the dreaded Sorceress of Craig Isaf. Hasten thither, seek the most potent in the magic art, and she will befriend you: *she* can command the powers of darkness.[9]

The two motherless de Beaulieu sisters are in effect becoming polarized as the good and the bad twin, as they ally themselves with these opposing alternative mother-figures: the rigid aunt obsessed with hierarchies and the anarchical sorceress, coupled with darkness. When Alice finally arrives in Craig Isaf, deep in the wilds of Wales, it is for her a luminous palace of delight. As she enters it, accompanied by a coven of fellow witch apprentices who have come out to meet her, a fanfare greets her approach: 'The martial music still sounded – the inspiring breath of the trumpet communicated an ardour, before unknown, to the bosom of Alice; and she proceeded with her companions rather with the march of a conqueror than the humility of a dependent.' Her new friends ask her how she feels about arriving at Craig Isaf: '"Happy! oh most happy!" exclaimed Alice; "till now I never lived – I feel existence for the first time!"' But according to her companions, more intense joy yet is in store for her: 'wait but a while,' they tell her, 'and you will experience the unspeakable happiness enjoyed by the votaries of liberty, who spurn all bonds.'[10]

This is the language of revolution, still dangerous in Britain in 1805, sixteen years after the storming of the Bastille, and ten years after the 'Reign of Terror'. After she has successfully undergone the rites of entry into the coven, which include plunging a dagger into the heart of a prostrate form she has been persuaded is her sister but is in fact a fawn, Alice is duly provided by the sorceress with an avenger, the Knight of the Panther. He rides forth to assail the Normans with whom Alice's father Reginald de Beaulieu fights, and wreaks havoc amongst them with the aid of his supernatural weaponry, telling them when accosted: "'My face must and shall remain unseen . . . but in me behold the avenger of the wrongs of a fair maid called Alice de Beaulieu.'"[11] Finally, he grapples in one-to-one combat with Reginald, only to be overcome. Reginald orders him to remove his visor and disclose his identity: "'Thy imperious will *must* be obeyed," said a soft female voice, and the mysterious Knight, lifting his beaver, exposed the delicate features of . . . Alice de Beaulieu! . . . the lost sister leagued with the denizens of hell!' "'Do I indeed behold my daughter Alice!'" exclaims the appalled father, but unrepentant to the end Alice tells him: "'I am indeed she who was once thy daughter, but I renounced thy blood – I renounced the human race . . . I am in alliance with the tremendous legion of Craig Isaf, and spurn the ties that bind timid hearts!'"[12] All the mistress of Craig Isaf has done for Alice is to give her a coat of mail and change her voice 'from the feeble female tone to manly strength': Alice has all along been her own knight in shining armour. In that Alice is soundly defeated and finally commits suicide by throwing herself off a castle's battlements, it is the Normans rather than the legions of Craig Isaf who triumph in this text, but its author's sympathies lie very obviously with the rebellious twin: the intrepid Alice is by far the bravest and most charismatic figure in the novel. With the aid of the sorceress she has overthrown not only family ties but also all social hierarchies, including gender roles; the attempt to force her into a dependent position has led to her adoption, in masculine guise, of the anarchic rebel's role, pitted against patriarchy and its systems of gender and rank division.

An equally anarchic struggle between a father and daughter is central to 'The school for witches', a short story by Dylan Thomas

(1914–53), first published in 1936. In a manner characteristic of his early prose it opens with a passage employing poetic techniques in its imagery and rhythms:

> On Cader Peak there was a school for witches where the doctor's daughter . . . had seven country girls. On Cader Peak, half ruined in an enemy weather, the house with a story held the seven girls, the cellar echoing, and a cross reversed above the entrance to the inner rooms. Here the doctor, dreaming of illness on the tubercular hill, heard his daughter cry to the power swarming under the West roots.[13]

The doctor is disturbed by his daughter's activities but rendered impotent to stop her by his obsession with sickness; the whole neighbourhood is diseased. On the evening on which the story takes place three tinkers come to the house; the doctor's daughter swoops down on one of them, the scissorsman, and takes him abruptly as her lover, thus confounding both social and gender proprieties, in that she makes the advances and does so across class boundaries. Then, she, her pupils and the tinkers enter into a wild celebratory dance in the cellar: 'Hand in hand the dancers spun . . . and lightly the doctor's daughter was among them. She drove them to a faster turn of foot; giddy as weathercocks in a hundred changing winds, they were revolving figures in the winds of their dresses.'

At this point the doctor enters the cellar; he is appalled at what he sees but had been expecting something like this: 'There had been nothing for that savage evening but an end of evil. The grave had yawned, and the black breath risen up. Here danced the metamorphoses of the dusts of Cathmarw.' The reference to the 'end of evil' is ambiguous: is this an evil end to the night, or the end of all evil? Cathmarw, that is 'Dead Cat', is the name of the local village, also dead and rotting like Cader Peak, but now changed, metamorphosized into new dancing figures of life, by the rhythms of witches' frolic. But at first the released energies are still too anarchic and upsetting for the doctor: '[W]oe unto Cader, into my nice, square house,' he laments as he stands by, 'grieving'. Then he, too, gets caught up in the swirling rhythm: 'One dancing past snatched at the doctor's hand; another dancing caught him around the waist, and, all bewildered by the white flesh of their arms, the doctor danced.' As he dances he becomes immersed in the circle, and abandons his separate perspective for theirs, identifying himself with the witches: 'A coven, a coven, cried the dancing doctor, and bowed in his measures.' His daughter and her pupils have triumphed: 'They had unloosed the spellbound . . . human skeleton, the flesh and heart out of the . . . valley roots . . . Their magic was done.'[14] The liberating energy embodied in the dance corresponds to the rejuvenating life force celebrated in many of Dylan Thomas's best-known poems: this is 'the force that through the green fuse drives the flower'. The whirling ring of dancers with its dark destructive aspects as well as its revitalizing force is representative of the cycle of nature, in which death and decay nourish living matter in readiness for the next birth, endlessly pushing up new life from the corpse-fed roots: death has no dominion in the school for witches.

The primary lesson taught in both of these schools for witches is the importance of liberating the self from the patriarchal order, from its confining gender roles and the rigidity of the social systems of private property and inheritance on which it depends. The 'nice square house' and tidy hierarchies of patriarchy are swept away by these anarchic daughters. Alice de Beaulieu, it is true, does not succeed in her fight against the patriarch in the earlier more conservative fiction, but at least she was given the tools with which to aim for that goal in her school at Craig Isaf and was taught the heady bliss of liberation and the energizing affect of defying the proprieties of gender roles. In both novels an aspiring life force, represented by the daughters, refuses repression and declares war on a patriarchy seen as inimical to it. This pattern evokes echoes of the long wars against the patriarchal ascendancy fought in primeval times, according to some influential historians and archaeologists; according to Marija Gimbutas, for example, during the Stone Ages European communities were matrilineal (that is, descent was traced through the female) and matrilocal (that is, families joined the clan of the mother not the father), and worshipped the mother goddess in her many aspects:

The primordial deity for our Paleolithic and Neolithic [that is, Old and New Stone Age] ancestors was female, reflecting the sovereignty of motherhood. In fact there are no images that have been found of a Father God throughout the prehistoric record. Paleolithic and Neolithic symbols and images cluster around a self-generating Goddess and her basic functions as Giver-of-Life, Wielder-of-Death and as Regeneratrix.

These cultures were apparently not matriarchal, but egalitarian; Gimbutas stresses that the evidence from Stone Age tomb burials indicates that men and women were treated with equal respect. The social order, she claims, eschewed hierarchies and militarization. But the peace-loving civilizations of the goddess lost power to patriarchal invaders during the fourth millennium BC. Yet, according to Gimbutas, the mother goddess's 'power was too ancient and deep to be altogether destroyed by succeeding patriarchal religions, including Christianity'.[15] Linguistic evidence also shows traces of the mother goddess's remains. The language codes embedded within Proto-Indo-European indicate that the culture of those who spoke it must from the first have been patriarchal, just as in Welsh the word *gwraig* (woman) derives from *gûr* (man), for instance, and the word *dynes* (woman) is clearly secondary to *dyn* (man). But in the ancient Celtic languages traces of another order remain. For example, the tribal goddess of the Brigantes, a British Celtic tribe, was Briganti, the 'Exalted One'. The Welsh word for king, *brenin*, derives from *brigantinos*, meaning consort of the goddess Briganti and had first arisen referring specifically to (male) leaders of the Brigantes.[16] Accordingly, Gimbutas argues that 'Celts . . . absorbed matricentric and matrilineal traditions from the rich substratum of Old Europe.'[17]

Mythological evidence also supports such arguments; the suggestion is that within some of the oldest myth cycles of Indo-European languages such as Greek and Celtic myth, the story of the degradation and loss of power of the old mother goddess civilizations is told. Thus, a tale like that of Ceridwen in *Hanes Taliesin* (History of Taliesin), first recorded in its entirety in the sixteenth century but with its origins in a much earlier oral tradition, is read as representing the passing of the goddess's power. Ceridwen is all-knowing, all-powerful and strongly maternal: she wants a full life for all her children, males as well females. But according to the myth, one of her sons, Afagddu, was born so ugly that she felt she must equip him with special skills to help him in life. In the words of Lady

Charlotte Guest (1812–95), who included the *History of Taliesin* in her 1838 translation of the *Mabinogion*, Ceridwen resolved 'to boil a cauldron of Inspiration and Science for her son, that his reception might be honourable because of his knowledge of the mysteries of the future state of the world'. The cauldron

> might not cease to boil for a year and a day until three blessed drops were obtained of the grace of inspiration. And she put Gwion Bach . . . to stir the cauldron . . . And she herself . . . in planetary hours, gathered every day of all charm-bearing herbs. And one day . . . as Caridwen [*sic*] was culling plants and making incantations, it chanced that three drops of the charmed liquor flew out of the cauldron and fell upon the finger of Gwion Bach. And by reason of their great heat he put his finger to his mouth, and that instant . . . he foresaw everything that was to come, and perceived that his chief care must be to guard against the wiles of Caridwen, for vast was her skill. And in very great fear he fled . . .
>
> Thereupon came in Caridwen and saw all the toil of the whole year lost . . . And she went forth after him, running. And he saw her, and changed into a hare and fled. But she changed herself into a greyhound and turned him. And he ran towards a river, and became a fish. And she in the form of an otter-bitch chased him under the water, until he was fain to turn himself into a bird of the air. Then she, as a hawk, followed him and gave him no rest in the sky. And just as she was about to stoop upon him, and he was in fear of death, he espied a heap of winnowed wheat on the floor of a barn, and he dropped amongst the wheat, and turned himself into one of the grains. Then she transformed herself into a high-crested black hen, and went to the wheat and scratched it with her feet, and found him out, and swallowed him. And, as the story says, she bore him nine months, and when she was delivered of him, she could not find it in her heart to kill him, by reason of his beauty.[18]

Gwion Bach thus lives on to become the famed bard Taliesin, who shows little gratitude to his mother but refers to Ceridwen as a 'hag' repeatedly in the verses included in his *History*. Her fall from all-powerful to hag was apparently a common decline for mother goddesses. According to Gimbutas,

The degradation of the goddess in all of her forms, which began during the period of Indo-Europeanization of Old Europe in the 4th and 3rd millennia B.C., continued . . . The Goddess of Death and Regeneration was demonized and degraded into the familiar and highly publicized image of the witch. She came to represent all that was denied and considered evil . . . No longer was the earth considered our Divine Mother, from whom we are born and to whom we return in death. Deity was removed into the heavens and earth became a place of exile.[19]

Thus, the powers of the goddess – her knowledge of the properties of plants and planets, her shape-shifting capacities and her cauldron cooking – became the trappings of the witch. For some, though, the myth of Ceridwen continues to resonate as a source of inspiration. Robert Graves, for example, claims that 'Cerridwen [*sic*] abides . . . I write of her as the White Goddess . . . Poetry began in the matriarchal age . . . with the breathing-in by the poet of . . . the *Awen* of the cauldron of Cerridwen';[20] in his *The White Goddess* (1948) Ceridwen is venerated as the source of all poetic inspiration.

But to what extent more generally speaking did those with access to these mythologies which include vestiges of the old religion continue to hold in awe the witch? Again, there is linguistic evidence of a difference in the conceptualization of the witch in Anglo-Saxon and Celtic cultures. There are two Welsh words for 'witch': *gwrach*, which can also mean 'old woman', and *gwiddon*, which is translated in the dictionaries as 'witch', but which includes within it the concept of knowing, of being one who knows: the *gwidd* in *gwiddon* apparently comes from the same root as the *gwydd* in *gwyddoniaeth* (science). And fictional accounts of witches in Welsh culture characteristically strongly emphasize her knowingness. A very typical Welsh witch is by far the most interesting female character in 'The youth of Edward Ellis', for example, one of the four novellas collected in Thomas Richards of Dolgellau's anonymously published *Tales of Welsh Society and Scenery* (1827). When Edward Ellis in his youth flees across the mid-Wales hilltops from the persecutions of his stepmother, he literally falls at the feet of the witch of Cae Coryn, in her little sunken cottage garden. Her first words to him are abrasive enough:

'Good mother!', said I . . .
'Call not *me* good,' interrupted she. '*Good* mother, truly! Go ask the
peasant in the valley how *good* I am, and he will tell thee, that I am
an imp of Beelzebub, and no earthly being: that I bewitch his cattle;
curdle his cream; blight his corn; and sour his ale.'[21]

But she then proceeds to feed Edward munificently like a good
mother indeed, from the bubbling cauldron, hanging above the fire
in her little cottage, before bundling him out of sight into the back
room of her hovel when another visitor begging her aid arrives.
Trapped in that back room, Edward is witness to her dealings with
an array of callers, thus providing the reader very naturally with a
detailed account of 'a day in the life of a late eighteenth-century
Welsh witch'. First in is the farmer John Roberts, bearing a pot of
butter as a gift and asking for the whereabouts of some lost sheep
for which he's searched low and high. 'Have you looked in the glen
by Moel Dûmog?' the witch asks, and no, he has not, but having
got his answer as to the sheep he's still unwilling to leave. Finally,
he reveals his more pressing need. 'David Williams has put me in
Fynnon Vawr, (the Great Well) and everything is going cross with
me,' he tells the witch; 'you can take me out of the *Fynnon* if you
will'.[22] This is a reference to the notorious 'cursing wells' of Wales,
into which one could, for a price, cast one's enemy's name; bad
luck would then follow the cursed one for the rest of his days, unless
he found a stronger power which could extract him from the well.
Charlotte Wardle (*c.*1790–1830), of Hartsheath, near Mold in Flintshire, published a long narrative poem, *St Ælian's, or the Cursing
Well* (1814) on the history of one such curse, thrown into Ffynnon
Elian in Llanelian on the county border between Denbighshire and
Caernarfonshire.[23]

At this second request the Cae Coryn witch becomes impatient
with her visitor: 'To-day ye come begging to me for a blessing;
to-morrow you will curse me over your ale-can! But go your ways,'
she says, relenting, 'you shall have your wish. I *will* take you out of
the well.' The grateful farmer offers her money but she replies, 'Put
up your money, man; I want it not', and instead gives him gratis
her good advice: 'Go home, and be more friendly with your neighbours, and more sparing of the ale-cup.'[24] After Roberts's departure,

two elegant young ladies with whom Edward Ellis, still in hiding, is acquainted, come to the cottage, wanting their fortunes told. Telling fortunes was one of the main ways in which so-called witches provided for themselves; the renowned fortune-teller Rebela, or Bela Fawr, of Denbigh, was also rumoured to be a witch. Once again the witch of Cae Coryn refuses cash payment – the local farmers, she tells her visitors, supply in kind all her needs – and once again she takes the opportunity to provide moral instruction, telling one of the girls as she looks at her hand, 'This is a fair hand, but it betokens levity of conduct, vanity, and forwardness, which, in a motherless child, are deeply dangerous to the possessor.'[25] Later, when the visitors have gone the witch tells Edward of her own background: born 'the daughter of a wealthy but a proud man' but disinherited by a male heir after her father's death, she chose her isolated cottage 'that I might live unmolested by mankind'. Her story is not dissimilar to that of another historical early nineteenth-century Denbigh witch, a Miss Lloyd who was left in poverty after the death of her clergyman father, and maintained herself by studying witchcraft, and carrying out such services for her neighbours as the discovery of lost objects and the detecting of robbers by apparently magical means. The witch of Cae Coryn, though, uses no magic; her knowledge is gained not through any charm but through close observance and a detailed acquaintance with the lives of the members of her small community. But she is aware that the 'poor credulous people' of the locality have 'endued me with the attributes of an infernal minister', and accepts that status because of the power it gives her not only to earn her keep but to do good: 'I humour their fancies,' she tells Edward, 'for by so doing I have settled many quarrels and quieted many angry minds'.[26]

A curious kind of 'double-talk' is in process here in which the villagers speak of the witch publically as 'Beelzebub's imp' but in private treat her reverently as a goddess, bearing gifts to her and respecting her advice. In point of fact, the Cae Coryn witch is very useful to her community as a herbalist, detective, fortune-teller and moral teacher; she is represented consistently as a *gwiddon*, a wise woman, rather than a *gwrach*, and as such has many successors in Welsh fiction. For example, Sara Spridion (Sarah of the Spirits) in Allen Raine's 1900 novel *Garthowen* is respected even

by the local Nonconformist minister who very candidly says of
her,

> She has wonderful spiritual insights . . . if I lay a subject before her
> upon which I have been pondering deeply but have not succeeded
> in elucidating, she grasps its meaning at once and explains it to me
> in simple words, and I come away wondering where the difficulty
> lay.[27]

Such a proficient teacher, whose intellectual capacity so far exceeded
the minister's, could obviously be very useful to her community,
and though they think of her as a witch, Sarah uses her skills, which
include clairvoyance, only in aid of her neighbours. Raine, who
participated in her age's interest in the occult, and attended seances,
describes the occurrences of this *gwiddon*'s clairvoyant trances with
reverence as 'seasons of refreshing to this strange woman's soul'.[28]
Sara Spridion is a figure of inspiration and solace in the novel in
which she appears, all-knowing and very maternal in her succouring
of the neighbourhood under her wing.

Another similar figure is Saro'r Wern who takes under her wing
the central female character in *Y Wisg Sidan* (The Silk Dress, 1939)
by Elena Puw Morgan (1900–73), a historical novel set in the mid-
nineteenth century. The novel includes a memorable account of
how Saro came to be seen as a witch in the first place. Saro had in
her youth spent some years in London; when she returned to her
natal village 'the people who knew about such things' announced
that in London she had 'sold herself to the devil' (*'wedi gwerthu ei
hun i'r diafol yno hefyd, meddai'r bobl a wyddai am bethau felly'*). In
London she had also learned fine sewing:

> *Pan ddaeth adref bu mynd mawr ar ei gwnïo . . . hyd oni aeth y si ar led fod
> anlwc yn dilyn ei gwaith. Bu farw un cyn gwisgo'r dillad priodas gwych a
> weithiwyd iddi. Taflwyd un arall oddi ar ei cheffyl, a gwisg o wneuthuriad
> Saro amdani hithau . . . Felly y gwnaethpwyd gwnïo Sara yn ddim amgen
> na thraddodiad, ond agorodd drws bywoliaeth arall iddi cyn bod y llall wedi
> gorffen cau. Ei thad oedd ffisigwr y plwyf. Yr hyn na wyddai ef am rin y dail
> a'r blodau at afiechyd nid oedd yn werth ei wybod . . . cafwyd fod ei ferch yr
> un mor hyddysg a medrus ag yntau. Eithr âi hi gam ymhellach nag ef, neu
> o leiaf fe'i gyrrwyd felly gan y cymdogion.*

When she came home her sewing was very popular until the rumour went round that bad luck followed her work. One woman died before wearing the fine wedding clothes which had been made for her. Another was thrown from her horse, wearing a habit made by Saro . . . So Saro's sewing became nothing but a tradition, but the door to another way of earning her living opened before the first had finished closing. Her father had been the physician of the parish. What he did not know about the virtues of leaves and flowers for healing was not worth knowing . . . his daughter, people realized, was just as knowledgeable and skilled as he. But she went one step further than he did, or at least she was driven to do so by her neighbours.[29]

That is, her neighbours want to believe that there is a special magic pungency to Sara's herbal brews as a result of her supposed close alliance with the Devil. Her witchery is constructed by her community to serve its purposes and she permits the process because it suits her needs, but her real skills are those of the *gwiddon*: she has a good herbalist knowledge combined with a sharp understanding of the community around her.

These *gwiddon* witches tend to dominate the texts in which they appear; the ostensible heroine of the plot may be the young women towards whom the *gwiddon* acts as surrogate mother, but the more memorable figure is the hag who holds their puppet strings. Very much the same can be said of the first witch to appear in a Welsh-language novel, though that one, Nansi'r Nant, from *Gwen Tomos* (1894) by Daniel Owen (1836–95) is as much an avenger in the anti-patriarchy tradition as she is a 'wise woman' and skilled herbalist. Nansi's main enemies are the two male figure-heads of her community, the squire and the parson, and she succeeds in confounding the two of them at once, and giving the squire a fatal stroke, when she halts at the altar the marriage of the squire's son and heir to his wealthy betrothed by producing in the church the proof that he is already a husband and father. Like the witches of Craig Isaf and Dylan Thomas's doctor's daughter, Nansi also refuses to recognize hierarchies of rank and transgresses gender boundaries for her own purposes. 'Nansi called everyone "Thou" from the highest to the lowest in the land' (*'"Ti" y galwai Nansi bawb, o'r uchaf hyd yr isaf yn y tir'*), says the narrator,[30] and he also more indirectly conveys to the reader the fact that Nansi gains her great knowledge of every detail of her neighbours' lives by moving amongst them incognito in so natural a male disguise that even those who know her best are deceived and think her a passing tramp. Nansi has also confounded the ties of blood and inheritance by using her role as local midwife to shuffle babies about at will, though in that role she cannot be said to function as an effective anti-patriarchy model, for she is as disdainful of female infants as any patriarch, and abandons her own daughters to other mothers, taking instead one of their sons in exchange. Interestingly, that son, the 'no-good-boyo' Twm Nansi, takes in common parlance his mother's name rather than his father's as his second name, in accordance with matrilineal practice.

Though such anarchical figures as Nansi'r Nant may be relatively rare in nineteenth-century and early twentieth-century fictions, in which the *gwiddon* type is more characteristic, since the 1970s the second wave of feminism has incited a more resolutely anti-patriarchal array of fictional witches in Welsh-language novels. In Bethan Gwanas's *Gwrach y Gwyllt* (Witch of the Wild, 2003), for example, a reincarnated seventeenth-century witch returns to her old Welsh battleground in the modern day to wreak havoc amongst the descendants of those who persecuted herself and her sisters.[31] But perhaps the best known of these contemporary witch-as-avenger fables is Angharad Jones's *Y Dylluan Wen* (The White Owl, 1995) in which Eirlys Hughes returns in disguise to her natal Welsh village in adulthood to avenge the savage beating she suffered as a child at the hands of the sadistic schoolteacher, Mr Gruffydd: her only crime was spilling milk, but that very feminine slip incensed the obsessive orderliness of the autocrat. Myfi, as she calls herself, enters the village on Hallowe'en, swinging her black PVC coat like a cloak, and surrounded by fluttering paper images of the schoolchildren's cut-out witches. Soon, she has succeeded in undoing the schoolteacher through making him her sexual slave and worshipper; she intends to kill him, but draws back from doing so at the close through her sympathetic identification with his young daughter, whom he has not abused. Another of the old Celtic myths, the tale of Blodeuwedd, made by the magician Gwydion from flowers but then turned into an owl by Gwydion when she chooses for herself a lover, functions as a key reference throughout the text. Myfi/ Eirlys experiences her maimed sense of self as having been created by the sadist, whose spell she must now undo. The schoolchildren under her guidance perform a play based on the Blodeuwedd story and in it they sing a song Myfi has composed, 'Eirlys's song', in which Blodeuwedd as the disgraced owl speaks:

> Tw-whit-tw-hw tw-whit-tw-hw
> Fe ddaw dial, ar fy llw,
> Ar Gwydion a'i wialen hud
> Am ddod â fi i mewn i'r byd.
>
> Pan o'n i'n flodau yn yr haul,
> Nid oeddwn byth yn teimlo'n wael,
> Ond rwân, deryn nos wyf i
> A'r byd o' nghwmpas i gyd yn ddu.
>
> Ond sychu wna fy nagrau prudd,
> A byddaf, byddaf eto'n rhydd,
> A Gwydion greulon, caiff o'i ladd,
> A byddaf eto'n flodau hardd.[32]

> Tw-whit-tw-hw tw-whit-tw-hw
> Vengeance cometh, that I vow,
> On Gwydion and his magic cane
> For bringing me into the world.
>
> When I was flowers in the sun
> Never sickness did I feel
> But now a night-bird's what I am
> And black's the world about me.
>
> But I shall dry my bitter tears
> And once more liberated be,
> And cruel Gwydion, he shall die
> And I'll again be pretty flowers.

The song refers back to the world of the Celtic mother goddess and her defeat and disgrace by a patriarchy which turned her into a creature of the night, the witch. But as if through a subversive identification with that older way of life, and with the natural forces her long-gone ancestor, the mother goddess, represented, the witch never was delivered up by Celtic communities for punishment to the same extent as she was elsewhere. That sense of identification with an alternative world also permeates these texts which celebrate the Welsh witch as heroine.

Unlike witches, other figures featured in Welsh Gothic are, however, indisputably Celtic from the outset: Druids, for example, as the priests of the religion which the Celtic tribes followed before the Roman conquest, are figures one would expect to find lurking in the Celtic twilight. One oddity about the literary representation of the Druid, however, is that though when he first features in anglophone Gothic fictions, plays and poems of the late eighteenth and early nineteenth centuries he is as likely to be Scottish, Irish or Cornish as Welsh, he subsequently becomes more and more decisively Welsh. This probably has to do with the embellishments added to the image of the Welsh Druid by Iolo Morganwg in the late eighteenth and early nineteenth centuries, and to the connections he forged between the Druids and the Welsh bards. The prestigious role given to the Druid in the Welsh cultural eisteddfod, as Iolo reconstructed it, must also have underlined the connection in the modern mind between Welsh bards and Druids. At any rate, when Druids feature in contemporary literature they are more likely than not to have Welsh origins. The Druids who make an appearance in the books based on the television series *Buffy the Vampire Slayer*, for example, have travelled from Wales to Sunnydale, USA, in order to seek the vampire slayer's aid in outwitting resurgent forces of evil trying to regain the dominion over the Earth they enjoyed 'before the Druids drove them out nearly five thousand years ago'.[33] The Welsh Druid arrived in late twentieth-century America via a literary trail followed in the next section of this chapter.

Druid sacrifice

The Irish poet and novelist Eliza Ryves (1750–97) begins her 1789 novel *The Hermit of Snowden* [*sic*] with a passage describing two antiquarians making an excursion into Wales, not merely to view . . . monuments of Druidical superstition . . . but to visit the villages . . . where they thought it probable the peasants might retain many traditions and customs which would throw light upon the imperfect account transmitted to us of their religious rites.[34]

The nature of druidic religious rites was indeed at the time under dispute, though it is unlikely that by 1789 any traces of them remained in Welsh villages fast turning Methodist. Druids had enjoyed a demonic reputation since Julius Caesar's account of them in his *De Bello Gallico* (*c.*50 BC). When they feared death through sickness or battle, the Gauls, he claimed, would 'either sacrifice human victims or vow to do so using the Druids as administrators to these sacrifices, since it is judged that unless for a man's life a man's life is given back, the will of the immortal gods cannot be placated'. Druids also, according to Caesar, administered at that dread ritual later reanimated in the twentieth-century imagination by the film *The Wicker Man* (1973):

> Others have effigies of great size interwoven with twigs, the limbs of which are filled up with living people who are set on fire from below . . . It is judged that the punishment of those who participated in theft or brigandage or other crimes are more pleasing to the immortal gods; but when the supplies of this kind fail, they even go so low as to inflict punishment on the innocent.[35]

Apparently, little archaeological evidence has been found to support Caesar's claims, and of course it behoved an imperial leader to present his empire's conquered peoples as much in need of the light of the civilization it could bring to them. But by the 1780s, as part of that movement from classicism to Romanticism which included the Celtic revival, Druids were being portrayed much more approvingly. The novel *Imogen* (1784) by William Godwin (1756–1836), anarchist and atheist philosopher and father of Mary Shelley, is set in prehistoric Clwyd, a choice of location possibly influenced by Godwin's Welsh descent: his paternal grandmother, Judith Weaver, was a Welsh woman, a member of a Radnorshire Nonconformist family. In the novel the druidic practice of human sacrifice is accepted as a fact, but the ritual is presented as appropriate, facilitated as it is in *Imogen* by the entire readiness of the heroic victim to accept his role in the rites. A bard, participating in a seasonal celebration, sings of a great drought in Arvon and describes the manner in which the wise Druids rescued the tribes from its threat:

> [The Bard] told of the dreadful famine, that laid waste the shores of the Menai . . . From the top of Penmaenmawr, as far as the eye could reach, all was uniform and waste . . . In this hour of calamity the Druids came forth from their secret cells, and assembled upon the heights of Mona . . . The shepherds . . . knew that at times like this the blood of a human victim was accustomed to be shed upon the altars of heaven . . . And now the holy priest had cast the lots in the mysterious urn; and the lot fell upon the generous Arthur . . . Terror sat upon every other countenance, tears started into every other eye: but the mien of Arthur was placid and serene. He came forward from the throng; his eyes glistened with the fire of patriotism. 'Hear me, my countrymen,' cried he, 'for you I am willing to die. What is my insignificant life, when weighed against the happiness of Arvon?'[36]

Imogen portrays those communities which adhered to druidic lore as regions of true liberty, fraternity and equality: in pagan Clwyd 'the iron hand of tyranny' had never 'taught care and apprehension to seat themselves upon the brow of its shepherds. They were strangers to riches and to ambition, for they all lived in happy equality.'[37] Both in their apparent acceptance of the rationality of the idea that to lose one's life for the sake of one's community is noble and in their eschewal of all social hierarchies, the Clwydians and their Druids prefigure those ideals of rational living recommended in Godwin's later philosophic work *Political Justice* (1793).[38]

In London in 1795 Godwin met and dined with Iolo Morganwg (Edward Williams, 1747–1826) and 'talked of God' with him.[39] By this time Iolo had already started on what was to became his abiding memorial – persuading the Welsh that their traditional strict-metre bards were the descendants of the Druids, and transforming the old bardic assemblies into a national institution, the Welsh National Eisteddfod, led by its Archdruid and his Gorsedd (court) of lesser Druids.[40] Iolo's Druids are not the administrators of sacrifice but the priests of an enlightened religion, and wise before their time. 'At an early period of the World the Cymmry became civilised by the moral, sentimental and instructive songs of their Bards,' he argued: 'The remains of their ancient and druidical learning are to this very day amongst us, and exhibit such high attainment of genuine wisdom as cannot be generally found amongst the Nations of this World.'[41] Modern scholarship has apparently shown conclusively that 'there is no historical foundation for Iolo's account of the development of the Gorsedd and for the alleged connection between the professional strict-metre bards and the ancient Druids';[42] it has also proven that the hundreds of triads infused with druidical learning which Iolo claimed to have found, and which he attributed to medieval bards, were in fact forgeries penned by Iolo himself.[43] But, during the early nineteenth century, the influence of his ideas was pervasive; their effect can be seen in such works as *Cona; or The Vale of Clwyd* (1814) by James Gray (1770–1830), for example, in which the Druid Mervyn acts as 'his country's rock' during the Roman invasion. All-knowing and all-seeing, the benevolent Druid 'held communion with the powers on high, / Who blaze on thrones of uncreated light, / In regions far beyond the starry sky.' At the same time, his loving-kindness is extended to the lowliest of his flock, to whom he brings the 'light of lore from heaven'.[44] Yet, though venerated by all – 'When he approached, even kings and heroes rose . . . / His presence quelled the rage of listed foes' – he can do little before the might of 'the conquering eagle', apart from establishing unequivocally that, when it came to comparing standards of civility, the barbarities were all on the invading Romans' side. For

> in their souls ambition, virtue's nurse,
> The mother of the arts, became a crime,
> A domineering pestilence, a curse,
> Withering the fertile plains of every clime.
> Ah! Why should man, whose destinies sublime
> Look heavenward, sink beneath oppression's sway,
> That fills with tears and woe his span of time,
> Shorn in his bloom, or dragged in bonds away,
> From kindred and from love, the haughty victor's prey![45]

There is no reference to any kind of druidical sacrifice, human or otherwise, in *Cona*; Mervyn is in all respects a fine upstanding pillar of his people's admirable civilization and the source of their wisdom.

The enthusiasm for all things druidic by which Iolo's many Welsh followers were infected led later in the century to the production of such curious works of fantasy scholarship as *Hynafiaeth Aruthrol y Trwn* (1875) by Myfyr Morganwg (Evan Davies, 1801–88), which argues that all religions stemmed from druidism, and *The Light of Britannia: The Mysteries of Ancient British Druidism Unveiled* in which his disciple Morien (Owen Morgan, 1836?–1921) claims that the bard Taliesin, he who was born of Ceridwen, was the true Jesus.[46] Myfyr and Morien after him both aspired to the status of Archdruid, but for that honour they had to do battle not only with the official eisteddfod which never accepted them in that role, but with their neighbour in Glamorganshire, Dr William Price (1800–93). A practising medic and an eccentric of the first order, who walked the streets of Pontypridd dressed in full druidic regalia, Dr Price had earlier been a Chartist leader, but gained lasting fame as the man who made cremation legal in Britain, after winning a court case brought against him in 1884 for cremating the body of his illegitimate infant son, named Iesu Grist (i.e. Jesus Christ).[47] In part through the activities of such neo-Druids as these, druidism by the close of the nineteenth century had once again gathered darker associations; as we saw in the second chapter of this book, it was hailed by the occult movement as a forerunner of their rites and beliefs. Dr William Price, in particular, appears to have served as a model for a pair of ominous druidical doctors in early twentieth-century Welsh Gothic fiction.

In 'The madness of Winifred Owen', included in *Picture Tales from Welsh Hills* (1912) by Bertha Thomas (1845–1918), a young woman from 'the heart of South Wales', in love with a suitor her parents reject, seeks aid from an eccentric neighbour, Dr Dathan, a vivisecting scientist who is reputed to practice black magic: local boys claim to have spotted him 'in his shirt-sleeves raising the devil'.[48] He makes her an offer which at first she thinks 'demoniacal', that he will inject her with a potion which will induce temporary madness and frighten away all suitors except the chosen one. In desperation she submits, and all goes well just as the doctor had promised, but she is aware that for him she was but another living subject on which to experiment. Remembering the event in maturity, Winifred comments, 'In the long after-years I have been in lands where they still offer up human sacrifices to their gods. I thought once or twice then of Dr Dathan.'[49] Thomas convincingly conveys the doctor's chilling combination of intense scientific intelligence and amorality; like Machen's experimenting doctor in *The Great God Pan* he accepts no responsibility for the human lives he tampers with. Given Dr William Price's continuing notoriety in the south Wales area at this time, he is a likely model for Dr Dathan, and was indisputably an influence on the depiction of the character Rhys Rhys in Dylan Thomas's story 'The burning baby' (1935). The story opens with Rhys Rhys attending his daughter at the pain-wracked birth of a child reputed to be his; the baby is apparently dead at birth and the doctor takes it out to a local hilltop to cremate it inside a druidical stone circle:

> 'Poor flesh' said Rhys Rhys as he . . . stacked the torn heathers in the midst of the circle where the stones still howled on the Sabbaths . . . Burn, child, poor flesh, mean flesh, flesh, flesh, sick sorry flesh, flesh of the foul womb, burn back to dust, he prayed. And the baby caught fire . . . A flame touched its tongue. Eeeh, cried the burning baby, and the illuminated hill replied.[50]

Whether or not the hills are here echoing to the last gasp of a living human sacrifice, or simply to the sound of gases leaving a corpse, is left undetermined, but the dark associations of this tale of incest and the repulsion of the flesh connect that druidic circle yet again with barbarities of an unholy order.

Any hope of returning to a more benign view of druidism was lost to a generation of horror fiction writers by the publication of Robert Bloch's 'The dark isle' in the American pulp fiction magazine *Weird Tales* in May 1939. Robert Bloch (1917–94), author of the novel *Psycho* upon which the Hitchcock film is based, was a disciple of the cult horror writer H. P. Lovecraft, who in his turn acknowledged the influence of Arthur Machen. In its account of the Roman invasion of Anglesey, as seen from the Roman point of view, 'The dark isle' presents Caesar's portrayal of the Druids as a whitewash. Bloch's Druids not only burn six 'wicker men', each one forty feet tall and stuffed with shrieking Roman legionaries, but they also have the capacity to metamorphose after death into blue-taloned monsters with faces 'shaped in Hell' and animal fangs.[51] At the heart of their 'Place of Mysteries', in an Anglesey cavern deep below ground into which the Roman Vincius penetrates, they guard 'something red and swollen – something that bled horribly, yet wobbled as though still pulsing with life. It was monstrous, gigantic, yet unmistakable – a swollen severed *tongue*.'[52] It is a dragon's tongue, no less, imbued with a poison which turns all those whom it touches instantly mad and shortly dead. By dint of repeatedly thrusting his sword into the tongue Vincius manages to arm himself effectively enough to kill not only all the Druids guarding the mystery, but also the (tongueless) dragon itself when it subsequently appears, dispatching it with its own poison. Thus, all supernatural obstacles are removed before the successful Roman advance into Anglesey, though whether or not Bloch is intentionally making the by now familiar metaphorical connection between the dragon's tongue and the Welsh language is unclear; elsewhere in his tale, he anachronistically differentiates between the Welsh and the Britons as two separate peoples, both living in fear of the Druid not as a figure of reverence or awe but as 'the furtive, bearded priest that stalked through the forests seeking stealthy counsel with voices that moaned in the night'.[53]

Nearly two thousand years later, the Druids' mystery returns to life again, though not as a dragon this time but as a 'great cowled shape' with 'no nose or chin: simply a hideous smile and grotesquely sightless eyes'.[54] Ivor Watkins's *Demon* (1983) is set in a modern-day Meirionethshire troubled by fighter planes practising overhead and an old avenger stirring underground. Unusually stormy weather precipitates an avalanche in the Moelwyn mountains which wakes out of its long sleep a demon hitherto 'undisturbed since Roman Legions marched the breadth of Britannica; undisturbed since Druids carried out their final orgiastic ritual; untouched since the last human sacrifice'.[55] The local Nonconformist minister Elliyn Price-Jones, a descendant of the Druids, tries to harness the demon's destructive powers to the needs of the chapels, 'to lay bare the sins of the wicked and condemn all who dishonour the ways of our fathers';[56] the novel attacks chapel culture much in the manner, though without the style, of Caradoc Evans, except that by now the minister is a woman. But even she cannot command the demon's obedience and is eventually killed by it, along with the fighter bomber pilots. Fortuitously, the heroine of the text, Hannah Frost, has inherited shamanic powers from her white witch Yorkshire mother and in a final confrontation, deep underground in an abandoned slate quarry, she challenges the demon. 'In the name of barbaric justice, I summon the essence of Druidical truth to avenge the death of its last surviving daughter, Elliyn of Tan-y-grisiau. In her name I seek the destruction of your selfish rancour,' she tells the demon: 'Where there are no eyes to put out, and no tongue to cut away, then shall the body be scorched' – at which the monster is consumed in flames.[57] The demon appears to represent the dark shadow which long years of human sacrifice have supposedly cast upon the land of Wales, leaving it uncontrollably unstable and yearning for fresh victims.

Fresh victims aplenty are available in Phil Rickman's *Candlenight* (1991), set in the modern-day village of Y Groes, not far from Aberystwyth in Cardiganshire, in which dark Druids are still sacrificing to their gods the would-be invaders of Wales. Within a year of their arrival all English men and women who settle in Y Groes are dead, of what in each case seems to be natural causes. Bethan McQueen's English husband has died in the village and in her grief she has come to appreciate that, for all its unclouded surface charm on which the sun never stops shining, there is something demonic about the place. With the help of a visiting American, Berry Morelli, she finally succeeds in unearthing its secrets. The parish church is built on a prehistoric tumulus, and the whole village is surrounded protectively by a circle of ancient oak trees which 'were one. An old entity. A fusion of consciousness, of now and then. More than trees. They had strong vibrant thoughts and the thoughts had sounds which came from far away, as if windborne.'[58] The trees themselves are imbued with a vengeful druidic spirit and they poison the air to visitors who decide to stay on, however positive their attitude towards the country they wish to adopt as their own. In this murderous aim, the Druid trees are assisted by the local *dyn hysbys* (wizard), the rector of the church, the Reverend ap Siencyn, and his *Gorsedd Ddu* (Black Court) of villagers whose families have lived in Y Groes since prehistoric times. Y Groes which, as Bethan says, 'is perhaps the only village in Wales where everyone is Welsh. And Welsh speaking',[59] is a shrine to the past, a zombie town, not dead to itself but death to outsiders who venture too close. At the same time, *Candlenight* through its representation of Bethan and her friend Guto, the local Plaid Cymru candidate, both of whom have been Welsh-language activists, understands the tensions besetting 1980s Wales. Bethan, explaining the situation to Berry, says:

> The English wanted more water for Liverpool and Birmingham, so they came into Wales and flooded our valleys. Whole Welsh villages at the bottom of English reservoirs . . . they're doing it again. Only this time they're flooding us with people and they're drowning our language and our culture.[60]

Eventually, the trees/Druids are gunned down by one of the villagers themselves, the inn-keeper Aled, who, grown sick of acting as host to visitors doomed to die, takes his gun and blasts 'both barrels into the night and into the company of ancient oaks gathered before him on the rectory lawn'.[61] Though Phil Rickman can sympathize with Plaid Cymru candidates and Welsh-language activists, to defend Druids would appear to constitute a step too far. As murderous in this novel as in any other written between the 1930s and 1990s, their image seemed irrevocably established as dark, as the stuff of horror movies. Whether or not the Druids ever practised human sacrifice, they have been themselves sacrificed to the gods of the modern entertainment industry, and look likely to remain figures of horror for some years to come.

In Y Groes, before its downfall, the village school's curriculum steeped its pupils in extreme versions of Welsh history and superstition; the children were taught when they heard thunder to think it 'the sound of Owain Glyndwr rolling about in his grave' and to look at storm-clouds 'not seeing formations of cumulonimbus but the Hounds of Annwn gathering for the hunt'.[62] Though it is unlikely that many schools in Wales today include the Hounds on their syllabi, they have featured in Gothic writing since the early days of the genre and like Welsh witches and Druids have evolved to suit their times, as the final section of this chapter aims to demonstrate.

Hunting with hellhounds

Cwn Annwn or the Hounds of Annwn make their first appearance at the very beginning of the first branch of the Welsh myth cycle, the *Mabinogi*. The supernatural adventures of Pwyll, prince of Dyfed, begin when, out hunting with his hounds one day, he sees a strange pack of dogs trap the stag his own dogs are chasing and is struck by their appearance: 'of all the hounds that he had seen in the world, he had never seen any that were like unto these. For their hair was of a brilliant shining white. And their ears were red; and as the whiteness of their bodies shone, so did their ears glisten.'[63] Undaunted, he drives away the strange hounds, and sets his own dogs on the stag, only to be chastised by the owner of the red-eared pack who suddenly appears and identifies himself as Arawn, king of Annwn, the Celtic Otherworld. The Hounds of Annwn, once adopted into folk culture, took on another role not mentioned in the *Mabinogi* itself: these, it was said, were the hounds who shepherd the souls of the dead to Annwn, lest they should lose their way as strangers in the afterlife. When pagan Annwn became associated in the Christian imagination with Hell, *Cwn Annwn* metamorphosed into hellhounds, hunting the reluctant fleeing souls of the damned to their eternal fiery pit. In that role they reappeared in sundry nineteenth- and twentieth-century Gothic texts.

In 1837, Taliesin Williams (1787–1847), born in Cardiff prison where his father the arch-forger Iolo Morganwg was at the time imprisoned for debt, published *The Doom of Colyn Dolphyn*, a long narrative poem on the life and death of a fifteenth-century pirate. Howel the Huntsman, who apparently witnessed Colyn Dolphyn's execution, tells the tale of Colyn's kidnapping of Sir Harry Stradling at sea, of the ransom he demanded, of his shipwreck and capture. The last canto of the poem is devoted to the account of his subsequent execution. Colyn is carried by cart to the scaffold and the noose is about his neck when he makes his last plea to 'the Sire of Sin' who had ruled his life:

> By murder'd infant's parting breath!
> By pleading Mothers, dash'd to death!
> By hands, thro' life, in blood imbrued!

> And by my soul! with thee imbued!
> Come to my aid! avert this fate! . . .
> Supreme of Darkness! nerve me now![64]

Fierce thunder rolls, and suddenly the chains binding the pirate's wrists snap apart; he flings up his arm and tries to undo the knot of the noose as the cart moves from under him. But a quick-thinking guard slices through his arm leaving the cut-off hand still clutching the rope 'in useless grasp' as the rest of Colyn hangs dangling from the noose. Enter 'Annwn's gaunt hounds . . . on fiendful scent' and in full cry:

> I've heard all sounds of mortal pain –
> The love-lorn swain's despairing strain;
> The shout of horror! – fever's moan;
> And varied torture's every groan:
> The craving voice when Famine speaks;
> The drowning seaman's gurgling shrieks,
> When lost to strength, with pallid face,
> He quiver'd in the flood's embrace;
> And call'd, – while onward! onward driven!
> In last appeal to man and Heaven!

> But such were music's sweetest quire
> To ears who heard the howlings dire,
> When guilty Colyn's worried soul,
> Freed from the body's gross control,
> Bade earth adieu: – and sped along
> Pursued by Annwn's hell-hound throng,
> To regions hopeless, – where alone
> Essential Anguish holds her throne.[65]

Taliesin Williams's hounds are accompanied not by Arawn, king of Annwn but by Mallt-y-Nos (Matilda of the Night), a witch frequently associated with the hounds in folklore. In her *Folk-lore and Folk-stories of Wales* (1909), Marie Trevelyan (Emma Mary Puclieu, 1853–1922) suggests that the original Mallt was a member of the Norman Welsh gentry who 'so passionately loved riding after the hounds that once she exclaimed: "If I cannot hunt in heaven I would rather not go there'",[66] and was subsequently doomed to ride with the hellhounds for eternity. In his notes to his poem 'Cwn Annwn', James Motley also refers to Mallt as the hounds' constant companion.[67] James Motley (1822–59) was born in Leeds but came to Wales in about 1840 with his father, an early investor in the Maesteg ironworks and Margam tin-works. The son worked as an engineer and manager of various coal, tin and ironworks in south Wales, then emigrated to manage a private coal-mine in Borneo where he, along with his wife and three children, was killed during an uprising, but not before he had won fame as a pioneer botanist.[68] 'Cwn Annwn', which appeared in *Tales of the Cymry* (1848), tells of another uprising, of the Welsh against the Normans; it opens with a young Welsh servant woman fleeing from Norman bloodhounds and closes with the Norman chieftain himself pursued by the Hounds of Annwn. The hellhounds are summoned, in this instance, by an anachronistic Druid, Idris, to whom the maidservant has brought news of her chieftain Madoc's struggle with the Normans. Druid and maid, looking out one stormy night from the Druid's retreat on Tor Curig above the Llyfni and Ogmore vales, hear 'a long fierce howl' above the tempest's blast. Idris exults:

> 'Ha, ha, right well my trusty spirits know
> To wreak dire vengeance on their Cambria's foe,
> The quarry's raised, the hounds are on their trail.'
> And as he spoke, a thin mist filled the vale,
> And a broad vivid flash, that scorching came
> O'er their seared eyeballs like a liquid flame,
> For one short, fearful moment glanced, to shew
> A huge red hound upon the mountain's brow.[69]

They then espy the figure of the Norman chieftain, 'with bloodbesprinkled mail and cloven crest', in furious haste dashing wildly down the mountainside:

> His glassy starting eyes behind were bent
> On his pursuers dread, that yelling came
> In close hot chase upon their ghastly game.

Twelve blood-red hounds, whose tangled shaggy hides
Hung loose upon their gaunt and bony sides
Dripping with gore . . .
Their small red angry eye-balls fiercely glare,
And as they raised their demon heads on high,
And the hills rang with their exulting cry,
From their black jaws dark clouds of vapour flowed,
And their huge fangs like heated iron glowed.[70]

Pursuers and pursued sweep through the parting waters of 'Ogmore's terror-stricken tide'. At this point a footnote helpfully informs the reader that 'although for the most part Welsh witcheries and deities are deemed to . . . melt into thin air before the disenchanting power of running water', yet 'there were some apparitions of too awful power to be thus dispelled; and from such unholy contact the shrinking waters were supposed to recoil, and leave a clear passage for the infernal procession'.[71] The watchers hear the chase proceeding over hill and dale, until at last 'the hounds' howl of joy and victim's wails / Were lost afar among the winding vales.' The morning dawns to reveal 'many a dark pool of curdling Norman blood' and the corpse of the dead chieftain, his 'glassy eyes' fixed 'in fierce but soulless stare'.[72] His soul is safe in the keeping of the hellhounds who have come to the aid of the embattled eleventh-century Cambrians much as the 'Angels of Mons', the ghostly Agincourt archers, defended British soldiers retreating from the First World War battle of Mons in 'The bowmen' (1914), the tale that first brought fame to Arthur Machen.[73]

James Motley's Cwn Annwn differ from their mythic originals not only in that they chase their victims to a Christian hell but also in their colouring: whereas the hounds that Pwyll saw were glistening white, with only their ears red, Motley's hounds are 'blood-red' from top to toe, including eyes and fangs. Marie Trevelyan in her anecdotal collection of folk stories records that the hellhounds were said to be not simply blood-red in colouring but 'dripping with gore, while their eyes resembled balls of liquid fire'.[74] A later author who was certainly familiar with Trevelyan's collections if not Motley's poem, was Ronald Chetwynd-Hayes who, when he included in his anthology *Welsh Tales of Terror* (1973) a hellhound story of his own devising, also painted his spectral dogs blood-red. Chetwynd-Hayes (1919–2001), born in Isleworth, Middlesex, was a prolific writer and anthologizer of ghost stories, who edited collections of Scottish and Irish tales of terror, as well as Welsh ones. In his 'Lord Dunwilliam and the Cwn Annwn', which is set on the Berwyn mountains above Bala during the early nineteenth-century Regency period, an arrogant English lord, lost on the mountains in a snowstorm when he comes to claim a Welsh estate he has just inherited, finds refuge in an isolated hovel inhabited by a surly peasant and his gazelle-like daughter. Silah Evans's beauty was 'so vivid and, in some inexplicable way, unearthly, that Dunwilliam experienced a spasm of pain' as he gazed at her.[75] He determines that she must be his forthwith, but soon learns that he has a rival; in the midst of the snowstorm, a huntsman's horn and the 'deep baying of many hounds' are heard outside, and Silah exits at the call, much to her father's discomfiture. 'Who is out there?' enquires Dunwilliam, and the father replies 'Arawn and his pack – the Cwn Annwn . . . the Dogs of Hell, and he rides behind them. 'Tis said he was once king of all the southern regions, but whatever he was, one thing is sure now, he does not breathe air.' Dunwilliam scorns the idea that he might be outrivalled by a ghost, though the father warns him that the dogs at any rate are physical enough: ''tis no phantoms that tear a man limb from limb, pull out his windpipe, then chase his soul to the underworld.'[76]

Undaunted, the English lord follows Silah out onto the snow-covered moors and tries to take her by force. On the distant mountainside, streaking straight towards them, appear 'a pack of swift-moving creatures that glittered bright red in the cold moonlight' led by a mounted huntsman of 'gigantic stature' garbed in 'a great black cloak that streamed out behind him like some monstrous wing'. They approach and the dogs form a ring around Dunwilliam, who sees that they are 'covered with blood': 'gore coated the great bodies, flowed down the long ears, oozed out of the drooling mouths, but the snow around them was virgin white'.[77] Soon, Dunwilliam's blood is also flowing as the dogs tear at his throat; he is killed but 'comes up from hell' to see for the first time the face of Arawn, 'dark, awful, evil, beautiful'. At that sight the reanimated English lord surrenders to 'a wave of fawning, self-effacing love'. Then,

Arawn, with Silah mounted in front of him, swings his horse around and sounds another 'arrogant blast' on his horn, in response to which Lord Dunwilliam 'climbed up on to his four feet, shook his blood-soaked hide, then streaked forth to join the pack'.[78] The rulers of the established order are metamorphosed to fawning beasts in this tale of arrogant English gentry laid low by the full frontal assault of Celtic mythology.

Today one can join the Hounds of Annwn pack less painfully by clicking on a website and signing up for membership of the *World of Warcraft* guild of that name; the hellhounds have become dramatis personae in the *Dungeons and Dragons* series of computer games. Streaking down through 3,000 years of human history, the pack looks set to endure for another millennium; long after Hell has become as much of a myth as Annwn, bloggers, or the equivalent, will be asking one another, 'How do you pronounce "cwn"? What language is it?', as they do now. According to James Motley 'the Cwn Annwn, or "Dogs of the Abyss", one of the most sublime of the ancient British superstitions', were by the time he came across them in the mid-nineteenth century 'almost forgotten', but they are as alive in the contemporary imagination as ever they were by today.

Even in 1848, however, Motley apparently came across 'a few old people who still cherished a belief in these infernal hounds', supposing them 'after dark to hunt the souls of the wretched to their allotted place of torment'.[79] For those superstitious believers, though, there was one infallible recourse: even after death the soul, however sin-laden, could be spared the dogs' hounding if in good time it received the services of the sin-eater, whose history, literary and otherwise, is traced in the next chapter of this book.

6

The Sin-eater

ॐ

One evening in the opening years of the eighteenth century, as darkness fell, a traveller lost his way on Cors Fochno, a large peat bog on the outskirts of the seaside village of Borth in Cardiganshire:

'I got lost,' says he, 'near nightfall, after being landed by the ferry-boat from the Aber of Dovey, on the Cardiganshire side of that estuary. A black turbary of great extent divided me from the road . . . I was cautioned to ride far round this pitchy morass, for no horse ever ventured among the peat pits – the whole being a quaking morass . . . At last, thanks to my stars, the good hard rock of a rough road rung to my horse's hoof, and I saw a pleasant cottage taper instead of that will-o'-wisp of the black bog, which was as ghastly as the Canwyll Corph [*sic*], the corpse-candle, carried by a figure of one (as these Welsh say) whose own burial will soon take place, in the spot it vanishes at . . .

Just as I came up [to the cottage], hoping lodging, I heard sounds of wailing within, and soon a woman came out into the dead night, late as it was, and cried a name to the top pitch of her wild voice . . . When I looked in, there lay a corpse of a man, with a plate of salt holding a bit of bread, placed on its breast. The woman was shouting to the Sin-Eater to come and do his office – that is, to eat the bread, lay his hand on the dead breast, place the dead man's on his own, after making a sign of the Cross, and then praying for a transfer of

whatever pains or penances in fire or 'thick-ribbed ice' or molten
lead, or what beside monastic belief attached to the perdition of
tormented souls, from that pardoned dead man for ever, to him that
more than dead alive, himself in his death of soul, but not of its pains,
for ever and for ever.'

The traveller's supposedly true tale is recorded in *The Mountain
Decameron* (1836), a curious collection of anecdote, folklore, fiction
and verse, published by Joseph Downes (1791–*c*.1860), a London-
born surgeon, who by 1836 had established himself in Builth Wells,
Brecknockshire. The account closes with the actual apparition of
the sin-eater:

> The traveller . . . had the curiosity to wait . . . After waiting long, he
> caught a far-out shout in reply to the woman's long unanswered . . .
> The Sin-Eater, he was told, lived alone in a hovel made of sea-wreck,
> and nails of such, between sea-marsh and that dim bog, where few
> could approach by day, none dared by night; whether for the footing,
> or the great fear, or at least awe, which all felt for that recluse . . . the
> wretched being he stood in the dark and wind expecting . . . [He] saw
> at last the motion of what seemed a foggy meteor moving towards
> their standing point.[1]

The 'foggy meteor' is all we glimpse in this anecdote of that
curious figure the sin-eater, but *The Mountain Decameron* is of interest
because it is probably the first literary text to include reference to
this phenomenon. Since then, however, from the last decades of
the nineteenth century to the present day, novels, short stories, plays
and poems featuring sin-eaters have proliferated. But contemporary
consumers of popular culture are more likely to have come across
him as a character in graphic fictions or computer games, or as the
name of a rock band or film title, than as a feature in literature or
folkloric historical annals. Sin-eaters have made guest appearances
in *Spiderman* and *Ghost Rider* comics, and feature in *Dungeons and
Dragons* computer games such as 'Forgotten realms'.[2] At least two
American heavy metal rock bands currently appear to be calling
themselves Sin-eaters (or Sineater), one from Tennessee and another
from Ohio. The feature film *The Sin Eater* starring the late Heath

Ledger opened in the States in 2003, though its title was changed to *The Order* when it was released in Britain; its sin-eaters are maverick priests of the Roman Catholic Church, and the action takes place mostly in Italy. As in the case of most other contemporary usages of the figure, no mention is made in this film of the sin-eater's Welsh origins. But another American film, *The Last Sin Eater* (2007), based on a 1998 novel of the same name by Francine Rivers, does account for the phenomenon of sin-eating through reference to Wales. Its story concerns a community of Welsh migrants who have settled in the Appalachian mountain range of the United States in the mid-nineteenth century, bringing their sin-eater with them; they are eventually shown the error of their ways by an American evangelist who tells them, 'No man can take away your sins. Only God . . . The man you call the sin eater is being used by Satan to stand in the way of truth. He is a scapegoat.'[3]

It would appear that a generation is growing up in America very familiar with the concept of sin-eating, which, if it knows anything at all about the origins of the concept, probably believes Welsh people to be well acquainted with the phenomenon. Gary D. Schmidt's *The Sin Eater* (1996), a novel for teenagers set in the Appalachian mountains in the 1990s, which has been on recommended reading lists in a number of American schools, begins: 'Some still recall the days of the Sin Eaters especially in the Welsh villages far from the sea where stone cottages cling to the hills and people hold to their ways.'[4] In fact, however far inland their natal villages may be, most Welsh people today know nothing about sin-eating, and if they come across the concept in popular culture are likely to think of it as an American export. In order to set the record straight, this chapter begins with an account of the historical sin-eater, before moving on in the second section to examine the numerous literary texts featuring Welsh sin-eaters, written from the close of the nineteenth century to the middle of the twentieth. Lastly, the more modern phenomenon of the migrant, frequently deracinated, sin-eater is examined to see what the differences between the sin-eater abroad and the sin-eater at home can tell us about the nature of the original and his role in Welsh culture.

The historical sin-eater

Sin-eating appears first to have been recorded by the antiquarian John Aubrey (1626–97) in 1686–7. It was 'an old Custome at Funeralls' in Wales and the border villages of England, wrote Aubrey, 'to hire poor people, who were to take upon them all the Sinnes of the party deceased':

> The manner was that when the Corps was brought out of the house and layd on the Biere; a Loafe of bread was brought out, and delivered to the Sinne-Eater over the corps, as also a Mazar-bowle of Maple full of beer, which he was to drink up, and sixpence in money, in consideration whereof he tooke upon him (*ipso facto*) all the Sinnes of the Defunct, and freed him from Walking after they were dead. This custome alludes, methinks, something to the scapegoat in the old lawe.

The 'old law' to which Aubrey refers is that passage in Leviticus which describes the ritual of creating scapegoats:

> And Aaron shall lay both his hands upon the head of the live goat, and confess over him all the iniquities of the children of Israel, and all their transgressions and all their sins, putting them on the head of the goat, and shall send him away . . . unto a land not inhabited.[5]

Giving instances of the ritual, Aubrey goes on to mention Llangors in Breckonshire, 'where Mr Gwin was minister about 1640', but 'could not hinder the performing of this ancient custom'. He concludes by remarking that 'In North-Wales, the Sinne-Eaters are frequently made use of . . . I believe this custom was heretofore used over all Wales.'[6]

Aubrey's manuscript, however, was not published until 1881, and it is a curious fact that, whereas in the years following its publication the sin-eater quite frequently features in Gothic fictions located in Wales and elsewhere, before that date there are no known references to sin-eating in literature, with the exception of Downes's *The Mountain Decameron*, and very few references to the practice in historical accounts of folkloric belief and superstitions. What is more, one of the few extant pre-1881 references apparently also owed its origins to Aubrey. A 1715 letter by John Bagford, which was published in 1770 as the preface to a new edition of John Leland's *Antiquarii De Rebus Britannicis Collectanea*, includes the following passage:

> Within the memory of our Fathers, in Shropshire, in those villages adjoyning to Wales, when a person dyed, there was notice given to an old Sire, (for so they call'd him), who presently repair'd to the Place where the deceased lay, and stood before the Door of the House, when some of the Family came out and furnished him with a Cricket [a low stool], on which he sat down facing the Door. Then they gave him a Groat, which he put in his Pocket; a Crust of Bread which he eat; and a full Bowle of Ale, which he drank off at a draught. After this he got up from the Cricket and pronounced, with a composed Gesture, *The ease and rest of the Soul departed, for which he would pawn his own Soul.* This I had from the ingenious John Aubrey.[7]

The question is, just how ingenious was John Aubrey? As the title of his manuscript – *Remains of Gentilisme and Judaisme* – indicates he was particularly interested in connections between the behaviour he observed in seventeenth-century Wales and Old Testament practices. It is possible that in his zeal to find such connections he misinterpreted certain existing funeral rites, and put his own exotic spin on them. Thomas Pennant in his *A Tour of Wales* (1780–1) gives an account of one ritual that could have led to Aubrey's error; Peter Roberts quotes from it in his 1815 volume *Cambrian Popular Antiquities*:

> 'Previous to a funeral,' says Mr. Pennant, 'it was customary, when the corpse was brought out of the house and laid upon the bier, for the next of kin . . . to give, over the coffin, a quantity of white loaves, in a great dish, and sometimes a cheese, with a piece of money stuck in it, to certain poor persons. After that, they presented . . . a cup of drink, and required the person to drink a little of it immediately.'[8]

There is no reference here to sin-eating, and other Welsh-language accounts of funeral rites, such as those included in the 1852 volume of Welsh folklore *Cymru Fu*,[9] similarly describe the same rite without mentioning sin-eaters as such. In his recent *History of Magic and Witchcraft in Wales* (2008), Richard Suggett states that such customs were 'accurately described but erroneously interpreted by Aubrey as "sin-eating"'.[10] Aubrey may have been misled by his own desire to see in Britain 'remains of Judaism', and may have mistakenly connected the funeral rites he witnessed with those passages in Leviticus which describe the ritual of creating scapegoats. Wirt Sikes apparently searched conscientiously for evidence of sin-eating when collecting material for his 1880 book *British Goblins: Welsh Folk-lore, Fairy Mythology, Legends and Traditions*, but found very little, and none before Aubrey. 'No other writer of Aubrey's time, either English or Welsh, appears to have made any reference to the Sin-eater in Wales,' he comments,

> and equal silence prevails throughout the writings of all previous centuries. Since Aubrey, many references to it have been made, but never, so far as I can discover, by any writer in the Welsh language a singular omission if there ever was such a custom, for concerning every other superstitious practice commonly ascribed to Wales the Welsh have written freely.[11]

And yet, if Aubrey was wrong, why should the Welsh ritual, as Pennant and *Cymru Fu* describe it, emphasize the importance of handing the poor the food and drink over the coffin? If the mourners had not some purpose directly relating to the deceased in mind why insist on passing food and drink over the body? Further, if the mourners were indeed employing sin-eaters to cleanse the souls of their dear departed, they had good reason not to refer to that fact openly. From the late eighteenth century on, the Nonconformist leaders of Welsh society would certainly have been strongly opposed to such pagan practices which openly flouted the teachings of the New Testament and its emphasis on the fact that Christ, through voluntarily dying on the Cross, had become the universal scapegoat for all humanity's sins. The rite, as described by Pennant and as illustrated in the *Cambrian Popular Antiquities* (and on the cover of this book), might well have been a sin-eating ritual, in which all those involved knew what was going on, though they did not name it to each other as such. As for the fact that, as Sikes pointed out, no mention was made of the phenomenon within the wealth of Welsh-language literature from the sixth century to Aubrey's time, it is possible that it was, indeed, not practised at that time and yet Aubrey was still not mistaken: sin-eating as a pagan ritual may have been in abeyance during the period of early Celtic Christianity and the Roman Catholic Church in Wales, but reverted to in certain areas in the sixteenth century, when the sudden state-enforced switch from Roman Catholicism to Protestantism under the Tudors entailed the loss of such Catholic cleansing rituals as death-bed confessions of sins and extreme unction, which can take place after death. Its heathen origins would then have meant that, once reintroduced, it was practised surreptitiously.

At any rate, sixteen years after the publication of *The Mountain Decameron*, in a meeting of the Cambrian Archaeological Association held in August 1852, Matthew Moggridge, of Swansea, spoke in detail of the act of sin-eating. It is very unlikely that Moggridge could have had access to Aubrey's manuscript; he may of course have read Bagford's published account of the ritual, but the details of his report are closer to Aubrey's than Bagford's, where they differ. Bagford did not make use of the term 'sin-eater', for example, but Moggridge does, just as Aubrey did, with the same capitalization and hyphenation. His report reads:

> When a person died, his friends sent for the Sin-eater of the district, who on his arrival placed a plate of salt on the breast of the defunct, and upon the salt a piece of bread. He then muttered an incantation over the bread, which he finally ate, thereby eating up all the sins of the deceased. This done he received his fee of 2s. 6d. and vanished as quickly as possible from the general gaze; for, as it was believed that he really appropriated to his own use the sins of all those over whom he performed the above ceremony, he was utterly detested in the neighbourhood regarded as a mere Pariah as one irredeemably lost.[12]

One of the association's members then apparently asked him 'if Sin-eater was the term used in the district where the custom prevailed, and Mr. Moggridge said it was'. He then mentioned the parish of Llandybïe, in Carmarthenshire, 'where the above practice was said to have prevailed to a recent period', and 'spoke of the survival of the plate and salt custom near Swansea, and indeed generally, within twenty years', that is, until the 1830s. His account was subsequently quoted by Ernest Silvanus Appleyard, in his *Welsh Sketches* (1853), where he comments: 'Sin-eating . . . seems to have been a perverted and perverse tradition, probably reaching Wales by an oriental channel, in which the Jewish scape-goat and Christian Eucharistic Sacrifice are blended in disguise and distortion,' making the same connection as Aubrey, though presumably without having had access to Aubrey's manuscript.[13] And Moggeridge's dating corroborates with evidence later supplied by Bertram S. Puckle who, in his *Funeral Customs* (1926), claims that 'Professor Evans of the Presbyterian College, Carmarthen, actually saw a sin-eater about the year 1825, who was then living near Llanwenog, Cardiganshire.'[14]

This accumulation of evidence would appear to suggest that sin-eating was no invention of Aubrey's but a historical practice that did not die out in Wales until at least the first half of the nineteenth century. As such its existence was hailed in certain quarters as further evidence of Welsh barbarism. In 1875, *Blackwood's Magazine* reported that: 'The scapegoat is a dark and narrow superstition still surviving in North and South Wales and on the borders.' After describing the ritual and adding that 'The scapegoat in this case is currently called a sin-eater', the report concludes 'It is hard to say who is the most degraded, the employers or those employed in the transaction.'[15] But the Nonconformist leaders of Welsh society refused to credit the idea that so 'perverted and perverse' a tradition had ever been a Welsh practice. Paxton Hood, the biographer of the Welsh Baptist preacher Christmas Evans, was much criticized for including the following sentence in his 1881 biography, in a passage in which he comments on the eighteenth-century era of religious revival in Wales:

> [W]hen the tides of a new spiritual life rolled over the Principality, the singular relics of even heathenish superstition were loitering still among the secluded valleys and mountains of the land . . . indeed, the superstition of the Sin-eater is said to linger even now in the secluded vale of Cwm-Aman, in Caermarthenshire.[16]

According to Huw Walters in his account of the uproar which ensued on the book's publication, at least three Nonconformist preachers, born and bred in the area, published articles in the Welsh and English journals of the day defending the honour of Cwmaman and protesting that neither they nor their congregations had ever seen or heard tell of sin-eating.[17]

Nevertheless, the idea that sin-eating was practised in Wales and on its borders as the remnant of a savage custom persisted. In *Ethnology and Folklore* (1892), George Laurence Gomme, then president of the Folklore Society, accepts the arguments for its existence, and sees in this 'gloomy and disgusting practice' a final remnant of cannibalism, in particular of 'the eating of dead kindred', a custom practised in classical times by the inhabitants of Ireland, according to Gomme.[18] He contrasts 'these horrid practices and theories of savagery' with Aryan culture, in which ancestors were worshipped and their corpses treated with a respect 'far removed, as a matter of development in culture, from the more primitive fear of dead kindred'.[19] Thus, sin-eating testifies to the continuing racial underdevelopment of the Welsh in contrast to their more civilized neighbours. Gomme also notes that evidence of sin-eating had also apparently surfaced elsewhere in Celtic Britain: in his *Folk Lore, or, Superstitious Beliefs in the West of Scotland*, published in 1879, James Napier recorded that there were in west Scotland 'persons calling themselves "*sin eaters*" who, when a person died, were sent for to come and eat the sins of the deceased'.[20] But Gomme finds Napier's account questionable, pronouncing himself 'not quite satisfied with this example. Mr. Napier evidently is not minutely describing an actual observance, and in his book he frequently refers to customs elsewhere.'[21] He suspects that Napier's account may be derived from the *Archaeologia Cambrensis* article which recorded Moggeridge's testimony.

Whether or not sin-eating was in fact practised, either in Scotland or elsewhere, Napier's description of it probably led, however, to one of its earliest fictional representations. In 1895, William Sharp (1855–1905), who published patriotic Scottish fiction under the pseudonym Fiona Macleod, produced a short-story collection entitled *The Sin-eater and Other Stories* in which the sin-eater features as part of a lament for the fallen greatness of the Celtic world. In her/his prologue to the 1895 collection, Macleod/Sharp presents Celticity as on the verge of fading into eternal night:

> A doomed and passing race . . . the Celt falls . . . Now, we are a scattered band. The Breton's eyes are slowly turning from the sea. And slowly his ears are forgetting the whisper of the wind around Menhir and Dolmen. The Cornishman has lost his language, and there is now no bond between him and his ancient kin. The Manxman has ever been the mere yeoman of Celtic chivalry; but even his rude dialect perishes year by year. In Wales, a great tradition survives; in Ireland, a supreme tradition fades through sunset-hued horizons to the edge o' dark; in Celtic Scotland, a passionate regret, a despairing love and longing, narrows yearly before a bastard utilitarianism which is almost as great a curse to our despoiled land as Calvinistic theology has been and is.[22]

This emphasis on the despairing Celt, dying and traumatized, is echoed in the title story of the collection. Set in Gaelic-speaking west Scotland, its central character, Neil Ross, is tricked into eating the sins of his dead enemy Adam Blair, much to the corpse's satisfaction according to the testimony of one witness to the deed, who tells Ross:

> After you ate the sins of Adam Blair . . . all there saw that the corpse had turned its head and was looking after you as you went down the heather. Then . . . Adam Blair that was dead put up his white face against the sky, and laughed.[23]

But quite apart from his enmity with Blair, Ross is doomed from the moment he acquiesces with the old tradition and carries out the ritual; before he leaves the corpse's side, he has become a social outcast. The deceased's relatives tell him, 'you had better not be trying to get work this side Iona; for it is known as the Sin-Eater you will be . . . you that are *Scapegoat* now!'[24] Ravaged by poverty, failure and isolation, Ross subsequently succumbs to incipient madness and commits suicide; his identity disintegrates, like that of his forlorn country as represented by Macleod/Sharp.

The features of this tale – its location in an isolated hill farming community, its bitter and impoverished characters and the profound abjection of the sin-eater himself – were soon to become familiar to readers of Welsh writing in English too. It is what has been made of the sin-eater as a figure in literature that is necessarily the primary concern of this chapter, and not the question of whether or not sin-eating was ever historically practised. Nevertheless, the arguments and counter-arguments of the antiquarians and folklorists interestingly reveal how ideas of ethnic difference and racial superiority were, during the nineteenth century, built upon this superstition. The sin-eater entered Welsh literature already heavily burdened with ethnic shame; he was the disgrace which proved the Welsh to be savages for all their protests to the contrary. The rest of this chapter explores the evolution of this shadowed figure as it emerges into the literary limelight.

The Welsh sin-eater in literature

In 1905, Allen Raine published *Hearts of Wales*, a historical novel set in Newcastle Emlyn in the period of Owain Glyndŵr's early fifteenth-century revolt against English rule in Wales, which, according to her biographer Sally Roberts Jones, she initially intended to entitle *The Sin Eater*.[25] Raine's sin-eater is by no means typical of his breed, however; he has not been thrust into the victim role of the scapegoat by others but has taken it voluntarily upon his own shoulders. He is introduced into the tale when the young noblewoman Eleri of Garth, who has been despatched to the home of her uncle Gwytheyrn of Twr-y-Graig, comes across the body of her maidservant Gwenna, killed by her uncle's henchman, and weeps for her: 'Oh, poor Gwenna! No shrift, no pader, but a sudden launching into eternity.' Heth, another of Twr-y-Graig's domestics, promptly responds, 'that trouble can be mended. I will fetch the Sin-eater.'[26] At this point Raine includes in her text a footnote which reads 'The last Sin-eater in South Wales lived near Llanwenog, in Cardiganshire. Professor Evans of the Presbyterian College, Carmarthen, and father of the Rev. George Eyre Evans, distinctly remembered seeing him about the year 1825.'[27] Supported by this evidence, her novel presents sin-eating as a practice with which many fifteenth-century Welsh people were familiar; Eleri, for one, 'had often heard of the Sin-eater', that terrible human being, who, for the sake of a small pittance and a good meal, was willing to eat the food that had lain on the dead body, and thus take upon himself the sins of the dead, and bear their consequence in the after-life . . . The loathing with which the scapegoat was regarded made his life one of the most terrible that can well be imagined. Shunned and abhorred, he lived alone . . . No word of greeting ever reached his ear, no voice of human sympathy, no touch of kindred hands; for the Sin-eater had voluntarily renounced every claim to human kinship.[28]

Her curiosity aroused, she looks out for his arrival to cleanse Gwenna of her sins, and finally sees him approach: 'into the grey shadows' of Tŵr y Graig 'glided a form as grey and almost as undefined as they. A tall slouching figure, whose tattered jerkin hung in shreds around him, his bare feet sandled by his long greaves of beaver skin – he was scarcely distinguishable from the grey ground of the courtyard.'[29] But though his abject appearance may accord with the tradition, his understanding of his role is most unorthodox, as Eleri later discovers when, fleeing from the house of her uncle who plans to incarcerate her in a nunnery, she finds a safe hiding-place in the sin-eater's isolated cottage. There she learns not only the sin-eater's name, Iestyn Mai, but that in fact he in no way believes in the superstitions surrounding his profession and is only pretending to perform it. During the ritual, he tips the supposedly sin-impregnated food from the corpse into a hidden pouch slung around his neck and later burns it as unclean. 'Think you that I could eat the food they bring the Sin-eater?', he tells Eleri; 'No – a thousand times, no! My soul would loathe the tainted garbage . . . not for the sin that dwells in it – for that I believe not – but because it might bring disease and death; and more, it is unnatural food for man.'[30] Later in the text, Iestyn, now recognized as the long-missing lord of Mathorwy, explains to his old friend Deraint, whom Eleri loves, why he took on so abject a role. As a Lollard, that is, a follower of the fourteenth-century heretic Wyclif, he had 'cast off the superstitious follies of my race', but masqueraded as sin-eater because the social exclusion and abjection of the role afforded him the opportunity to make private penance for his own sin, as he saw it. During Glyndŵr's wars, Iestyn Mai had fought at his prince's side with his friend Seithyn, and had later, after Glyndŵr's defeat, shared Seithyn's purse, only to find that it was Seithyn himself who betrayed Glyndŵr to the English, receiving from them in payment the gold on which Iestyn Mai too, for a period, had lived. As an act of contrition, he has taken upon himself the sin-eater's role: 'I have lived all these years as Sin-eater,' he tells Deraint, 'weighted sore with shame to think that I once lived upon the price of that betrayal which every Cymro hates.'[31]

At the novel's close, however, its contrite sin-eater gives his life for Deraint's in a self-sacrificial manner resembling that of Sidney Carton at the close of Dickens's *Tale of Two Cities*; in so doing he frees Deraint from incarceration and threatened death, and allows him to rejoin Eleri, whom Iestyn Mai by now also loves. His voluntary death in Deraint's place will give the beloved her desire and finally cleanse him of his shame: 'For me, nor fight nor venture, nor castle hall nor banqueting-room, holds out such promise of relief and such escape from shame and sorrow as does this dungeon dark,' he tells Deraint.[32] ''Twas ever thy fate to be the scapegoat,' Deraint concludes, thinking of his friend after his own escape.[33] Raine introduces the figure of the sin-eater with its supernatural associations only in effect to de-Gothicize it: no actual sin-eating in fact takes place in her novel. Yet, the shame associated with the role and the concept of transferring culpability through a scapegoat are central to the text. Iestyn would appear to stand as scapegoat not only for his friends Seithyn and Deraint but also for all those who failed sufficiently to support Glyndŵr in his valiant struggle for Welsh freedom. In so far as it can be said to have a message for its readers, *Hearts of Wales* suggests that the national disgrace of not having been stalwart enough in the support of independence movements is at the heart of Wales. As it was published in 1905 just after the collapse of the late nineteenth-century Welsh Home Rule movement, its message may have had contemporary as well as historical implications. At any rate, its suggestion that sin-eating could be voluntarily adopted as a practice by which one could atone for one's own sense of shame set a pattern for some of the Welsh sin-eating novels which followed it.

The uncertainty as to the origins of the sin-eater's role – what faith he originated from, what beliefs he represented – made him a

usefully malleable figure in these novels; he could be used to arouse
the reader's repulsion against the enemy of a multiplicity of different
causes. Henry Elwyn Thomas, a Wesleyan minister born *c.*1858 in
Llandybïe, Carmarthenshire, who wrote under the pseudonym
'Elwyn', represented sin-eating as a relic of the Roman Catholic
faith. In *The Forerunner* (1910), a novel set in the seventeenth century
just prior to the civil war, which includes historical and fictional
characters, Nell, the granddaughter of the Puritan martyr John
Penry, is kidnapped by her rejected lover, Shôn Jones, and incarcerated in a nearby convent. Shôn has been persuaded to take up sin-
eating by a Catholic priest in order to atone for the crimes of his
father, who was none other than the well-known Welsh Robin
Hood equivalent, Twm Siôn Cati, highway robber of the rich. His
son believes that 'I am atoning for all my sins and my father's sins
and my grandfather's sins as a Sin-eater.'[34] (The inclusion of the
grandfather's sins appears to refer to the fact that Twm Siôn Cati
was illegitimate.) Shôn takes Nell to Gellyforwynion Priory in order
that she should be converted, against her will of course, to Catholicism, and in so doing acts, it would appear, as an emissary for the
church: the nuns tell her that 'as a faithful son of the Church, its
appointed Sin-eater in the district, had practically sacrificed his
earthly happiness in his zeal to win a convert, and had brought her
to the Priory . . . she was there for aye'.[35] A year later, Elwyn published a Welsh-language novel, *Ifor Owain*, set in the Newport area
in the 1640s, in which once again sin-eating is associated with
Roman Catholicism. Gwladys Ifan, the daughter of another early
Welsh Puritan, remembers at one point that 'her father had often
informed her that "Sin eaters" were pretty well established institutions in Catholic Wales; and though the belief in them was dying
in those areas where . . . the light of Protestantism was spreading,
thousands of Catholics still believed in them.' (*'Daeth i gof Gwladys
fod ei thad wedi ei hysbysebu droion fod "Pechod-fwytawyr" yn sefydliadau
digon cyffredin yng Ngymru Babyddol; ac er fod y gred ynddynt yn marw
yn yr ardaloedd lle . . . y taenid goleuni Protestanaidd, yr oedd miloedd
o'r Pabyddion yn parhau i gredu ynddynt.'*)[36] Arthur Vaughan, the
sin-eater in this novel, has adopted the role in order to atone for
having, as he erroneously believes, brought about the death of the
Catholic priest who had murdered his betrothed. *Ifor Owain* may

be of particular interest as the only known work of Welsh-language fiction in which mention is made of sin-eating, but its interpretation of seventeenth-century Welsh history is strongly biased towards the Puritan cause: Elwyn makes use of the sin-eater motif to support Nonconformity and blacken its Papist enemies. Had sin-eating indeed been so central to the Catholic Church's activities, then it would have flourished more in Ireland rather than Wales but there is no mention of the practice in accounts of Irish funeral rites.

Three years later, however, another novelist made use of the same figure to support an opposing cause. *Ffynon, the Sin-eater* (1914), published by Eleanor Nepean under the pseudonym 'A Whisper', is a critique of the manner in which Welsh Nonconformity supported the sexual double standard, making scapegoats of its women and afflicting them with a dread of their own sexuality. Ffynnon Morgan, the novel's heroine (whose name is spelt with two 'n's in the text, but only one on the title-page), is the daughter of a Nonconformist lay preacher who rules over an isolated, rural congregation with his fiery sermons: 'death, judgement, hell and damnation were his themes'.[37] When the novel opens Llywelyn Morgan is already dead and Ffynnon is the devoted mother of a sickly child. A visiting Englishman, Paul Lethbridge, notices her beauty, and questions his host about her. Owen Humphreys replies: 'Ffynnon's devoted to her child.' When Paul asks, 'Is she married?', his host is offended:

> 'Do you suppose' – haughtily – 'she would have one if she wasn't?'
> Paul was amused and said teasingly with assumed innocence: 'I really didn't know; in Wales I thought –'
> 'You thought wrong then,' said Owen, with some show of temper. 'The morals of Wales are no worse and no better than any other country.'[38]

Paul is clearly familiar with the stereotype of the wanton Welsh woman, popularized by the 1847 English government *Report on Education* in Wales which went way beyond its brief to castigate the sins of Wales, attributing them to a lack of sufficient civilizing acquaintance with the English language; it cited as the greatest of these sins the sexual incontinence of Welsh women. The accusation provoked the Welsh Nonconformist chapels into punitive policing of the sexuality of their female members, in order to refute the report. But in Nepean's novel, the Englishman's supposition is in fact proved correct: Ffynnon is not only unmarried, but it was his intense fury at her pregnancy which killed her father. She is living with a heavy consciousness of sin, much increased when her ailing child dies. In accordance with the creed in which she was reared she takes all the blame upon herself, but the text protests, saying, 'Why should a woman always imagine the fury of God was all for her, and, if there was a man in it, that he should go free?'[39] At the close of the text, pregnant once again, this time by Paul, who has since deserted her, Ffynnon commits suicide. The sexual morality of Welsh Nonconformity and the predatory nature of the visiting upper-class English tourist combine to destroy the naive Ffynnon, the scapegoat for sins not her own and in that symbolic sense a sin-eater though she does not literally eat the bread of the dead.

These texts are using the motif of the sin-eater to explore aspects of Welsh identity as they, very differently, see it. One facet of the role they all in common stress, however, is the sin-eater's profound abjection. That shame is more pronounced still in 'The sin eater: a Welsh legend', a long narrative poem by Septimus G. Green published in 1920, in which the 'human spider' Black Evan, a wrecker, glumly calls for the bread and salt to be placed on his chest as he prepares to die. Morgan the sin-eater, a 'gaunt, ghastly, lean, miserable, and poor' marsh-dweller described here as 'the devil's priest', duly appears to take Evan's sins for the sake of his gold, though he knows that one of his own brothers has been amongst the human spider's many victims.[40] Next morning, Evan's widow finds the sin-eater's body lying on her threshold 'scorched as if with heaven's bolt / His greedy hands still clutching at the gold,' which she quietly retrieves for her own purposes.[41] The whole community is abject here, not just the sin-eater but those he serves as well, and the same is also true in the short story 'The sins of the fathers' (1939) by Christianna Brand (Mary Christianna Milne Lewis, 1905–97), the Malayan-born wife of a Welsh surgeon. After its republication in the *Fifth Pan Book of Horror Stories* in 1964, Brand's story was filmed in the 1970s as part of the popular US TV *Night Gallery* series, which did much to popularize the idea of sin-eating in the States.

In the tale, a messenger approaches an isolated and seemingly un-inhabitable ruined cottage, and 'in their native Welsh' asks the woman who comes to the door for the sin-eater: 'He must come! I've been searching for three days,' he says. 'The sin-eater from Tregarron [*sic*] is sick, the one at Cilycwm died yesterday.'[42] But the woman's husband, the sin-eater, is also seriously ill, and his wife and son are both starving. In desperation she persuades her son to take the father's place:

> She looked into his face: a strange look, intent, compassionate, yet fiercely resolute. 'Ianto,' she said, '*you* must go with the man.'
> 'I?' He was terrified, panic-stricken . . . 'I couldn't! I couldn't! To eat a dead man's sins . . . I'd rather starve – I'd rather starve.'[43]

By tricking the mourners and bringing the food away with him he can eat it and yet be sinless, she assures him: 'To take the sins, you must eat from the body . . . Eat nothing there, Ianto . . . Bring it here . . . You shall eat it all.' Ianto duly accompanies the messenger, carries out the ritual, stuffs the food secretly into his pockets and inside his shirt, and returns besmeared with it. The mother 'took it from him, silently, piece by piece, scrapped with a cupped palm the melting butter from the hollow of his waist' and turned with it into the hovel's inner room:

> The sins of the simple farmer – what are they? . . . But the sins of the sin-eater – the long accumulation of sin upon sin, of sins unrepented, unshriven, unforgiven, of sins stolen from dead men's souls for gain: who shall take on the sins of the sin-eater?
> She had known all along that he was at the point of death; and now the mother came out and took her son's hand and led him, innocent, through to the inner room where the father lay: with the food spread out upon his naked breast.[44]

In effect the mother in Brand's tale plays a double trick: as well as tricking the mourners of their sin-eating, she also tricks her son into inheriting his father's profession. Starving as he is, he will eat the food spread out on his father's breast, and in so doing will not only save his father's soul but also provide for his mother and himself in the only way that is open to him, pariah by association as they both are within that community. But the reader is encouraged to sympathize with this strong-minded mother, who has no choice if she is to save her son's life but to act as she does. It is their circumstances within the community which has entrapped and damned them. Welsh sin-eating fictions tend to represent not only the sin-eaters but also their Welsh communities as trapped in a primitive darkness, with their members battling to save their lives and souls under adverse circumstances which have in effect made scapegoats of them all.

For the next twenty years or so, during the Second World War and well after it, very few literary sin-eaters of any kind appeared from the presses, either in Wales or elsewhere; it is as if the tragic reality and unprecedented scale of scapegoat-making during those war years rendered it too terrible to serve as a fit subject for fiction. In the early 1960s, however, the Welsh sin-eater resurfaced in a very different guise, but still serving similar communities. Gwyn Jones, in his novel *The Walk Home* (1962) set in nineteenth-century Wales, includes an unusual portrayal of a sin-eater. Rather than being forced into the role through poverty, through inheriting it from a father or through a personal desire to do penance, Jethro Coleman has voluntarily taken upon himself what he sees as a necessary cleansing and healing act in the service of others. He is first introduced by the novel's young narrator, David Rowlands, who sees striding in front of him as he walks across mountainous mid-Wales 'a tall, thinnish man in black, who walked one of the steadiest gaits I ever beheld. He walked, I noticed, in isolation.' David assumes that the stranger is a peripatetic preacher and grows 'curious to see his face, imagining it stern, melancholy, forbidding, prayerful'.[45] But after he has become acquainted with Coleman he realizes that the man in black is motivated by something other than Christian evangelism: 'His on-driving, unfaltering gait – why had I not noticed this before? – was the gait of one who flees and must not rest.'[46] Finally, he learns the secret of his mysterious new friend's profession:

'I am a Sin-Eater, David Rowlands.' . . .
'It's horrible, Mr Coleman. Why do you do it?'
'I meet a need.' . . .

'You mean you believe in that – that blasphemy?'
'Put it in another way. I believe in sin. And I believe that man's sin
is now mine, as many other men's sins are mine.' He tapped his bag.
'Which is why I carry my pistol and keep my wits about me. I am a
man, David Rowlands, who cannot afford to die.' . . . What must he
feel? I wondered . . . Power – great power – and authority; but what
loneliness![47]

Mr Coleman on his long walk is heading towards Cors Fochno (the
same Cardiganshire location as that in which Downes's *Mountain
Decameron* sin-eating took place), where a sin-eater is needed for a
particularly serious case, and David Rowlands accompanies him,
having agreed out of curiosity to act as his helper in the ritual. For
all his admiration of his new friend what strikes him as he observes
the event is the way in which sin-eating encourages not so much
the abjection of the sin-eater himself but of the community he
serves; the Borth inhabitants' grotesque relish of the ritual is to him
repulsive:

> I could not endure the blank face, averted eye and anxious mutter,
> nor the servile welcome that was ours at Gors Fochno . . . There was
> a lip-licking quality about the mourners: the Sin-Eater was a relish
> on their meat, a Sunday extra. Some of them, I believe, thought he
> would enter with his forked tail on high and his cloven hoofs tapping
> like drumsticks on the pitch-and-cobble floor . . . It looked to me
> then, and appears to me still, a ghastly and blasphemous performance,
> which invested the Sin-Eater with a Cain-like corrupted majesty and
> made the rest of us slimy and vile.[48]

After the ritual has been completed the sin-eater prepares to leave
rapidly: '"This", he said to me quietly, "is a bad place, and these
are bad people. Get your pack. We should move."'[49] But they do
not manage to avoid a hail of stones thrown at their backs by the
mourners, and when David returns to Borth later in the tale, and is
recognized there as 'the sin-eater's boy', he's badly beaten up and
urinated upon by the villagers.

Gwyn Jones's sin-eater is less abject than most, but his very dignity
and self-respect seem to expose the communities he serves as that

much more vicious and primitive by comparison, and his willingness to perpetuate the role but maintains them in their abjection. It is characteristic of sin-eating fictions that they should take place in isolated locations, where the unsophisticated inhabitants are miserably aware of their decline, through poverty and depopulation. The mid-Wales mountain village of Nant-glyn, the birthplace of the protagonist in Gerry Jones's *The Sin Eater* (1971), is another such characteristically bleak, inaccessible and impoverished spot. The theme of this novel, which takes place during the First World War, is similar to that of *Ffynon, the Sin-eater*; no sin-eating as such takes place, but David James, returning home to Wales for the burial of his sister who, pregnant and unmarried, has committed suicide, feels as if all the family guilt is being laid upon his own shoulders. He himself blames his sister's death on the harsh coldness of their mother, supported, as he sees it, by the inflamed preaching of their local pastor who every Sunday 'burns his glare into the congregation' while they 'shout their delight at the lash of his tongue'.[50] But before the close of the novel that mother is mad, David's father is dead, also possibly of suicide, and another brother, Iorwerth, who had taunted the lost sister with her 'crime', is discovered to be himself illegitimate and not the father's son. High standards of moral propriety set by the chapel culture are presented here as perversely encouraging falls from grace, after which the unfortunate guilty party is too much burdened by shame to sustain life or reason; and in Gerry Jones's *Sin Eater* this pattern is presented as essentially Welsh. 'What in God's name is it about Wales? What terrible primeval power seems to lurk in the place?' laments David, seeing the whole country as abject and glad to flee from it to the less complex evils of world war.[51]

Similarly, in Alice Thomas Ellis's *The Sin Eater* (1977), though the novel is set in 1970s Wales when the 'cold respectable grip of the chapels had lost its power', Welsh families can still be doomed by the slow decline of the patriarchs and what they had stood for.[52] To witness his passing, Captain Ellis's family – his two sons, his daughter and two daughters-in-law – gather together in his north Wales home, the *Plâs*, along with his housekeeper Phyllis, her son Jack and her doted-upon grandson Gomer. Apart from Phyllis, however, none of them mourn nor indeed pay much attention

to the dying man, whose strongest characteristic had been his iras-
cible, illiberal anger. Rose, the sardonic Irish daughter-in-law,
'affected to believe that Phyllis had made a pact with the Captain,
and would serve the funeral baked meats from his chest, herself
eating up the crumbs, together with all his sins, according to the
old Welsh custom'.[53] Phyllis does indeed appear to become more
and more consumed by anger as the family waits for the death, incensed as she is by the realization that Michael, one of the captain's
married sons, has seduced her grandson Gomer. Finally, she tampers
with the brakes of Michael's car, so that when he drives down the
steep hills of the neighbourhood it will be to his death. Ermyn, the
captain's daughter, witnesses the act, but is too passively entram-
melled in her depressed sense of the futility of life to intervene. In
the event it is not Michael who drives off in the damaged car, but
Henry, the older son and Rose's husband, on his way to pick up
his own two young children and Gomer and bring them home over
the dangerous Pass. The novel closes, then, not only with the death
of the patriarch but the imminent extinction of the family's younger
generation and their hope for the future. For the most part this is a
black comedy of manners, satirizing both the Welsh as a group and
the English tourists who are increasingly taking over Llanelys, the
local village, but in its use of the sin-eater theme, it suggests, more
sombrely, the way each generation inherits the poison of past generations to the destruction of innocence and youth, the scapegoats for
sins not their own.

Earlier in the novel, Ermyn recalls that when Phyllis's husband
had died,

> Phyllis had put two glasses of British port on the coffin, handed them
> to Gomer and Jack, and watched while they drank it. Rose had been
> enthralled – could hardly wait for the service to end. 'Did you see
> that?' she kept saying. 'Did you see? The *cwpan y meirw*, the cup of
> death. Some loony aborigines and the Welsh are the only people who
> ever did that, and the aborigines have stopped.'[54]

Of course, the Welsh too had in fact abandoned sin-eating (if they
ever practised it) at least a century before the period in which this
text is set, but the connection drawn here between aboriginal and

Welsh cultures is suggestive. The abjection which is inherent in the act of sin-eating as represented in Welsh texts may not be unrelated to the abjection experienced by all colonized peoples. That a community should be in the habit of making scapegoats for itself from some of its own more vulnerable members is described by Frantz Fanon, in his analyses of the psyche of the African under Western colonialism, as one of the consequences of colonization. 'Every colonized people,' he argues,

> in other words, every people in whose soul an inferiority complex has been created by the death and burial of its local cultural originality – finds itself face to face with the language of the civilizing nation; that is, with the culture of the mother country. The colonized is elevated above his jungle status in proportion to his adoption of the mother country's cultural standards.[55]

The indigenous inhabitants of the colony, once they have lost the battle to the invaders, are indoctrinated in the colonialists' disparaging view of themselves and will interiorize it. But the more powerful amongst them dissociate themselves from it, projecting the humiliation instead on the less privileged members of their own community. '[T]he Negro,' Fanon concludes, 'identifying himself with the civilising power, will make the nigger the scapegoat of his moral life.'[56] Such a postcolonial analysis may be pertinent in the case of the sin-eater as scapegoat also. The act of sin-eating seems physically to represent the colonized people's propensity to project its sense of inferiority and self-loathing onto one of its own less successful members, who is then marked as pariah and cast out, leaving the more powerful members of the tribe cleansed and superior.

At any rate, after the 1970s there are few further references to sin-eating in anglophone Welsh writing, though apparently in the 1980s Raymond Williams had intended to include a sin-eating episode, set in 1879, in the final uncompleted volume of his *People of the Black Mountains* trilogy.[57] Earlier in the first half of the twentieth century, however, sin-eating narratives had started to proliferate elsewhere. The next section of this chapter traces the development of the sin-eater as a figure in literature outside Wales and considers in what ways the emigrant sin-eater differs from the Welsh originals.

Sin-eating beyond Wales

In the 1920s, sin-eaters featured in literary texts set on the eastern side of Offa's Dyke, including one of the best-known fictional sin-eaters, Gideon Sarn of Mary Webb's novel *Precious Bane* (1924). Mary Webb (née Mary Gladys Meredith, 1881–1927), who was born in the village of Leighton, Shropshire, to a Welsh school-teacher and his English wife, set most of her fictions in the border region;[58] in *Precious Bane*, set in Shropshire, the sin-eater is not Welsh, though it would appear that according to local custom he was expected to be. After the sudden death of his father during a family brawl, Gideon Sarn objects to the expense of hiring a sin-eater. 'In our time', explains the narrator, Gideon's sister Prue Sarn, 'there were none left around Sarn. They had nearly died out, and they had to be sent for to the mountains [i.e. to Wales]. It was a long way to send, and they asked a big price.'[59] Much to his mother's distress, Gideon decides 'We'll save the money.' At the funeral, however, 'a strange, heart-shaking thing came to pass. Gideon stepped up to the coffin and said, "There is a Sin Eater . . . I ool be the Sin Eater . . . Oot turn over the farm and all to me if I be the Sin Eater, Mother?"'[60] His mother protests initially before eventually agreeing and the ritual takes place, but all the family, including Gideon himself, pay a far greater price for that act of sin-eating than they would have had to give any Welsh scapegoat coming down from the mountains. Gideon senior was a miser, and his son not only inherits the father's failings but appears to his sister to have multiplied them in himself after eating the father's sins. His extreme avarice leads to the downfall of his family, the wrecking of his personal happiness and the loss of the farm.

Nevertheless, Gideon is not abject, and neither is the sin-eater in another border text published in the same year as *Precious Bane*, the political satire *The Sin Eater's Hallowe'en* (1923) by Francis Neilson, a play that mocks European politicians for the manner in which they abandon their principles once in office. A Mr Makepeace, whose name suggests his good intentions, constructs an elaborate charade, in which the leaders of the West are lured on false pretences to a tavern on the English side of the Wales-England border. They each appear at the inn accompanied by an appropriately dressed personification of their principles. Taffy, for example, clearly a caricature of Lloyd George, is accompanied by his principles in the form of a young girl dressed in Welsh costume. At one point the following exchange takes place between them:

> *Taffy's Principles*: Abandon that vampire power and return to me, your first love. Oh! let me dream once more that you will be the champion of the people; that you will fight against war, abolish armaments, free the land from the tyranny of the squirearchy, disestablish and disendow the Church, institute free trade, peace and good will amongst the nations –
> *Taffy*: What nonsense you are talking! . . . Have I not over and over again, on ten thousand platforms, to millions and millions of people, said I was in favour of all these things? . . .
> *Taffy's Principles*: You used your principles – you trampled on them to gain power.
> *Taffy*: Of course, I used my principles. What good were they if I didn't gain power?[61]

– at which one of the locals drinking in the tavern comments ''ere's a job for Timothy Sinniter'. The political leaders, drugged by the tavern fare, fall into a stupor, food is placed on their sleeping chests, and Timothy Sinniter is ushered in to perform his role. 'Taffy, rest at ease,' he tells Lloyd George, 'I've eat your sin.'[62] The ceremony over, all the leaders awake to a revived sense of joy; Taffy says: 'I feel like a young Liberal. Full of hope and large in faith! . . . I haven't felt like this since the Boer War.'[63] Their rejuvenation is short-lived, however; the sound of prolonged vomiting is heard offstage, and the sin-eater's wife, Mrs Patience Sinniter, rushes in to announce, 'He's vomited most awful!' before the sin-eater himself re-appears to issue an apology: 'I'm sorry, but it was too much for me to swallow . . . Now, I'm afraid you've all got to go to 'ell in the reg'lar way.'[64] Mr Makepeace's trick has misfired, but this mock-Gothic satire makes evident the sin-eater's potential as a comic figure, though – surprisingly, perhaps – no further literary exploitation of this possibility has as yet appeared.

Sin-eating is not, however, at the centre of this play, for all its title; the ritual acts merely as a plot device about which the play's political satire is worked. Its role is also secondary in Elizabeth

Walter's short story 'The sin-eater' (1967), which primarily belongs to the more macabre branches of the detective fiction genre. An architectural draughtsman, Clive Tomlinson, the compiler of a book on *English Church Interiors in the Middle Ages*, while on his rambles in search of striking church interiors is persuaded against his inclination to enter an isolated farmhouse he passes in the hamlet of Penrhayader on the Wales–England border. He has arrived, the farmer says, just in time 'to take a glass of wine with my son', that is, to drink and eat over the corpse of the farmer's son, Eddie Preece.[65] Later, Tomlinson discovers not only the meaning of the ritual into which he was inveigled but that Eddie had been accused of the murder of his wife, who had been having an illicit affair with a neighbour, Dick Roper; Eddie's plea that it was Roper who had murdered his wife, not he, was not accepted. Fascinated by the story, Clive returns to the farmhouse, to find it empty and deserted except for a stranger who Clive intuits must be Dick Roper himself, returned to the scene of his crime. Roper admits the fact, adding that he must now kill Clive as well, but before he can do so the dark vengeful shadow of Eddie Preece materializes and strangles Roper. The tale dryly concludes: 'So it was that Eddie Preece's sin-eater was arrested, charged with murder, and in due course tried and condemned.'[66] But though Tomlinson thus becomes the scape-goat for a ghost's vengeance, at no point in the tale is he presented to the reader as abject; he does not interiorize the false guilt laid upon him and his only weakness is the polite urbanity which made it difficult for him to refuse the farmer's request that he should grieve with him over his son.

Though Gideon Sarn knew what he was doing while Clive Tomlinson did not, in neither text is there much sustained focus on the sin-eater as pariah: their sin-eating is a singular event; they do not inhabit the role for any extended period, though they do suffer some of its consequences. The same can be said of the sin-eater in a story published in 1938 in the American pulp fiction magazine *Weird Tales*, written by G. G. Pendarves, the pen-name of Gladys Gordon Trenery (1885–1938), and set in Cornwall – unexpectedly perhaps, given that there is no historical evidence of Cornish sin-eating. Pendarves's 'The sin eater' would appear to have been influenced by Fiona Macleod/William Sharp's Scottish story of the same name; it opens with a lament similar to his/hers on the passing of Celtic cultures: 'Old gods, old worships, old forgotten races have died hard and lingeringly in this ancient haunted land of Cornwall . . . On this wild coast the breaking tides boom one continuous knell – death!'[67] In the story that follows, sin-eating becomes part of an act of vengeance carried out in accordance with the malign wishes of the corpse, again as in Sharp/Macleod's 'The sin-eater'. Mark Zennor, black magician of the port of Trink, is the dark villain of the tale: on his death-bed he 'watched the pair of young lovers with hard, merciless eyes. His young wife Rosina, and Stephen Lynn, his nephew.' '*I wish you to be my sin-eater,*'[68] he says to Stephen, who duly carries out the request, but the vows which Mark has written for Stephen to recite over his corpse involve more than the transference of sins. '*I receive the great darkness of your sins. I give the light of my soul that your own may walk in it forever,*' Stephen is made to swear as sin-eater,[69] thus allowing the dead Mark to take possession of his body, so that henceforth when Stephen speaks, 'It was Mark Zennor's voice . . . calling on his dark gods, reiterating his impious vows, drawing to his service a vast army of the damned.'[70] In revenge for his illicit affair with his aunt, Stephen, or rather his body, is forced by Zennor to practice black arts rituals which are intended to culminate in human sacrifice, with Rosina as the victim; he is saved only at the last moment by the exorcizing power of Rosina's love which draws him back 'from hell'. This is a tale of demonic possession, rather than of sin-eating per se, but it appears to have served to alert the readers of *Weird Tales* to the marketable weirdness of the sin-eating motif. Pendarves's 'The sin eater' was later reproduced in a 1979 US collection of 'classic' pulp magazine stories; its evident popularity may well have been one of the reasons why home-based versions of sin-eaters soon started to appear in the pages of these American journals.

At any rate, four years later in 1942 another such magazine, entitled *Spicy Mystery*, published 'The sin-eater' by Lew Merrill, the pen-name of Victor Rousseau Emanuel; the hero of this tale is a young government official sent to the northern reaches of the Appalachian mountain range in New York state to supervise the building of a dam. The area is inhabited by 'descendants of the primitive American pioneers' who have brought their native customs with them from their unspecified homeland; naturally enough, they are much angered by the intended drowning of their new territories, but Craig feels little sympathy for them.[71] He is outraged, however, when he happens to witness a scene in which the Appalachian community, or the hillbillies as he calls them, project their frustrated resentment and grief upon a scapegoat, Tess, who has only recently arrived in their midst, and drive her out, with whips and blows, as a sin-eater. He is told by one of them,

> We're drivin' Tess outer this community, because we're God-fearin' people . . . It's writ in the Holy Book . . . about drivin' the scapegoat into the wilderness, to bear the sins of the people. Tess is the sin-eater for this settlement, and we're drivin' her out, seein' as she's a furriner, and brung all this trouble upon us, losin' our homes.[72]

Some later texts which feature Appalachian sin-eaters, such as, for example, Garry Schmidt's 1996 *The Sin-Eater*, or Francine Reeves's *The Last Sin Eater*, specify Wales as being these emigrants' country of origin. Indeed, many Welsh people did in fact emigrate to the Appalachians during the second half of the nineteenth century, because of the similarities between their homeland and that locality – a mountainous country, with coal-mining as its main industry along with hill farming. But the details of the sin-eater's role seem to have become lost in transit here, for Tess in this story takes the sins of the living rather than the dead, and does so not through any act of mastication but through telepathically acquiring knowledge of their intended crimes and then carrying them out herself, as if hypnotically induced to do so. Caught within this pattern, she is on the verge of killing Craig at her neighbours' behest, before being awoken from her trance by the sudden realization that she loves him. Both Lew Merrill's and G. G. Pendarves's stories are tales of supernatural possession rather than traditional sin-eating, and both move into the romance genre before the close, bringing about a happy ending for the sin-eater in each case.

Nevertheless, as what would appear to be the first tale to portray a so-called sin-eater in an American location, Lew Merrill's story set a precedent. From the early 1960s sin-eaters have featured in about thirty literary or popular culture US texts, but the term is often used quite loosely without much reference to the original superstition. In *Sin Eater* (1960), for example, a pulp-fiction novel by Glenn Low (Glenn Dale Lough, 1906–1991) located in the Appalachians, the sin-eater is a psychotic serial killer who exterminates women as carriers of sin. He patrols the swamps, and kills like a swamp snake, by injecting poison held in his mouth into his victims' throats through biting them. The communities upon which he preys may be isolated, primitive and abject – one inhabitant comments: 'People just do what they feel like up here – kill a feller and throw his body into some slough . . . A powerful lot of people turns up missing and ain't ever heard tell of again here on the high river' – but otherwise there is little to connect this novel in which no sin-eating takes place, either literally or symbolically, with the Welsh originals.[73] The sin-eater in the graphic fiction *Ghost Rider* also operates in an isolated mid-American town, called Holly, but sin-eating here is once again but another name for demonic possession, this time of the living by a local pastor, Ethan Domblue. One of the town's inhabitants, Roxanne Simpson, explains Domblue's evolution to Johnny Blaze, the series' hero:

> The town pastor was Ethan Domblue, a quiet, almost timid soul. That's why it was such a surprise when, one day, he seemed . . . transformed. He started calling himself the Sin Eater . . . and swearing during his fiery sermons that he was empowered to devour all the sins that stain the human heart. And one by one the people of Holly turned to the Sin Eater, submitting to the absolution ceremony that they believed would free them from evil. That ceremony changed them, Johnny. They radiated a sense of peace and contentment all right . . . But it seemed more hellish than divine.[74]

In 1985, a character called Sin-eater also surfaced in *Spiderman* comics, this time in the role of a demented policeman turned vigilante killer, murdering those whom he deemed too liberal towards criminals. Strengthened by the sin-eating act, not shamed by it, these American sin-eaters refuse the scapegoat aspect of the role. They relate differently to their communities, surviving with assurance outside them or tyrannizing over them, unlike the abject Welsh sin-eaters who interiorize the community's view of them.

The same can also be said of another group of American sin-eaters who function in effect as psychotherapists. In these cases the precedence was probably set by the Canadian writer Margaret Atwood in her 1977 short story 'Sin eater' in which, for once, the sin-eater's Welsh origins are mentioned. The unnamed narrator recollects conversations with her psychoanalyst Joseph when, after his sudden death from a fall from a tree, she attends his funeral. He had once talked to her of sin-eaters, comparing their work favourably with his own profession: 'In Wales,' he had said,

> 'mostly in the rural areas, there was personage known as the Sin Eater . . . In point of fact I think Sin Eating has a lot to be said for it . . . think of the time saving . . . A couple of hours per patient, sum total, as opposed to twice a week for years and years, with the same result in the end . . . You wouldn't even have to listen to them,' he says. 'Not a blessed word. The sins are transmitted in the food.'[75]

During the funeral the narrator becomes reluctantly aware that the three-times married Joseph had led a troubled life, and may have killed himself: his second wife tells her, '"He didn't fall,"' and the narrator knows that 'what she wants me to infer is that he jumped'. But she resists the idea: 'I want Joseph to remain as he appeared: solid, capable, wise and sane. I do not need his darkness.'[76] That night, however, she has a dream in which she is sitting at a table with Joseph when they are approached by his first wife, carrying a platter of cakes similar to those which had earlier in the day been served to the guests at the funeral:

> She sets a large plate in front of us . . . The plate is filled with cookies . . . cut into the shapes of moons and stars . . . They look too rich. 'My sins,' Joseph says . . . I have a moment of panic: this is not what I ordered, it's too much for me, I might get sick. Maybe I could send it back; but I know this isn't possible.
>
> I remember now that Joseph is dead. The plate floats up towards me, there is no table, around us is dark space. There are thousands of stars, thousands of moons, and as I reach out for one they begin to shine.[77]

The narrator was in analysis because she could not rid herself of her cynical anger at having been cheated, she felt, by an unsatisfactory, empty life. In her dream she is in effect being told that pain, weakness, hatred, the dark processes of the psyche, both one's own and that of others, have to be recognized and ingested if life is to be found fulfilling. The suggestion is that men and women are all required to be one another's sin-eaters in the figurative sense, if they are to see the stars shine.

A similar message is conveyed in Bradley Denton's 'The sin eater of the Kaw' (1989), in which an apparently derelict 'hobo' of a sin-eater has a store of humane wisdom, as well as sins, to pass on, as he journeys through life relieving the living of their burden of guilt and unhappiness.[78] Similarly, in Elizabeth Rollins's *The Sin Eater* (2003) it is taken for granted that sin-eaters serve the living rather than the dead, and that they discuss with them the nature of their sin and guilt, in a therapeutic manner. In both tales the sin-eaters eat food supposedly impregnated with sin as part of the healing process, but only as part; at the close of Elizabeth Rollins' tale, her sin-eater, a woman whose appearance deteriorates from smart to derelict as the sin-eating proceeds, literally draws the sin of selfishness out of her patient's body, like 'a giant white root, a tendon, a bone'.[79] Another female sin-eater is the heroine of Alex Kava's *A Necessary Evil* (2006); in this crime fiction, the sin-eater is a nun who uses a computer game she has devised to elicit disclosures from choirboys about child-abusing priests; she then tracks the abusers down and quietly dispatches them herself, before cleansing them of their evil by performing the sin-eating act on their corpses.[80] Sin-eaters, then, appear to have changed and evolved like characters in some Chinese whispers game, owing more to their immediate fictional predecessors than to the original superstition. Their émigré characteristics seem by now to be better known than their Celtic ones, even in Britain. The Scottish Arts Council recently funded a 'quick read' novel by the Scottish writer Deborah J. Miller, for example, in which the sin-eater lurks in a swamp inhabited by crocodiles, suggesting that the otherwise unspecified setting of the tale is certainly not Scotland, or Wales for that matter. He does not eat food impregnated with sin, but gulps down 'something that looked like a bubble made from slimy muddy water', which issues from a corpse's mouth and hangs 'suspended in the air, polluting the room' until it dries 'into a thin, papery film', a description evidently drawn from the central scene in the US film *The Sin Eater* (2003), in which sin manifests itself very similarly.[81]

But whether they be killers or healers, once beyond Wales all sin-eaters share one central characteristic: they are not usually abject. One telling exception to this rule, however, occurs in the Native American writer Sherman Alexie's short-story collection *The Toughest Indian in the World* (2000). In his tale 'The sin eaters' the children of a Native American reservation are abruptly rounded up and taken away by the authorities to serve as sin-eaters to white men: the tale serves to highlight the degradations the colonizers' culture forced upon the Indians. One of their company explains to the bewildered children why they are held prisoners in a morgue: John tells them,

> There's a feast on the chest of every one of those dead white people out there. And that food is soaking up all of the hate and envy and sloth in those white people. That food is soaking up all of the anger and murder and thievery . . . Children, they're going to force us to devour those feasts, devour those sins.[82]

The natives are about to be forced literally to interiorize the colonizers' harmful ideologies with their food. Into them will be projected the failings of the dominant mother country; they will become the receptacles of their conquerors' darkness and they will be formed in that image and interiorize it as their own. This story is much closer to the Welsh fictions explored in the second part of this chapter than to the majority of the more recent tales which bear the same title. The abjection which is the dominant trait of Alexie's unfortunate sin-eaters was, as we have seen, also common to the Welsh sin-eater, from his first appearance in literature in the 1830s to his eventual demise in the second half of the twentieth century. By that time, however, a more self-assertive spirit was developing within Welsh culture, as it finally shed itself of its collusion with English rule. What remains to be considered in the last chapter of this study is the forms which Welsh Gothic took after the second referendum on Welsh devolution finally secured a positive result in 1997.

Epilogue

Post-devolution Gothic

Though Welsh devolution was won by the narrowest of margins in the second referendum of September 1997, the measure of autonomy it brought made a significant difference to Welsh cultural as well as political life. Now, Wales was for the first time a nation with a border marking out the fact that those living to the west of that line, under the governance of the Welsh National Assembly, had a straightforward civic identity which differed from that of England; no longer would it have to struggle to survive as a separate entity through emphasizing its ethnic difference and encouraging a pre-occupation with past grievances. Consequently, since 1997, the spirits of Llywelyn, Glyndŵr or Arthur, urging their descendants on with the fight, are less likely to manifest themselves in Gothic fictions written by Welsh-born authors. Indeed, Welsh Gothic writers today do not necessarily concern themselves with any specifically Welsh themes. Pembrokeshire-born Sarah Waters, for example, currently one of the best-known British novelists, has not as yet located any of her dark fictions in Wales, though it could be argued that her interest in the class conflicts which dominate her 2009 novel *The Little Stranger* has Welsh origins. Apparently, one of the historical events behind the novel's first conception was the case of a young Welsh woman from Neath, Elizabeth Jones, who aspired to make her fortune in London as a striptease artist but in October 1944 was found guilty of having with an accomplice committed robbery with violence, culminating in murder.[1] Young Welsh women seeking employment over the border during the first half of the twentieth century more usually ended up in domestic service; in *The Little Stranger*, set in the immediate post-war period, the unreliable narrator's recollection of his mother's role as maid-servant disquiets him to such an extent that he feels a 'dark dislike' for her former employers and appears to have brought about their downfall.[2]

Even when a text is located in Wales, it need not necessarily, post-devolution, share the characteristic preoccupations of earlier Welsh Gothic. Anglesey-born Dyfed Edwards has published Gothic novels in both Welsh and English, the latter under his pen-name Thomas Emson, but his themes in both languages are international. The vampires who attempt to take over a Welsh city in his *Dant at Waed* (A Taste – literally, a tooth – for Blood) have arrived there from all over the globe; their tale could have taken place in any European city, except for the fact that all its characters speak Welsh. Similarly, in Edwards/Emson's *Zombie Britannica* (2010), the zombies who successfully conquer Britain have no connection with Wales apart from the fact that one human character's knowledge of the sewage system in Beaumaris Castle, Anglesey, helps a group of their victims to make an attempted escape bid.[3]

One strand evident in pre-devolution Welsh Gothic continues to flourish in the post-devolution era, however: the re-telling of Welsh myth is as popular as ever. Blodeuwedd, Ceridwen and other characters from the Mabinogi continue to live on in twenty-first-century fictions, but in these more recent tales the way in which the resurrected power of myth can shed light as well as darkness is often emphasized. In *Darkhenge* (2005), for example, a young adults' fiction by Catherine Fisher from Newport in Gwent, the shape-shifting Taliesin who stole knowledge and inspiration from Ceridwen's cauldron intervenes in the contemporary world to aid the promising young writer, Chloe, paralysed by her family's neglect of her talent as much as by a road accident. Prone in a coma in the human world, Chloe is wandering through the forests of Annwn when her brother Rob, guided by Taliesin, arrives in the Otherworld through an ancient wooden henge excavated by archaeologists in their locality; the brother is alerted to the Darkhenge's role as gateway to Annwn when he sees a bird 'coming out of the earth alive' at the centre of the henge.[4] In effect, *Darkhenge* restores the gender balance distorted by 3,000 years of patriarchy by making its Taliesin, penitent for his inadvertent theft from Ceridwen, the promoter of Chloe's talent. It is he who reveals to Rob his unconscious resentment of his sister, telling him,

> 'You want her to die . . . all [your parents'] attention, all their love, would come back to you . . . there is a place inside you that feels these things . . . Dark as coal, a ring round your heart, like this henge. But maybe inside that, deeper and darker, is something else, and it would emerge if you let it, if you scraped at it and dug away at it, let all the creatures of your imagination come out of it, birds and beasts from depths you have no knowledge of. That's where Chloe is, Rob.'[5]

Enlightened by the bard/Druid's teachings, Rob finally succeeds in finding Chloe and persuading her to return from Annwn. In so doing he also saves himself from what the text suggests would otherwise have been a lifetime's corrosive unconscious guilt as well as conscious sorrow.

The corrosive effects of self-obsession are also healed by insights drawn from myth in Gwyneth Lewis's *The Meat Tree* (2010), one of the 'New Stories from the Mabinogion' series of myth re-writes commissioned by Seren Press. *The Meat Tree* re-engages with the fourth branch of the *Mabinogi*, which includes the story of Blodeuwedd, but its focus is not so much on Blodeuwedd herself as on the manner in which the myth appears to have intuited the theory of evolution. Just as animal and subsequently human life evolved from plant life according to Darwin, with every species sharing similar DNA patterns, so, in the myth, flowers become a woman in the form of Blodeuwedd and a tree sheds flesh, the flesh of the wounded Lleu, Blodeuwedd's cheated husband, in his metamorphosis as eagle. In *The Meat Tree*, which is set in the year 2210, an ageing and initially misanthropic inspector of wrecked spaceships and his angry young female apprentice come to realize that they, too, are caught up in an evolutionary process. A Virtual Reality system on an old apparently abandoned wreck draws them into the fourth branch of the *Mabinogi*; they act out its scenes and both become aware of the manner in which this myth too, like Ceridwen's story, illustrates the subjugation of women. More darkly, they also slowly grow to realize that myth feeds on the human imagination for its own survival. The fabric of the myth is the fabric of the spacecraft itself, which has never been abandoned but is nourished by the humans on whom it casts its spell, devouring them as they devour the plants from which they evolved. The inspector and his apprentice learn hidden truths of their own nature as they live out the myth, until the apprentice decides of her own volition to offer herself to the evolutionary process, thus freeing the inspector to return to base a wiser man, his misanthropy shattered. 'I've seen a rogue cell of alien imagination that consumed a living girl,' he thinks as he flees, but he also carries with him, as an abiding inspiration, the internalized voice of his apprentice reborn as living myth.[6]

Dark and light materials combine in this retelling, which is also hybrid in a generic sense, amalgamating as it does science-fiction and fantasy materials with Gothic shadowing. In so doing it illustrates another prevalent trend in modern Gothic: the genre as it evolves in new directions has shown a marked propensity to cross genre boundaries and emerge in hybrid forms. In texts like Malcolm Pryce's *Aberystwyth Mon Amour* (2001) and its numerous sequels, for example, Gothic materials are deployed ironically within detective fiction plots. Parodying Raymond Chandler's writing style, Pryce's private-eye narrator recounts his *noir* adventures in an Aberystwyth overrun by corrupt Druids who have metamorphosed into Mafia, managing not only the eisteddfod but organized crime and 'those people put into office to stop it'.[7] With their Witches' Co-ops and rune translation classes for schoolchildren, Price's novels are entertainingly mock-Gothic. Macabre mock-Gothic is also the dominant tone of many of the stories collected in Gwen Davies's recent anthology of Welsh Gothic short fiction, *Sing Sorrow Sorrow* (2010). Jon Gower's 'The pit', for example, revisits the underworld of the deep coal pits, those 'halls of lost kings, troglodyte rulers of the darkness under the land', in this tale of a collier buried underground in the 1920s who survives by turning cannibal and eating first his own severed arm, then the bodies of his dead co-workers.[8] His appetite for human flesh aroused, he stays underground, tunnelling from pit to pit throughout the south Wales coalfield, on the scent of the next disaster and the next store of fresh fodder. Finally, he is forced to the surface in the 1980s, as Thatcher closes the last Welsh pits, but manages to survive in the post-industrial valleys by 'stalking unwitting prey along the empty aisles of late night supermarkets'.[9]

Since the Thatcher era, authors writing in both of Wales's languages have also in all sober seriousness introduced into more realist texts a distinct strain of post-industrial and what might be termed post-rural Gothic, characteristically focusing on the broken lives of those left behind after the collapse of those occupations which formerly shaped their identity and that of their communities. In Rachel Trezise's *In and Out of the Goldfish Bowl* (2000), for example, the protagonist describes her upbringing in the Rhondda of the late 1980s: sexually abused by her stepfather, an unemployed collier sinking into alcoholism, she experiences herself as trapped in a 'glass coffin . . . where I could see and hear life going on around me, but where participating would not be possible. Speaking was not possible.'[10] Her surroundings in Penrhys council estate, 'the drug and crime capital of the valleys . . . a prison for the innocent and a haven for the criminal', reflect her hidden inner trauma: all day she paces 'around and around the bedroom in circles, circles, circles, too scared to go out but too scared to stay in, and all hours of the day I heard smashing in the distance. Why wouldn't someone shatter my glass?'[11] Though it is set in very different rural surroundings, the same pattern of lives haunted by hidden personal trauma lived out in communities disintegrating economically is also predominant in Caryl Lewis's *Martha, Jac a Sianco* (2004), in which a woman experiences herself as entombed alive on the failing farm in which she was reared. Because she has secretly buried on its land her still-born infant, the result of an unreported rape, she cannot bring herself to leave Graig-ddu (Black-rock). Omens of doom proliferate on the farm – a cow bites off its own teats, a raven knocks frenziedly at its windows – but still Martha stays on, even after her mentally damaged brother steals the poison she had intended for the *aderyn y drycin* (storm bird, foretelling death) and uses it to put out of his misery their older brother, a stroke victim, before taking the rest of it himself, leaving the sister alone at last, like a 'ghost of light in the darkness' of her home (*'fel ysbryd gole yn y tywyllwch'*).[12]

Like the post-industrial valleys, the rural Welsh-language heartlands of the north and west are currently in economic decline: 50
per cent of Welsh dairy farms have recently been forced to give up
the struggle, a fact reflected in *Martha, Jac and Sianco* when Martha
has to sell the farm's dairy stock as her brother sickens. Twenty-
first-century anglophone as well as Welsh-language novelists have
also focused on rural decline; farming communities are similarly
ossifying in Tristan Hughes's *Send My Cold Bones Home* (2006), in
which a newcomer to Anglesey makes the acquaintance of the local
recluse, Johnny, an 'Ancient Mariner' figure doomed to recount
the trauma of his and his ancestors' losses. 'I'd become . . . the
caretaker of all my pasts,' says Johnny; 'And being the last one I
couldn't just shut the gates and leave them behind. So I've stayed
locked in here with them, almost my whole life, thinking that if
only I could pass them on I'd be free.'[13] After Johnny's suicide, his
friends take his body back for burial to his parents' home village,
Llanysgerbwd (Skeleton's Parish), only to find it deserted and falling
into slow ruin. The title story in Glenda Beagan's short-story collection *The Great Master of Ecstasy* (2009) is also located on dying
farms, on the Anglo-Welsh border this time. The Vaughans of Maes
Derwen have traditionally acted as the guardians of their mountain
area, walking its boundaries and 'noticing and blessing all the plants
and animals in the old way and stopping in special places like
Ffynnon Wna and Craig Rwlff to repeat the rhymes'.[14] Hidden in
the chimney breast of the farm is a human skull which 'represents
the Guardian',[15] and in each generation of the family one of its
members has been blessed or cursed with shamanic gifts, marking
them out as the reincarnated guardian for that generation. But
the last two gifted members, Olwen and her son Kieran, flee the
responsibility as too complex and conflicted a burden for them to
carry without the traditional community support, and both die in
England with the farms left to perish or fall into strangers' hands.

In Lloyd Jones's apocalyptic dystopia *Y Dŵr* (The Water, 2009),
however, farmlands globally, not those of Wales alone, are threatened by ecological changes which have already made an island of
Wales and wrecked the country's infrastructure and economy, leaving its populace desperately scratching a living as subsistence farmers
or marauding pirates. The novel's central characters have fled the

violent city and returned to the old family farm, where they live in isolated ignorance, not even knowing that the dark water continually inching up the slopes of their fields and the walls of the old cottages is not a lake but the encroaching sea. The water's inexorable progress and 'overwhelming power' over their lives strikes them as uncanny: they fear it 'in a primitive fashion, beyond reason' (*'Roedd arnyn nhw ei ofn o mewn ffordd gyntefig, heb fod ganddynt reswm. Roedd ganddo . . . rym aruthrol drostyn nhw.'*)[16] Dark water also rules in Mihangel Morgan's *Pantglas* (2011), though it is set not in the future but in the 1880s when Welsh villages like Llanwddyn and Cwmtaf were drowned under reservoir waters with little public protest. Pantglas, an imaginary village whose tale combines the histories of Llanwddyn and Cwmtaf, is slowly emptied of its population as the 'dam walls grew around them every day' (*'muriau'r argae a dyfai o'u cwmpas bob dydd'*).[17] The village witch, Pedws Ffowc, warns the dam-builders that disaster will befall them if they move Carreg Einion (the Stone of Einion), a massive druid stone set above the village reputedly by its guardian spirit. But the builders ignore her, though bitter personal losses do indeed beset them, and the walls encircling the village continue inexorably to rise. The village blacksmith commits suicide, the aged opt for earlier than expected natural deaths and slowly Pantglas becomes 'a skeleton, a dead place', its few remaining inhabitants left musing 'how strange it is to think that a place so full of life as a village can be swept away and leave nothing behind it but ruins, remnants, traces' before they also leave (*'Roedd y pentre yn sgerbwd, yn lle marw . . . Rhyfedd meddwl bod modd sgubo i ffwrdd beth mor llawn bywyd â phentre a gadael ar ei ôl dim ond adfeilion, gweddillion, olion.'*).[18]

Pantglas in fact incorporates many of the themes introduced in this book. Its druid stones are emblems of those Celtic antiquities the rediscovery of which in the eighteenth century fuelled the beginnings of Welsh Gothic, just as its witch evokes Welsh folklore and mythology and their continuing influence upon the genre. Like many of the laments for the demise of rural Welsh communities, it also focuses on the issue of linguistic death. In contemporary Wales, though the census figures indicate that the decline in the number of Welsh speakers overall has slowed down, they also show that in many of the heartland communities, where Welsh speakers used to be in the majority, the numbers are still falling, a fact that imperils the longevity of the language. Pantglas is Welsh-speaking, but whether its villagers can take their language with them when they are forced out is uncertain. The village shopkeeper marries one of the dam builders, an Englishman, and as she prepares to leave, happily aware that she carries new life within her, she tells her unborn child: 'I will learn to speak proper English with you, won't I?' (in English in the original).[19] Drowned Welsh villages under reservoirs owned by municipal authorities in England also evoke more recent memories of Capel Celyn in Cwm Tryweryn, of course, which was not drowned without some protest and yet the protest was insufficient. Reservoirs in Wales, as R. S. Thomas said, function as 'the subconscious / Of a people, troubled far down / With gravestones, chapels, villages even.'[20] They evoke the 'long terror' of the conquered, the paralyzing fear of being impotent to control one's destiny and of having already betrayed and lost that which should have been precious.

And yet *Pantglas* is a book full of humour which wears its Gothic colouring ironically, expecting its readers to find Pedws Ffowc and her curses amusing as much as frightening. In that, too, as we have seen, it resembles contemporary Gothic, as the genre keeps changing and evolving. At the close of the novel, when the reservoir is full and there are few who remember the village of Pantglas, Pedws appears once more as a shape-shifting witch/goddess, like Ceridwen: she is a hare leaping along the reservoir's shores, then turning into a jackdaw, a black cat, a rat, a buzzard, a swan, and plunging under its waters as an otter, then a fish darting between the drowned village's old walls, before in the end becoming part of the water itself. Her backward evolution is a reminder of the shape-shifting vitality of the genre of which she is part, a genre which will no doubt continue to give imaginative expression to the future hidden dreads of Wales.

One category of Welsh Gothic has, however, proved remarkably resistant to any post-devolutionary changes: border-crossing novels recounting the misadventures which can befall tourists or would-be settlers in Cambria Gothica continue to be published, little changed in essence from the 'first-contact' narratives of the Romantic period, apart from an increased tendency towards violent sensationalism.

The wild Welsh landscape and the array of dark materials associated with it, along with subjugated spectral inhabitants still avid for vengeance, continue to provide a setting for contemporary 'imperial Gothic' fictions. Though the dead princes no longer haunt post-devolutionary Welsh-language Gothic, they are still potent in these texts primarily intended, presumably, for readers in England. In Trevor Dalton's *The Possession Legacy* (2006), for example, the blood of Llywelyn the Last Prince lives on, ever ready to attack the English invader. Before his death in the thirteenth century Llywelyn apparently drank of a chalice containing the blood of Merlin which turned him into a vampire; a mosquito drew his immortal blood and procreated a long-lived swarm of giant insects which in this novel continue in the twenty-first century to exact his vengeance on modern-day English visitors to Wales. Druids rather than princes keep the English at bay in Welsh-born Sally Spedding's *A Night with No Stars* (2004), in which Lucy Mitchell arrives from London intending to settle in Rhayader and grow organic vegetables, only to find that a secret neo-Druidic cult, the Dagda, still rules the area, its semi-insane members raping unwary English women. At the close Lucy escapes back to sanity in London where she warns her friends never to go to Wales, 'not any part of it': it is the 'Land of the Dead. The damned.'[21]

Wales is still an 'underworld' in such narratives, still seething 'under the hatches' with revengeful animosities. The longevity of such motifs, persisting after they have lost their historical rationale and been generally abandoned in fictions directed towards Welsh readers, alerts us to their function within the British imagination generally, as opposed to that of the Welsh alone. The term 'Welsh', when it was first coined by the Anglo-Saxon invaders, meant not simply 'foreigners' but 'Roman-colonized foreigners'; that concept of the Welsh, as both 'other' and subjugated, continues to tincture these modern-day Gothic representations of the Cymry. But of course when it was first coined the term referred to all Britons who had lived under Roman rule, not merely the inhabitants of Cymru. The violent 'return of the colonized repressed' fictionalized in these border-crossing Welsh Gothic novels can thus be read as reflecting at base a British historical trauma, experienced by the isle as a whole, south of Hadrian's Wall, but exteriorized before it could be fully surmounted and projected onto the image of the Cymry alone. That the trauma of its own experience of being colonized was not, until recently fully surmounted in the British consciousness is amply demonstrated by its history of compulsively repeated aggressive colonizing acts, following the pattern of the abused child who without therapeutic help can become the abusing adult.

It is some time now, though, since the sun set on the British Empire; Britain is changing and so is a devolved Wales, as it grows in confidence and shows readiness for increasing self-rule. The old 'underworld' motifs of Welsh Gothic may for a little longer persist, both in terms of how Wales sees itself and how it is seen by others, but they have lost their former virulence. The genre itself paradoxically helped to promote such changes; through repetitively instancing specifically Welsh patterns of the uncanny, it drew them into full consciousness, thus making it possible to analyse and understand them, dispersing much of their darkness. The aim of this book has been to further such a process by evidencing the existence not simply of Welsh Gothic but of its characteristic patterns as they have been made manifest to date.

Notes

༄

1: Prologue

1   Gruffudd ab yr Ynad Goch, 'Marwnad Llywelyn ap Gruffudd', in
     Thomas Parry (ed.), *The Oxford Book of Welsh Verse* (Oxford: Oxford
     University Press, 1962), pp. 45–8; 'Lament for Llywelyn ap Gruffudd,
     the Last Prince', trans. Tony Conran, *Welsh Verse* (1976; Bridgend:
     Poetry Wales Press, 1986), pp. 161–4.
2   [Anon.], 'Stafell Cynddylan', *Oxford Book of Welsh Verse*, p. 12; 'Cyn-
     ddylan's Hall', trans. Conran, *Welsh Voices*, p. 127.
3   Thomas Gray, 'The Bard' [1757], *The Complete English Poems of Thomas
     Gray*, ed. James Reeves (London: Heinemann, 1973), pp. 78–9.
4   Patrick Brantlinger, *Rule of Darkness: British Literature and Imperialism
     1830–1914* (Ithaca, NY: Cornell University Press, 1988), pp. 227–53.
5   See, for example, Murray G. H. Pittock, *Celtic Identity and the British
     Image* (Manchester and NY: Manchester University Press, 1999),
     pp. 94–116; Stephen Knight, *One Hundred Years of Fiction: Writing
     Wales in English* (Cardiff: University of Wales Press, 2004); Kirsti Bohata,
     Postcolonialism Revisited (Cardiff: University of Wales Press, 2004); Dai
     Smith, 'Psycho-colonialism', *New Welsh Review*, 66 (2004), 22–9; Jane
     Aaron, 'Postcolonial change', *New Welsh Review*, 67 (2005), 32–6;
     Jane Aaron and Chris Williams (eds), *Postcolonial Wales* (Cardiff: Uni-
     versity of Wales Press, 2005); Kirsti Bohata, '"Psycho-colonialism"
     revisited', *New Welsh Review*, 69 (2005), 31–9.
6   William Hughes and Andrew Smith, 'Introduction: defining the relation-
     ships between Gothic and the postcolonial', *Gothic Studies*, 'Postcolonial

Gothic' special no., 5/2 (2003), 1; see also Andrew Smith and William Hughes (eds), *Empire and the Gothic: The Politics of Genre* (Basingstoke: Palgrave Macmillan, 2003).

7   See, for example, Seamus Deane, *Strange Country: Modernity and Nationhood in Irish Writing since 1790* (London: Oxford University Press, 1997); Jim Hansen, *Terror and Irish Modernism* (NY: SUNY Press, 2009).

8   Kirsti Bohata 'Apes and cannibals in Cambria: images of the racial and gendered other in Gothic writing in Wales', *Welsh Writing in English: A Yearbook of Critical Essays*, 6 (2000), 119–43, and '"Unhomely Moments": Reading and Writing Nation in Welsh Female Gothic', in Diana Wallace and Andrew Smith, eds., *The Female Gothic: New Directions* (Basingstoke: Palgrave Macmillan, 2009), pp. 180–95; Darryl Jones, 'Borderlands: spiritualism and the occult in fin de siècle and Edwardian Welsh and Irish horror', *Irish Studies Review*, 17/1 (2009), 31–44; Jane Aaron, 'Twentieth-century and Contemporary Welsh Gothic', *Literature Compass*, 7/4 (2010), 281–9. *www3.interscience.wiley.com/journal/123338358*.

9   See Sigmund Freud, 'The "Uncanny"' [1919], *The Standard Edition of the Complete Psychological Works of Sigmund Freud: An Infantile Neurosis and Other Works (1917–1919)*, XVII, ed. James Strachey (1955; London: Vintage, 2001), pp. 241–51.

10 Robert Mighall, *A Geography of Victorian Gothic Fiction: Mapping History's Nightmares* (Oxford: Oxford University Press, 1999), p. xxv.

11 See Knight, *One Hundred Years of Fiction*, pp. 1–49, for an account of 'first-contact texts', penned by colonial travellers portraying 'the mysterious, magical, even sinister elements of the colony and its people' (p. 3).

12 Sion Eirian, 'Welsh Gothic' in Marie Mulvey-Roberts (ed.), *The Handbook to Gothic Literature* (Basingstoke and London: Macmillan, 1998), pp. 251–2.

13 Kelly Hurley, 'British Gothic fiction, 1885–1930', in Jerrold E. Hogle (ed.), *The Cambridge Companion to Gothic Fiction* (Cambridge: Cambridge University Press, 2002), pp. 189–90.

1: Cambria Gothica (1780s–1820s)

1   [Julia Ann Hatton], Ann of Swansea, *Cambrian Pictures; or, Every One Has Errors*, 3 vols, i (London: E. Kerby, 1810), p. 76.

2   Ibid., p. 77.

3   Ibid., pp. 78–9.
4   Ibid., pp. 80 and 85.
5   Ibid., p. 86.
6   Ibid., p. 89.
7   See Richard Holland, *Haunted Wales: A Survey of Welsh Ghostlore* (Ashbourne: Landmark Publishing, 2005), pp. 111–13; Ken Radford, *Tales of South Wales* (London: Skilton & Shaw, 1979), pp. 56–7; Eirlys Gruffydd, *Gwrachod Cymru* (Caernarfon: Gwasg Gwynedd, 1980), pp. 57, 82–3.
8   [Isabella Kelly], *The Abbey of St Asaph*, 3 vols (London: Minerva Press, 1795), i, p. 50.
9   Ibid., ii, p. 28.
10   Ibid., ii, pp. 38, 157, 218–19.
11   Ibid., ii, pp. 223–4.
12   Ibid., iii, p. 92.
13   See ibid., iii, pp. 13–15, 127–8.
14   Ibid., ii, pp. 159–61.
15   Sarah Lansdell, *The Tower; or the Romance of Ruthyne*, 3 vols (London: printed for the author, 1798), i, pp. 5–6, 31.
16   Ibid., p. 11.
17   Ann Howell Ann, *Anzoletta Zadoski. A Novel*, 2 vols (London: Minerva Press, 1796), ii, pp. 124–5.
18   Ibid., pp. 122–3, 128–9.
19   Matthew G. Lewis, *The Castle Spectre: A Drama. In Five Acts* [1797] (London: I. Bell, 1798), p. i. M. G. Lewis also profited more directly from the African slave trade; his family's vast fortune was established on the basis of their colonial estates.
20   Ibid., pp. 101–2.
21   Charles Lucas, *The Castle of Saint Donats: or, The History of Jack Smith*, 3 vols (London: William Lane, 1798), i, pp. 84–5.
22   Emily Clark, *Ianthé, or the Flower of Caernarvon*, 2 vols (London: printed for the author, 1798), i, pp. 9, 92.
23   Andrew Davies, '"The Gothic novel in Wales" revisited: a preliminary survey of the Wales-related Romantic fiction at Cardiff University', *Cardiff Corvey: Reading the Romantic Text*, 2 (1998), *www.cardiff.ac.uk/encap/journals/corvey/articles/cc02_n01.pdf*, accessed 6 October 2012; the article constitutes a critical revision of James Henderson, 'The Gothic novel in Wales', *The National Library of Wales Journal*, 11 (1959–60), 244–54.
24   R. C. Hoare (ed.), *Itinerary of Bishop Baldwin in Wales* [1806], quoted in Philip Jenkins, *The Making of a Ruling Class: The Glamorgan Gentry 1640–1790* (Cambridge: Cambridge University Press, 1983), p. 249.

25 See, for example, Linda Colley, *Britons: Forging the Nation 1797–1837* (New Haven and London: Yale University Press, 1992); Katie Trumpener, *Bardic Nationalism: The Romantic Novel and the British Empire* (Princeton, NJ: Princeton University Press, 1997); Murray Pittock, *Celtic Identity and the British Image* (Manchester and NY: Manchester University Press, 1999).

26 See Colley, *Britons*, p. 156.

27 Anna Maria Bennett, *Ellen, Countess of Castle Howel* (London, 1794; 2nd edn, 2 vols, Dublin: Jones, Colbert, Fitzpatrick & Milliken, 1794), i, pp. 2–3.

28 Ibid., pp. 192, 259, 277; the text italicizes.

29 Sarah Prescott, *Eighteenth-century Writing from Wales: Bards and Britons* (Cardiff: University of Wales Press, 2008), p. 145.

30 Mary Robinson, *Angelina; A Novel*, 3 vols (London: Hookham & Carpenter, 1796), iii, pp. 272–3.

31 [Robert Evans], *The Stranger; or, Llewellyn Family: A Cambrian Tale*, 2 vols (London: Minerva Press, 1798), ii, pp. 38, 40.

32 Ibid., p. 41.

33 Ibid., i, pp. 70–1.

34 Sigmund Freud, 'The "Uncanny"' [1919], *The Standard Edition of the Complete Psychological Works of Sigmund Freud: An Infantile Neurosis and Other Works (1917–1919)*, XVII, ed. James Strachey (1955; London: Vintage, 2001), p. 235.

35 [Evans], *The Stranger*, i, p. 29.

36 Ibid., p. 33; the text italicizes.

37 Ibid., pp. 33, 34–5; the text italicizes.

38 Cecil Price, *The English Theatre in Wales in the Eighteenth and Early Nineteenth Centuries* (Cardiff: University of Wales Press, 1948), p. 40.

39 For further biographical information, see Ivor J. Bromham, '"Ann of Swansea" (Ann Julia Hatton: 1764–1838)', *Glamorgan Historian*, 7 (1971), 173–86; and James Henderson, 'An edition of the poems of Ann of Swansea (Ann Julia Hatton, née Kemble, 1764–1838) including unpublished material' (unpublished M.Phil. thesis, University of Glamorgan, 2005).

40 Ann of Swansea, *Cambrian Pictures*, i, pp. 163 and 169.

41 Ibid., i, p. 179.

42 Ibid, ii, p. 17.

43 Ibid., i, pp. 113–14.

44 Jim Hansen, *Terror and Irish Modernism: The Gothic Tradition from Burke to Beckett* (Albany, NY: SUNY Press, 2009), p. 16.

45 1536 Act of Union between England and Wales; quoted in Norman Davies, *The Isles: A History* (London: Macmillan, 1999), pp. 492–3.

46 Anna Maria Bennett, *Anna: or Memoirs of a Welch Heiress: interspersed with anecdotes of a Nabob*, 4 vols (London: William Lane, 1785; 2nd edn, London: William Lane, 1786), i, p. 89.

47 Bennett, *Ellen; Countess of Castle Howel*, i, pp. 24–5; the text italicizes.

48 Ann of Swansea, *Cambrian Pictures*, ii, pp. 348–9.

49 Ibid., iii, pp. 33–4.

50 Ibid., p. 157.

51 J. C. Horner, 'Richards, Thomas (1800–1877)', *Australian Dictionary of National Biography*, http://adb.anu.edu.au/biography/richards-thomas-4472/text/297, accessed 17 August 2011.

52 See *www.british-fiction.cf.ac.uk/guide/authorlist.html*, 'ANWYL, Edward Trevor [pseud?]', accessed 6 October 2012.

53 [Thomas Richards], *Tales of Welsh Society and Scenery*, 2 vols (London: Longman, Rees, Orme, Brown and Green, 1827), ii, p. 212.

54 Ibid., p. 239.

55 Ibid., p. 248.

56 Ibid., pp. 257 and 260.

57 Ibid., p. 275.

58 Ibid., p. 281.

59 Ibid., p. 284.

60 Ibid., p. 286.

61 Ibid., p. 287.

62 Ibid., p. 310.

63 Ibid., p. 314.

64 See Lady Charlotte Guest, *The Mabinogion Translated from the Red Book of Hergest*, 3 vols (1838–49; London: T. Fisher Unwin, 1902), iii, p. 143.

65 [William Owen Pughe], 'Preface', *The Cambrian Register*, i ([1796] 1795), v.

66 William Earle, Jnr, *The Welshman, a Romance*, 4 vols (London: Earle and Hemet, 1801); for further information on Earle's career, see Andrew Davies, 'The reputed nation of inspiration: representations of Wales in fiction from the Romantic period, 1780–1830' (unpublished Ph.D. thesis, Cardiff University, 2001), 130.

67 Earle, *The Welshman*, iv, pp. 184–5

68 Ibid., p. 244.

69 David Punter, 'Scottish and Irish Gothic', in Jerrold E. Hogle (ed.), *The Cambridge Companion to Gothic Fiction* (Cambridge: Cambridge University Press, 2002), pp. 110, 113, 122–3.

70 Earle, *The Welshman*, iv, pp. 1–2; the text italicizes.

71 See Davies, '"The Gothic novel in Wales" revisited'; the text italicizes.

72 [William Earle], 'The knight of the blood-red plume', *Welsh Legends: A Collection of Popular Oral Tales* (London: J. Babcock, 1802), p. 65.

73 Ibid., pp. 67–8.

74 Ibid., p. 66.

75 The name is absurd in Welsh, as it means Iolo of the Wash (i.e. laundry); Earle is probably thinking of Iolo Goch, a fourteenth-century poet.

76 [William Earle], 'The Mountain Bard', *Welsh Legends*, p. 275.

77 Ibid., pp. 277–8, 279, 280.

78 Evan Jones, *The Bard, or, The Towers of Morven. A Legendary Tale* (London: printed for the author, 1809), p. 56.

79 Ibid., p. 104.

80 Richard Llwyd, *Beaumaris Bay, a Poem: with Notes, Descriptive and Explanatory* (Chester: J. Fletcher, n. d. [1800]), pp. 13–15.

81 Thomas Pennant, *A Tour in Wales*, 2 vols (1778–81; London: Wilkie and Robinson, et al., 1810), ii, pp. 232–4.

82 I. D. Hooson, 'Y Gwylliaid Cochion', *Cerddi a Baledi* (Dinbych: Gwasg Gee, 1936), p. 94.

83 Nella Stephens, *The Robber Chieftain, or, Dinas Linn*, 4 vols (London: A. K. Newman, 1825), i, p. 126.

84 Ibid., ii, p. 131.

85 Ibid., iv, pp. 222–3.

86 Ibid., ii, p. 75.

87 Ibid., ii, p. 85.

88 Diana Wallace, *Female Gothic Histories* (Cardiff: University of Wales Press, 2013), p. 1.

2: An Underworld of One's Own (1830s–1900s)

1 Robert Mighall, *A Geography of Victorian Gothic Fiction: Mapping History's Nightmares* (Oxford: Oxford University Press, 1999), p. xviii.

2 Patrick Brantlinger, *Rule of Darkness: British Literature and Imperialism 1830–1914* (Ithaca, NY: Cornell University Press, 1988), pp. 227–53.

3 Thomas Love Peacock, *The Misfortunes of Elphin* [1829], in *Novels of Thomas Love Peacock*, ed. Barbara Lloyd Evans (London: Pan, 1967), p. 175.

4 For an account of the Rebecca riots, see David J. V. Jones, *Rebecca's Children: A Study of Rural Society, Crime and Protest* (Oxford: Clarendon Press, 1989).

5 See David Howell, 'The Rebecca riots', in Trevor Herbert and Gareth Elwyn Jones (eds), *People & Protest: Wales 1815–1880* (Cardiff: University of Wales Press, 1988), p. 129.

6   Quoted in Ieuan Gwynedd Jones, *Mid-Victorian Wales: The Observers and the Observed* (Cardiff: University of Wales Press, 1992), p. 123.

7   Quoted in W. Gareth Evans, 'Y ferch, addysg a moesoldeb: portread y Llyfrau Gleision 1847', in Prys Morgan (ed.), *Brad y Llyfrau Gleision* (Llandysul: Gwasg Gomer, 1991), p. 95.

8   *Report of the Commission of Inquiry into the State of Education in Wales . . . In Three Parts. Part I, Carmarthen, Glamorgan and Pembroke. Part II, Brecknock, Cardigan, Radnor and Monmouth. Part III, North Wales* (London, 1847), ii, p. 66.

9   Joseph Conrad, 'Heart of darkness' [1902], *Youth and Heart of Darkness* (London: Dent, 1965), p. 50.

10   Sigmund Freud, 'The "Uncanny"', *The Standard Edition of the Complete Psychological Works of Sigmund Freud: An Infantile Neurosis and Other Works (1917–1919)*, XVII, ed. James Strachey (1955; London: Vintage, 2001), p. 244.

11   Matthew Arnold, quoted in Saunders Lewis, *Tynged yr Iaith* (1962; Llandysul: Gwasg Gomer, 2012), p. 42.

12   See Dot Jones, *Statistical Evidence relating to the Welsh Language 1801–1911* (Cardiff: University of Wales Press, 1998), p. 221.

13   Joseph Downes, *The Mountain Decameron*, 3 vols (London: Richard Bentley, 1836), i, p. 4; the text italicizes.

14   See, for example, David Punter and Glennis Byron, 'Victorian Gothic', in *The Gothic* (Oxford: Blackwell, 2004), p. 27.

15   See Philip Jenkins, *The Making of a Ruling Class: The Glamorgan Gentry 1640–1790* (Cambridge: Cambridge University Press, 1983).

16   'Beuno', 'Legend of Iolo ap Hugh', *The Cambrian Quarterly Magazine and Celtic Repertory*, i (1829), 41.

17   Ibid., 42.

18   'Beuno', 'Legend of Bala Lake', *The Cambrian Quarterly Magazine and Celtic Repertory*, i (1829), 53–4; in this case, as opposed to the 'Legend of Iolo ap Hugh', the legend is traditional.

19   See, for example, Mighall, *A Geography of Victorian Gothic Fiction*, pp. 78–103.

20   Downes, *The Mountain Decameron*, i, p. 299.

21   Ibid., i, p. 211.

22   Ibid., p. 213.

23   Ibid., pp. 235–6; the text italicizes.

24   Ibid., p. 267. 'The tragical passion of Marmaduke Paull' bears interesting resemblance to Mary Shelley's novel *Mathilda*, written in 1819, but as *Mathilda* was not in fact published until 1959, that similarity is presumably coincidental.

25 See Sigmund Freud, 'From the history of an infantile neurosis' [1918], in *The Standard Edition of the Complete Psychological Works of Sigmund Freud: An Infantile Neurosis and Other Works (1917–1919)*, XVII, ed. James Strachey (1955; London: Vintage, 2001), pp. 101–2.

26 William Shakespeare, *Henry IV: Part I*, Act I, sc iii, l.82 and Act III, sc. i, l. 50.

27 Elizabeth Gaskell, 'The doom of the Griffiths', *Harper's Magazine* [1858], repr. in Laura Kranzler (ed.), *Gothic Tales* (Harmondsworth: Penguin, 2000), p. 104.

28 Ibid., p. 108.

29 Ibid., p. 113.

30 Ibid., p. 124.

31 Ibid., p. 138.

32 Sarah Williams (Sadie), *Twilight Hours: A Legacy of Verse* (London: Strahan & Co, 1868), p. 37.

33 Ibid., p. 47.

34 Ibid., p. 58.

35 Ibid., p. 56.

36 *Report of the Commission of Inquiry into the State of Education in Wales*, ii, 56.

37 Jarlath Killeen, *Gothic Literature 1825–1914* (Cardiff: University of Wales Press, 2009), p. 124.

38 Ernest Rhys, *Welsh Ballads and Other Poems* (London, Carmarthen and Bangor: David Nutt, W. Spurrell and Jarvis and Foster, 1895), p. x.

39 Ibid., pp. 4–5.

40 Ibid., p. 105.

41 Ibid., pp. 38 and 40.

42 T. Gwynn Jones, 'Ymadawiad Arthur' [1902], *Caniadau* (Wrecsam: Hughes a'i Fab, 1934), p. 32; trans. 'Arthur's Passing', Tony Conran, *Welsh Verse* (1976; Bridgend: Poetry Wales Press, 1986), pp. 258–9.

43 [Annie Harriet Hughes] Gwyneth Vaughan, 'Breuddwyd nos Nadolig', *Cymru*, 29 (1905), 246; my translation. All translations from the Welsh throughout this volume are its author's, unless otherwise stated.

44 Frantz Fanon, *The Wretched of the Earth*, trans. C. Farrington (New York: Grove Press, 1963), p. 240.

45 See, for example, Cadwalader Griffiths, 'In search of that which was lost', *The Red Dragon: The National Magazine of Wales*, i (1882), 563–7; Thomas Davis, 'Cymric rule and Cymric rulers', *The Red Dragon*, ix (1886), 113–14. For a further account of Charles Wilkins's career as editor, see Malcolm Ballin, *Welsh Periodicals in English: 1882–2000* (Cardiff: University of Wales Press, 2012).

46   Charles Wilkins, *Kilsanos: A Tale of the Welsh Mountains* (Cardiff: Daniel Owen, 1894), pp. 31 and 38.

47   Ibid., p. 70.

48   Ibid., pp. 7 and 76; the text italicizes.

49   Ibid., p. 78.

50   Ibid., p. 99

51   Peter Lord, *Winifred Coombe Tennant: A Life through Art* (Aberystwyth: Llyfrgell Genedlaethol Cymru, 2007), pp. 19, 25 and 27.

52   Frances Mary Owen, *Across the Hills* (London: Kegan Paul, Tench & Co., 1883), pp. 5 and 7.

53   Ibid., p. 24.

54   Ibid., p. 30.

55   Ibid., pp. 16 and 25.

56   See Miranda J. Green, *Exploring the World of the Druids* (London: Thames & Hudson, 1997), pp. 170 and 178.

57   Owen, *Across the Hills*, p. 19.

58   [Anon], 'Druidism and popular Welsh occultism', *The Platonist* (1890s; repr. Largs, Scotland: The Banton Press, 1991), p. 300.

59   Ibid., p. 109.

60   Ibid., p. 300.

61   Ibid.

62   Ibid., pp. 298 and 107.

63   Ibid., p. 302.

64   See Geraint H. Jenkins (ed.), *A Rattleskull Genius: The Many Faces of Iolo Morganwg* (Cardiff: University of Wales Press, 2005); Mary-Ann Constantine, *The Truth against the World: Iolo Morganwg and Romantic Forgery* (Cardiff: University of Wales Press, 2007); and Catherine A. Charnell-White, *Bardic Circles: National, Regional and Personal Identity in the Bardic Vision of Iolo Morganwg* (Cardiff: University of Wales Press, 2007), for more information on Iolo's forgeries and druidism.

65   See John Harris, 'Queen of the Rushes: Allen Raine and her public', *Planet*, 97 (1993), 64–72; and Hutchinson's tabulations published as frontispieces to their 1906 and 1911 editions of Raine's novels.

66   Sally Roberts Jones, *Allen Raine* (Cardiff: University of Wales Press, 1979), p. 16.

67   Allen Raine, *Where Billows Roll* (London: Hutchinson, 1909), p. 23.

68   Ibid., pp. 81–2.

69   Ibid., p. 24.

70   Ibid., p. 54.

71   Ibid., p. 57.

72   Ibid., pp. 299–300.

73   Ibid., pp. 339 and 337.
74   See Arthur Machen, *The Secret Glory* (London: Martin Secker, 1922).
75   See 'Things near and far', in Arthur Machen, *The Autobiography of Arthur Machen* (London: The Richards Press, 1951), p. 287.
76   Quoted in Mark Valentine, *Arthur Machen*, Border Lines series (Bridgend: Seren, 1995), p. 71.
77   Kirsti Bohata, 'Apes and cannibals in Cambria: images of the racial and gendered other in Gothic writing in Wales', *Welsh Writing in English: A Yearbook of Critical Essays*, 6 (2000), 126; and Darryl Jones, 'Borderlands: spiritualism and the occult in fin de siècle and Edwardian Welsh and Irish horror', *Irish Studies Review*, 17/1 (2009), 38.
78   Arthur Machen, *Far Off Things* [1922], in *The Autobiography of Arthur Machen*, p. 18.
79   See, for example, Arthur Machen, *The Three Impostors* (London: John Lane, 1895; repr. Mineola, NY: Dover Publications, 2007), p. 53.
80   Valentine, *Arthur Machen*, p. 57.
81   Ibid., p. 14.
82   Machen, *Far Off Things*, in *The Autobiography of Arthur Machen*, p. 18.
83   Arthur Machen, *The Hill of Dreams* [1907], repr. *The Great God Pan and The Hill of Dreams* (Mineola, NY: Dover Publications, 2006), p. 83.
84   Ibid., pp. 85–6.
85   Ibid., pp. 109, 112.
86   Ibid., p. 113.
87   See Kirsti Bohata, *Postcolonialism Revisited* (Cardiff: University of Wales Press, 2004), p. 33–4, on the 'little people' as the 'vestiges of an aboriginal British race'.
88   Machen, *The Hill of Dreams*, pp. 133–4.
89   Ibid., pp. 183–4.
90   Ibid., p. 195.
91   Arthur Machen, *The Great God Pan* [1894], repr. *The Great God Pan and The Hill of Dreams* (Mineola, NY: Dover Publications, 2006), pp. 20 and 22.
92   Ibid., p. 26.
93   Fred Botting, *Gothic* (London: Routledge, 1996), p. 143.
94   Machen, *The Great God Pan*, pp. 61–2.
95   Mighall, *A Geography of Victorian Gothic Fiction*, pp. 202 and 207.
96   Machen says as much in his 1916 'Introduction' to the novel; see *The Great God Pan and The Hill of Dreams*, pp. 3–4.
97   Ibid., pp. 63–4.
98   Arthur Machen, 'The novel of the black seal', *The Three Impostors*, p. 53.
99   Ibid., p. 76.

100 Ibid., p. 82.
101 Ibid., p. 83.
102 Arthur Machen, 'The shining pyramid' [1895], repr. in R. Chetwynd-Hayes (ed.), *Welsh Tales of Terror* (London: Fontana, 1973), p. 69.
103 Ibid., pp. 69–70.
104 Ibid., pp. 63–4.
105 Ibid., p. 64.
106 Machen, 'Far off things', in *The Autobiography of Arthur Machen*, pp. 27–8.
107 Ibid., p. 121.
108 Arthur Machen, 'Introduction' [1923], in *The Great God Pan and The Hill of Dreams*, p. 70.
109 Arthur Machen, 'A fragment of life', *The House of Souls* (London: Grant Richards, 1906; repr. US: Blackmask, 2007), pp. 24 and 58.
110 Ibid., pp. 58 and 66.
111 Ibid., pp. 60, 66–7.
112 Ibid., p. 61.
113 Ibid., p. 69.
114 Ibid., pp. 3 and 75.
115 See Arthur Machen, *The Great Return* (London: The Faith Press, 1915).
116 See Valentine, *Arthur Machen*, p. 80.

3: Haunted Communities (1900s–1940s)

1 Avery F. Gordon, *Ghostly Matters: Haunting and the Sociological Imagination* (1997; new edn, Minneapolis: University of Minnesota Press, 2008), p. xvi.
2 Walter Benjamin, 'What is epic theatre?' [1939], *Understanding Brecht* (London: New Left Books, 1977), pp. 18–19.
3 For these figures, see W. J. Rees, 'Inequalities: Caradoc Evans and D. J. Williams', *Planet*, 81 (1990), 77.
4 Harri Webb, *The Green Desert: Collected Poems 1950–1969* (Llandysul: Gwasg Gomer, 1969).
5 Dot Jones, *Statistical Evidence relating to the Welsh Language 1801–1911* (Cardiff: University of Wales Press, 1998), pp. 17–18, 23 and 28.
6 Graham Day, 'The sociology of Wales', in I. Hume and W. T. R. Pryce (eds), *The Welsh and their Country* (Llandysul: Gomer Press, 1986), pp. 163–4.
7 Quoted in Bill Jones and Beth Thomas, *Coal's Domain* (Cardiff: National Museum of Wales, 1993), pp. 37, 47.

[8] Glyn Jones, *The Dragon Has Two Tongues: Essays on Anglo-Welsh Writers and Writing* (London: J. M. Dent, 1968), p. 55.

[9] Edward Wright, *The Bookman*, October 1917; quoted in T. L. Williams, *Caradoc Evans* (Cardiff: University of Wales Press, 1970), p. 12. The likely truth of this tale has since been queried, however: see David Jenkins, *Anglo-Welsh Review* (winter 1974), 50–1.

[10] See John Harris, 'Introduction: "The Banned, Burned Book of War"', in Caradoc Evans, *My People* (1915; Bridgend: Seren Books, 1987), pp. 41–2.

[11] Tony Conran, 'A note on Caradoc Evans', in *The Cost of Strangeness* (Llandysul: Gwasg Gomer, 1982), pp. 156–7.

[12] Arthur Machen, 'Caradoc Evans', in Oliver Sandys, *Caradoc Evans* (London: Hurst & Blackett, 1945), p. 146.

[13] M. Wynn Thomas, *In the Shadow of the Pulpit: Literature and Nonconformist Wales* (Cardiff: University of Wales Press, 2010).

[14] Lewis Morris, 'Young Mends the clothier's sermon' [*c*.1743], National Library of Wales MS 67A, 57–68; quoted in Geraint H. Jenkins, 'The new enthusiasts', in Trevor Herbert and Gareth Elwyn Jones (eds), *The Remaking of Wales in the Eighteenth Century* (Cardiff: University of Wales Press, 1988), pp. 56 and 69–70.

[15] William Roberts, *Ffrewyll y Methodistiaid* [*c*.1747], ed. A. Cynfael Lake (Caerdydd: Gwasg Prifysgol Cymru, 1998), p. 39.

[16] Valentine Cunningham, *Everywhere Spoken Against: Dissent in the Victorian Novel* (Oxford: Clarendon Press, 1975), pp. 199–225.

[17] Anna Maria Bennett, *Anna, or, Memoirs of a Welch Heiress: interspersed with anecdotes of a Nabob*, 4 vols (1785; 2nd edn, London: William Lane, 1786), i, pp. 12, 13 and 15.

[18] Robinson claimed that her mother hailed from the Seys family of Castle Boverton in the Vale of Glamorgan; see Moira Dearnley, *Distant Fields: Eighteenth-century Fictions of Wales* (Cardiff: University of Wales Press, 2001), p. 172.

[19] Mary Robinson, *Walsingham, or, The Pupil of Nature*, 4 vols (London: T. N. Longman, 1797); repr. facs. edn, with intro. by Peter Garside (London: Routledge/ Thoemmes Press, 1992), ii, p. 328.

[20] Ibid., ii, p. 317; the text italicizes.

[21] Mary Robinson, *Memoirs of the late Mrs Robinson, written by herself. With some posthumous pieces*, ed. Maria Elizabeth Robinson, 4 vols (London: Richard Phillips, 1801; first two vols repr. as *Perdita: The Memoirs of Mary Robinson*, ed. M. J. Levy (London: Peter Owen, 1994)), p. 50.

[22] [Robert Evans], *The Stranger; or, Llewellyn Family: A Cambrian Tale*, 2 vols (London: Minerva Press, 1798), ii, p. 150.

23 William Frederick Williams, *Fitzmaurice: A Novel*, 2 vols (London: J. Murray and S. Highley, 1800), ii, p. 79.

24 Ibid., p. 80.

25 Ibid., pp. 128, 129, 132.

26 Brutus [David Owen], *Wil Brydydd y Coed* (1863–66; Caerdydd: Gwasg Prifysgol Cymru, 1949), p. 244.

27 Allen Raine, *Queen of the Rushes: A Tale of the Welsh Revival* (1906; Dinas Powys: Honno Press, 1998), p. 258.

28 *Report of the Commission of Inquiry into the State of Education in Wales . . . In Three Parts. Part I, Carmarthen, Glamorgan and Pembroke. Part II, Brecknock, Cardigan, Radnor and Monmouth. Part III, North Wales* (London, 1847), ii, p. 56.

29 Max Baring [Charles Messent], *A Prophet of Wales: A Story* (London: Greening & Company, 1905), pp. 170, 291.

30 Andrew Melrose, on the dust-jacket of *My People* (1915), quoted in John Harris, 'Introduction' to Evans, *My People*, p. 34.

31 Caradoc Evans, *Western Mail*, 23 January 1917.

32 Lloyd George quoted in Williams, *Caradoc Evans*, p. 21.

33 Evans, *My People*, p. 143.

34 Caradoc Evans, *Capel Sion* (1916; Bridgend: Seren, 2002), p. 25.

35 Ibid., p. 43.

36 Caradoc Evans, 'Self portrait', *Wales* (1944), 3; see also on Caradoc Evans's style, Thomas, *In the Shadow of the Pulpit*, pp. 129–34.

37 Evans, *My People*, pp. 64–5.

38 Ibid., p. 112.

39 For a thorough-going analysis of Caradoc Evans's writings, and of the story 'Be this her memorial' in particular, in the light of Julia Kristeva's concept of abjection, see Harri Garrod Roberts, *Embodying Identity: Representations of the Body in Welsh Literature* (Cardiff: University of Wales Press, 2009), pp. 45–69, and his 'The body and the book: Caradoc Evans's *My People*', *Welsh Writing in English: A Yearbook of Critical Essays*, 11 (2006–7), 188–209.

40 Evans, *Capel Sion*, p. 68.

41 Richard Hughes, *A Moment of Time* (London: Chatto & Windus, 1926), pp. 83–4.

42 Rhys Davies, *The Withered Root* (1927; Cardigan: Parthian, 2007), p. 123. For further analysis, see Stephen Knight, '"On Stony Ground": Rhys Davies's *The Withered Root*', in Katie Gramich (ed.), *Mapping the Territory: Critical Approaches to Welsh Fiction in English* (Cardigan: Parthian, 2010), pp. 11–34.

43 Alun Llewellyn, *The Deacon* (London: G. Bell & Sons, 1934), p. 351.

44 Margiad Evans, *Creed* (Oxford: Basil Blackwell, 1936), p. 233.

45 W. H. Taylor, quoted in David Egan, *Coal Society: A History of the South Wales Mining Valleys 1840–1980* (Llandysul: Gomer Press, 1987), p. 30.

46 Freud, 'The "Uncanny"' [1919], *The Standard Edition of the Complete Psychological Works of Sigmund Freud: An Infantile Neurosis and Other Works (1917–1919)*, XVII, ed. James Strachey (1955; London: Vintage, 2001), p. 244.

47 Gwyn Jones, 'The pit', *Collected Stories of Gwyn Jones* (Cardiff: University of Wales Press, 1998), pp. 21 and 23.

48 Jones, *The Dragon Has Two Tongues*, p. 32.

49 Glyn Jones, 'The kiss', *Collected Stories of Glyn Jones*, ed. Tony Brown (Cardiff: University of Wales Press, 1999), p. 41.

50 Ibid., p. 43.

51 Ibid., p. 45.

52 Ibid., p. 46.

53 Ibid., p. 48.

54 Rhys Davies, *Print of a Hare's Foot* (London: Heinemann, 1969), p. 89.

55 Rhys Davies, 'The last struggle', *Collected Stories*, ed. Meic Stephens, 3 vols (Llandysul: Gomer Press, 1996–8), ii, pp. 35 and 36.

56 Ibid., i, p. 262.

57 Ibid., i, pp. 264–5.

58 Dot Jones, 'Counting the cost of coal: women's lives in the Rhondda, 1881–1911', in Angela V. John (ed.), *Our Mothers' Land: Chapters in Welsh Women's History 1830–1939* (1991; Cardiff: University of Wales Press, 2010), p. 126.

59 Rhys Davies, 'The dark world', *Collected Stories*, i, p. 248.

60 Ibid., p. 251.

61 Ibid., pp. 252–3.

62 Ken Etheridge, *Songs for Courage* (Llandysul: Gomerian Press, 1940), p. 32.

63 Karl Marx, letter to Arnold Ruge, May 1843.

64 Karl Marx, 'The eighteenth Brumaire of Louis Bonaparte' [1852], in Karl Marx and Friedrich Engels, *Selected Works* (London: Lawrence & Wishart, 1968), p. 96; Marx, quoted in Chris Baldick, *In Frankenstein's Shadow: Myth, Monstrosity and Nineteenth-century Writing* (Oxford: Clarendon Press, 1987), pp. 128 and 130.

65 Gwyn Thomas, 'Oscar', in *The Dark Philosophers* (1946; Cardigan: Parthian, 2006), p. 44.

66 Ibid., p. 70.

67 Ibid, p. 35.

68 Ibid., p. 42.
69 Ibid., p. 58.
70 Ibid., p. 84.
71 Ibid., pp. 88–9.
72 Ibid., p. 101.
73 Gwyn Thomas, 'Simeon' [1946], in *The Dark Philosophers*, p. 264.
74 Ibid., p. 252.
75 Ibid., p. 269.
76 Ibid., p. 294.

4: Land of the Living Dead (1940s–1997)

1 Ruth Bidgood, 'The Zombie-makers' (1969–70), published in Matthew Jarvis, *Ruth Bidgood* (Cardiff: University of Wales Press, 2012), 'Appendix B. Two unpublished early poems', pp. 133–4.
2 R. S. Thomas, 'Reservoirs', in *Not That He Brought Flowers* (London: Hart-Davis, 1968), p. 26; repr. in *Collected Poems 1945–1990* (London: Dent, 1993), p. 194.
3 Gwenallt, 'Cymru', *Ysgubau'r Awen* (Aberystwyth: Gwasg Aberystwyth, 1935), p. 84; trans. J. P. Clancy, 'Wales', in Menna Elfyn and John Rowlands (eds), *The Bloodaxe Book of Modern Welsh Poetry: Twentieth-century Welsh-language Poetry in Translation* (Tarset: Bloodaxe Books, 2003), p. 94.
4 T. H. Parry-Williams, 'Hon', *Ugain o Gerddi* (Aberystwyth: Gwasg Aberystwyth, 1949), p. 12.
5 Meuryn [Robert John Rowlands], *Chwedlau'r Meini: Gwib i Fro'r Cysgodion* (Dinbych: Gwasg Gee, 1946), p. 6.
6 Ibid., pp. 8, 14–15.
7 Ibid., p. 10.
8 Caradog Prichard, *Un Nos Ola Leuad* (1961; Talybont: Y Lolfa, 2008), pp. 203–5; *One Moonlit Night*, trans. Philip Mitchell (Edinburgh: Canongate, 1995), pp. 173–4.
9 Saunders Lewis, 'Tynged yr iaith', 'The fate of the language' [1962], trans. G. Aled Williams, in Alun R. Jones and Gwyn Thomas (eds), *Presenting Saunders Lewis* (Cardiff: University of Wales Press, 1983), pp. 127 and 141.
10 Islwyn Ffowc Elis, *Y Gromlech yn yr Haidd* (Llandysul: Gwasg Gomer, 1970), pp. 90, 91, 92.
11 Ibid., pp. 93, 96; the text italicizes.

[12] See, for further biographical information, Rhian Davies, 'Scarred background: Nigel Heseltine (1916–1995), a biographical introduction and a bibliography', in *Welsh Writing in English: A Yearbook of Critical Essays*, ii (2006–7), 69–101.

[13] M. Wynn Thomas, '" A Grand Harlequinade": the border writing of Nigel Heseltine', in *Welsh Writing in English: A Yearbook of Critical Essays*, ii (2006–7), 61.

[14] Nigel Heseltine, 'Cam-Vaughan's shoot', *Tales of the Squirearchy* (Carmarthen and Dublin: The Druid Press, 1946), pp. 7–8.

[15] Ibid., p. 10.

[16] Ibid., p. 11.

[17] See Rob Gossedge, 'Tales of the *Boneddigion*: Nigel Heseltine's gentry context', *Almanac: Yearbook of Welsh Writing in English*, 13 (2008–9), 68.

[18] C. E. [Colwyn Edward] Vulliamy, *The Proud Walkers* (London: Chapman & Hall, 1955), pp. 91–2.

[19] Ibid., p. 239.

[20] [D.] Griffith Jones, *Ofnadwy Ddydd* (Abercynon: Cwmni'r Cyhoeddiadau Modern Cymreig, 1966), pp. 12–13.

[21] Ibid., p. 25.

[22] Ibid., pp. 33–4.

[23] See D. Griffith Jones's defence of his novel in *Llais Llyfrau* (winter 1964), repr. in *Ofnadwy Ddydd*, pp. 6–7.

[24] D. Griffith Jones, *Y Clychau* (Llandybïe: Llyfrau'r Dryw, 1972), p. 38.

[25] Ibid., pp. 91, 108, 111.

[26] Ibid., p. 109.

[27] Ibid., pp. 111, 112, 114.

[28] Julia Kristeva, *Powers of Horror: An Essay on Subjection* (New York: Columbia University Press, 1982), p. 4.

[29] Christopher Lockett, *newnewfie.blogspot.com/2010/04/i-haz-seen-teh*, accessed 6 October 2012. For a more extensive discussion of Julia Kristeva's theories in relation to Welsh writing in English, see Harri Garrod Roberts, *Embodying Identity: Representations of the Body in Welsh Literature* (Cardiff: University of Wales Press, 2009).

[30] Kristeva, *Powers of Horror*, p. 4.

[31] 1536 Act, quoted in Norman Davies, *The Isles: A History* (London: Macmillan, 1991), pp. 492–3.

[32] Gerallt Lloyd Owen, 'I'r Farwolaeth', *Cerddi'r Cywilydd* (Caernarfon: Gwasg Gwynedd, 1972), p. 20; 'To the Death', trans. Gillian Clarke, in Menna Elfyn and John Rowlands (eds), *The Bloodaxe Book of Modern Welsh Poetry*, pp. 285–6.

33 Gwyn Thomas, 'O'r ddaear hen', *Drychiolaethau* (Caernarfon: Gwasg y Bwthyn, 2010), p. 164.

34 Ibid., p. 165.

35 Roy Lewis, 'Y bwystfil', *Dawns Angau* (Talybont: Y Lolfa, 1981), pp. 26–7.

36 Angharad Tomos, *Yma o Hyd* (Talybont: Y Lolfa, 1985), pp. 107–8.

37 Angharad Tomos, *Hen Fyd Hurt* (Talybont: Y Lolfa, 1982), pp. 13, 28; the text italicizes.

38 Ibid., pp. 49 and 53.

39 Ibid., p. 58.

40 Mary Jones, *Resistance* (Belfast: The Blackstaff Press, 1985), p. 102. See M. Wynn Thomas, *Internal Difference: Literature in Twentieth-century Wales* (Cardiff: University of Wales Press, 1992), pp. 156–70, for further comparison of Angharad Tomos's and Mary Jones's fictions.

41 Ibid., pp. 123–4.

42 Ibid., p. 149.

43 Margiad Evans, *Country Dance* (1932; Cardigan: Parthian, 2006), p. 102.

44 Guy N. Smith, *The Knighton Vampires* (London: Piatkus, 1993), p. 27.

45 Ibid., p. 113.

46 Raymond Williams, *Politics and Letters* [1979], repr. in *Who Speaks for Wales? Nation, Culture, Identity*, ed. Daniel Williams (Cardiff: University of Wales Press, 2003), pp. 49–50.

47 Darryl Jones, 'Borderlands: spiritualism and the occult in fin de siècle and Edwardian Welsh and Irish horror', *Irish Studies Review*, 17/1 (2009), 37.

48 Kristeva, *Powers of Horror*, p. 4.

49 Phil Rickman, *Curfew* (New York: G. P. Putnam's Sons, 1993); published as *Crybbe* in the UK (London: Macmillan, 1993), p. 407.

50 Ibid., pp. 24–5.

51 Ibid., p. 45.

52 Ibid., p. 159.

53 Regan Forest, *Bridge across Forever* (New York: Silhouette Books, 1993), pp. 9–10.

54 Ibid., pp. 223 and 239.

55 Alice Thomas Ellis, *Fairy Tale* (1996; Harmondsworth: Penguin, 1997), pp. 36 and 191.

56 Ibid., p. 170.

Part II

1 David Pryce-Jones, *Shirley's Guild* (1979; London: Capuchin Classics, 2009), p. 130.

5:*Witches, Druids and the Hounds of Annwn*

[1] Eirlys Gruffydd, *Gwrachod Cymru* (Caernarfon: Gwasg Gwynedd, 1980), p. 34.
[2] Ibid., pp. 39–40.
[3] Ibid., p. 47.
[4] Ibid., p. 36.
[5] See Lady Charlotte Guest, 'Peredur the Son of Evrawc' in *The Mabinogion Translated from the Red Book of Hergest*, 3 vols (1838–49; London: T. Fisher Unwin, 1902), i, pp. 71–105.
[6] Tudur Penllyn, 'Dychanu'r wrach', in T. Roberts (ed.) *Gwaith Tudur Penllyn ac Ieuan ap Tudur Penllyn* (Caerdydd: Gwasg Prifysgol Cymru, 1958), pp. 45–6; quoted in Gruffydd, *Gwrachod Cymru*, p. 12.
[7] Ellis Wynne, *Gweledigaethau y Bardd Cwsg* (1703; Caerdydd: Gwasg Prifysgol Cymru, 1960), p. 120. This reference has been censored from the English translation of Ellis Wynne's masterpiece. When Lucifer receives in hell the souls of the courtiers and flatterers of recent kings, he disposes of them in the original as follows: *'Bwriwyd y rhain bob un tan din ei frenin ei hun, fel yr oedd y breninoedd tan dineu'r diawliaid, ynghachty Lucifer. Ond yr oedd rhann o'r bawdy o tan y Diawliaid gwaela, lle'r oedd y Witsiaid . . . fyth yn cusanu tineu'r Ellyllon.'* ('These were thrown each one under his own king's arse, in the same way as the kings were under the devils' arses, in Lucifer's shit-house. But part of the dirt-house was under the worst Devils, where the Witches were . . . eternally kissing the Fiends' arses.') According to the 1897 translation, the courtiers and their kings merely 'lay beneath Lucifer's feet'; see Robert Gwyneddon Davies, *Visions of the Sleeping Bard* (London and Caernarfon: Simpkin, Marshall & Co. and The Welsh National Press, 1897), p. 95.
[8] William Frederick Williams, *The Witcheries of Craig Isaf*, 2 vols (London: Minerva Press, 1805) i, p. 37; the text italicizes.
[9] Ibid., i, pp. 117–18.
[10] Ibid., ii, pp. 181 and 227.
[11] Ibid., ii, p. 243
[12] Dylan Thomas, 'The school for witches' [1936], *The Collected Stories*, ed. Walford Davies (London: Dent, 1983), pp. 67–8, 72–3.
[13] Ibid., pp. 72–3.
[14] Marija Gimbutas, *The Civilization of the Goddess* (San Francisco: Harper San Francisco, 1991), pp. x, 270.
[15] J. T. Koch (ed.), *The Celtic Heroic Age: Literary Sources for Ancient Celtic Europe, Early Ireland & Wales* (Aberystwyth: Celtic Studies Publications, 2000), p. 45.

16   Gimbutas, *The Civilization of the Goddess*, p. 344.

17   Guest, *The Mabinogion*, iii, pp. 118–20.

18   Gimbutas, *The Civilization of the Goddess*, p. 244.

19   Robert Graves, *The White Goddess: A Historical Grammar of Poetic Myth* (1948; New York: Farrar, Straus and Giroux, 1966), pp. 401, 439.

20   [Thomas Richards], *Tales of Welsh Society and Scenery*, 2 vols (London: Longman, Rees, Orme, Brown, and Green, 1827), i, p. 53.

21   Ibid., pp. 60–1.

22   Charlotte Wardle, *St Ælian's, or the Cursing Well. A Poem in Five Cantos* (London: printed for the author, 1814); see also Richard Suggett, *A History of Magic and Witchcraft in Wales* (Stroud: The History Press, 2008), pp. 118–26, for a further account of activities at Ffynnon Elian.

23   [Richards], *Tales of Welsh Society and Scenery*, i, p. 61; the text italicizes.

24   Ibid., p. 63.

25   Ibid., pp. 71–3.

26   Allen Raine, *Garthowen: A Story of a Welsh Homestead* (London: Hutchinson, 1900), pp. 98.

27   Ibid., p. 137.

28   Elena Puw Morgan, *Y Wisg Sidan* (Caernarfon: Clwb Llyfrau Cymreig, 1939), pp. 23–4.

29   Daniel Owen, *Gwen Tomos* (1894; Wrecsam: Hughes a'i Fab, 1907), p. 112.

30   Bethan Gwanas, *Gwrach y Gwyllt* (Llandysul: Gwasg Gomer, 2003).

31   Angharad Jones, *Y Dylluan Wen* (Llandysul: Gwasg Gomer, 1995), p. 87.

32   Craig Shaw Gardner, *Buffy the Vampire Slayer: Return to Chaos* (London, Sydney, New York: Pocket Books, 1998), p. 89.

33   [Eliza Ryves], *The Hermit of Snowden* [*sic*]: *or Memoirs of Albert and Lavinia* (London: Logographic Press for Literary Society, 1789), pp. i–ii.

34   Julius Caesar, *De Bello Gallico*, *c.*50 BC, trans. Anne Lea in Koch (ed.), *The Celtic Heroic Age*, p. 22.

35   [William Godwin], *Imogen: A Pastoral Romance . . . From the Ancient British* (London: William Lane, 1784), pp. i, 35, 36, 37, 39.

36   Ibid., pp. 2 and 4.

37   But see Moira Dearnley, *Distant Fields: Eighteenth-century Fictions of Wales* (Cardiff: University of Wales Press, 2001), pp. 114–129, for an interesting discussion of this novel which argues that Godwin's representation of druidism was more conflicted and contradictory.

38   Godwin, diary entry for 2 January 1795, quoted in Damian Walford Davies, '"At Defiance": Iolo, Godwin, Coleridge, Wordsworth', in Geraint H. Jenkins (ed.), *A Rattleskull Genius: The Many Faces of Iolo Morganwg* (Cardiff: University of Wales Press, 2005), p. 154.

39 See Ceri W. Lewis, 'Iolo Morganwg and strict-metre Welsh poetry', in ibid., pp. 88 and 91.
40 Iolo Morganwg, address to the Cambrian Society Carmarthen eisteddfod, 1819, quoted in Geraint H. Jenkins, 'The Unitarian firebrand, the Cambrian Society and the eisteddfod', in ibid., p. 298.
41 Lewis, 'Iolo Morganwg and strict-metre Welsh poetry', p. 91.
42 See Geraint H. Jenkins, 'On the trail of a "Rattleskull Genius": introduction', in Jenkins (ed.), *A Rattleskull Genius*, pp. 19–20.
43 [James Gray], *Cona; or The Vale of Clwyd* (London: Longman, Hurst, Rees, Orme and Brown, 1814), pp. 7 and 10.
44 Ibid., pp. 9 and 43.
45 See Huw Walters, 'Myfyr Morganwg and the rocking-stone Gorsedd', in Jenkins (ed.), *A Rattleskull Genius*, pp. 481–500.
46 See Cyril Bracegirdle, *Dr William Price: Saint or Sinner?* (Llanrwst: Gwasg Carreg Gwalch, 1997).
47 Bertha Thomas, *Picture Tales from Welsh Hills* (London: T. Fisher Unwin, 1912); repr. in *Stranger within the Gates*, ed. Kirsti Bohata (Dinas Powys: Honno, 2008), the page nos are from this edn, pp. 1 and 7.
48 Ibid., pp. 15 and 17. See Kirsti Bohata, *Postcolonialism Revisited* (Cardiff: University of Wales Press, 2004), pp. 34–5, for further material on the Gothic elements in Bertha Thomas's short stories.
49 Dylan Thomas, 'The burning baby' [1935], *Collected Stories*, pp. 40–1.
50 Robert Bloch, 'The dark isle', *Weird Tales* [May 1939], repr. in Peter Haining (ed.), *Great Welsh Fantasy Stories* (Llanrwst: Gwasg Carreg Gwalch, 2000; first published as *The Magic Valley Travellers* (London; Victor Gollancz, 1974)), pp. 243–4.
51 Ibid., pp. 262–3; the text italicizes.
52 Ibid., p. 240.
53 Ivor Watkins, *Demon* (London: Macdonald, 1983; London: Futura Publications, 1994), pp. 187 and 195.
54 Ibid., p. 5.
55 Ibid., p. 206.
56 Ibid., pp. 217–18.
57 Phil Rickman, *Candlenight* (London: Macmillan, 1991; London: Pan Books, 1993), p. 388.
58 Ibid., p. 273.
59 Ibid., pp. 288–9.
60 Ibid., p. 424.
61 Ibid., p. 68.
62 Lady Charlotte Guest, *The Mabinogion*, iii, p. 12.

[63] Taliesin Williams, *The Doom of Colyn Dolphyn. A Poem; with notes illustrative of various traditions of Glamorganshire* (London: Longman, Rees, Orme, & Co., 1837), pp. 67–8.

[64] Ibid., pp. 70–1.

[65] Marie Trevelyan, *Folk-lore and Folk-stories of Wales* (London: Elliot Stock, 1909), p. 49.

[66] James Motley, *Tales of the Cymry: With Notes Illustrative and Explanatory* (London, Swansea and Llanelly: Longmans, Hughes, Cambrian Office and Thomas, 1848), p. 61.

[67] For further biographical details, see A. Raymond Walker, 'James Motley, the life story of a collector and naturalist', *Swansea Historic Journal*, 13 (2005).

[68] Motley, *Tales of the Cymry*, p. 36.

[69] Ibid., p. 37.

[70] Ibid., p. 63.

[71] Ibid., pp. 37, 38, 39.

[72] Arthur Machen, *The Bowmen and Other Legends of the War* (London: Kent, Simpkin, Marshall, Hamilton, 1915).

[73] Trevelyan, *Folk-lore and Folk-stories of Wales*, p. 47.

[74] R. Chetwynd-Hayes (ed.), *Welsh Tales of Terror* (London: Fontana, 1973), p. 171.

[75] Ibid., pp. 178–9.

[76] Ibid., pp. 184–5.

[77] Ibid., pp. 187–8.

[78] Motley, *Tales of the Cymry*, p. 58.

6: The Sin-eater

[1] Joseph Downes, *The Mountain Decameron*, 3 vols (London: Richard Bentley, 1836), iii, pp. 232–6.

[2] Peter David (scripter) and Rich Buckler (penciler), *The Death of Jean DeWolff*, from *The Amazing Spider-man* series, originally published in magazine form as *Peter Parker, The Spectacular Spider-man* (1985; New York: Marvel Comics, 1990) , 107–10; J. M. DeMatties (scripter) and Bob Budinasky (penciler), *Ghost Rider*, i, 80 and 81 (New York: Marvel Comics Group, 1983); for 'Forgotten realms', see James Jacobs, 'Forgotten realms: sin eaters of Eilistrae', *Dragon*, 315, xxviii/8 (January 2004), 28–31.

[3] Francine Rivers, *The Last Sin Eater: A Novel* (Wheaton, Illinois: Tyndale House, 1998), pp. 146–7.

4   Gary D. Schmidt, *The Sin Eater* (New York: Lodestar Books, 1996), p. i.

5   Leviticus, 16, 21–2.

6   John Aubrey, *Remains of Gentilisme and Judaisme* (1686–7; London: Folklore Society, 1881), pp. 35–6; repr. in *John Aubrey, Three Prose Works*, ed. J. Buchanan-Brown (London: Centaur Classics, 1972), pp. 179–80.

7   John Bagford, 'A letter to the publisher, written by the ingenious Mr. John Bagford, in which are many curious remarks relating to the City of London, and some things about Leland', in John Leland, *Antiquarii De Rebus Britannicis Collectanea*, vol. i, ed. Thomas Hearne (London: William and John Richardson, 1770), p. lxxvi; the text italicizes.

8   Peter Roberts, *The Cambrian Popular Antiquities; or, an account of some Traditions, Customs, and Superstitions of Wales* (London: E. Williams, 1815), pp. 175–6.

9   See [Anon.], 'Defodau angladd', *Cymru Fu; yn cynwys Hanesion, Traddodiadau, yn nghyda Chwedlau a Dammegion Cymreig* (Wrexham: Hughes & Son, 1862), pp. 91–2.

10   Richard Suggett, *A History of Magic and Witchcraft in Wales* (Stroud: The History Press, 2008), p. 144.

11   Wirt Sikes, *British Goblins: Welsh Folk-lore, Fairy Mythology, Legends and Traditions* (London: Sampson Low, Marston, Searle & Rivington, 1880), p. 327.

12   *Archaeologia Cambrensis*, iii (October, 1852), 330–2.

13   E.S.A. [Ernest Silvanus Appleyard], *Welsh Sketches*, 3rd ser. (London: James Darling, 1853), p. 187.

14   Bertram S. Puckle, *Funeral Customs: Their Origin and Development* (London: T. W. Laurie, 1926), p. 69.

15   *Blackwood's Magazine* (1875), quoted in *Country Quest*, 28/5 (1987), 25.

16   Paxton Hood, *Christmas Evans: The Popular Preacher of Wild Wales* (London: Hodder & Stoughton, 1881), p. 23.

17   Huw Walters, *Canu'r Pwll a'r Pulpud: Portread o'r Diwylliant Barddol Cymraeg yn Nyffryn Aman* (Abertawe: Cyhoeddiadau Barddas, 1987), pp. 36–7; see also Huw Walters, 'Bwyta pechod yng Nghwmaman', *Y Genhinen*, xxviii (1978), 96–9.

18   George Laurence Gomme, *Ethnology and Folklore* (London: Kegan Paul, Trench, Trubner & Co., 1892), p. 120.

19   Ibid., pp. 127–8.

20   James Napier, *Folk Lore, or, Superstitious Beliefs in the West of Scotland within this Century* (1879; repr. Wakefield, Yorkshire: EP Publishing, 1976), pp. 60–1; the text italicizes.

21   Gomme, *Ethnology and Folklore*, p. 118.

22   Fiona Macleod [William Sharp], *The Sin-eater and other Tales* (Edinburgh and Chicago: Patrick Geddes and Stone & Kimball, 1895), pp. 8, 9, and 13.

23   Ibid., pp. 53–4.

24   Ibid., p. 44; the text italicizes.

25   See Sally Roberts Jones, *Allen Raine* (Cardiff: University of Wales Press, 1979), p. 51.

26   Allen Raine, *Hearts of Wales: An Old Romance* (London: Hutchinson, 1905), p. 121.

27   Ibid., p. 294.

28   Ibid., pp. 122–3.

29   Ibid., p. 123.

30   Ibid., pp. 168–9.

31   Ibid., p. 233.

32   Ibid., p. 234.

33   Ibid., p. 239.

34   [Henry] Elwyn Thomas, *The Forerunner* (London: Lynwood & Co., 1910), p. 306.

35   Ibid., p. 310.

36   Elwyn [Henry Elwyn Thomas], *Ifor Owain: Nofel am Gymru yn Amser Cromwel* (Gwrecsam: Hughes a'i Fab, 1911), p. 128.

37   A Whisper [Eleanor Nepean], *Ffynon, the Sin-eater* (London: Holden and Hardingham, 1914), p. 34.

38   Ibid., p. 19.

39   Ibid., p. 61.

40   Septimus G. Green, 'The sin eater: a Welsh legend', in *A Vision of Time, the Sin Eater, Cecilia, and Other Poems* (London: Erskine Macdonald, 1920), pp. 49–50.

41   Ibid., p. 57.

42   Christianna Brand, 'The sins of the fathers . . .', in *What Dread Hand: A Collection of Short Stories* (London: Michael Joseph, 1939; repr. Hornchurch: Ian Henry Publications, 1977), p. 123.

43   Ibid., p. 125; the text italicizes.

44   Ibid., p. 131.

45   Gwyn Jones, *The Walk Home* (London: Dent, 1962), p. 44.

46   Ibid., p. 73.

47   Ibid., p. 82.

48   Ibid., pp. 73–4, 77, 80.

49   Ibid., p. 81.

50   Gerry Jones, *The Sin Eater* (1971; London: New English Library, 1972), p. 10.

[51] Ibid., p. 48.

[52] Alice Thomas Ellis, *The Sin Eater* (London: Duckworth, 1977), p. 7.

[53] Ibid., p. 32.

[54] Ibid., p. 100.

[55] Frantz Fanon, *Black Skin, White Mask* (1952; London: Pluto Press, 1986), p. 19.

[56] Ibid., p. 194.

[57] See Joy Williams, 'Postscript', in Raymond Williams, *People of the Black Mountains 2: The Eggs of the Eagle* (London: Chatto & Windus, 1990), p. 321.

[58] For further biographical information on Mary Webb, see Gladys Mary Coles, *Mary Webb* (Bridgend: Seren, 1990).

[59] Mary Webb, *Precious Bane* (London: Jonathan Cape, 1924), p. 35.

[60] Ibid., p. 36.

[61] Francis Neilson, *The Sin-eater's Hallowe'en: A Fantasy in One Act and Two Scenes* (1923; New York: B. W. Huebsch, 1924), p. 64.

[62] Ibid., p. 74.

[63] Ibid., p. 76.

[64] Ibid., p. 80.

[65] Elizabeth Walter, *The Sin-eater and other Scientific Impossibilities* (London: The Harvill Press, 1967), p. 18.

[66] Ibid., p. 44.

[67] G. G. Pendarves [Gladys Gordon Trenery], 'The sin eater', *Weird Tales* [1938]; repr. *Weird Tales* [1952]; repr. *Lost Fantasies*, 9 (1979), 7–8.

[68] Ibid., 11; the text italicizes.

[69] Ibid., 15; the text italicizes.

[70] Ibid., 22.

[71] Lew Merrill [Victor Rousseau Emanuel], 'The Sin-eater', *Spicy Mystery*, 12/4 (1942), 20.

[72] Ibid., 21.

[73] Glenn Low, *Sin Eater* (Chicago: Novel Books, 1960), p. 138.

[74] DeMatties, *Ghost Rider*, 3.

[75] Margaret Atwood, 'The sin eater', *Dancing Girls* (1977; London: Virago, 1984), pp. 213, 214–15.

[76] Ibid., pp. 220–1.

[77] Ibid., p. 224.

[78] Bradley Denton, 'The sin-eater of the Kaw', *Fantasy & Science Fiction*, 76/6 (1989), 6–39.

[79] Elizabeth Rollins, *The Sin Eater* (Beverly, Mass.: Corvid Pres, 2003), p. 19.

[80] Alex Kava, *A Necessary Evil* (Richmond: MIRA Books, 2006).

81 Deborah J. Miller, *The Sin Eater* (Dingwall, Ross-shire: Sandstone Press, 2007), p. 66.

82 Sherman Alexie, 'The sin eaters', *The Toughest Indian in the World* (New York: Atlantic Monthly Press, 2000), p. 107.

Epilogue

1 See Sarah Waters, 'The lost girl', *The Guardian*, 30 May 2009.

2 Sarah Waters, *The Little Stranger* (London: Virago, 2009), p. 27.

3 Thomas Emson [Dyfed Edwards], *Zombie Britannica* (Kirtlington: Snowbooks, 2010).

4 Catherine Fisher, *Darkhenge* (London: Bodley Head, 2005), p. 54.

5 Ibid., pp. 99–100.

6 Gwyneth Lewis, *The Meat Tree* (Bridgend: Seren Books, 2010), p. 245.

7 Malcolm Pryce, *Aberystwyth Mon Amour* (London: Bloomsbury, 2001), p. 21.

8 Jon Gower, 'The pit', in Gwen Davies (ed.), *Sing Sorrow Sorrow: Dark and Chilling Tales* (Bridgend: Seren, 2010), p. 236.

9 Ibid., p. 241.

10 Rachel Trezise, *In and Out of the Goldfish Bowl* (2000; Cardigan: Parthian, 2002), p. 37.

11 Ibid., pp. 46–7.

12 Caryl Lewis, *Martha, Jac a Sianco* (Talybont: Y Lolfa, 2004), p. 190.

13 Tristan Hughes, *Send My Cold Bones Home* (Cardigan: Parthian, 2006), p. 303.

14 Glenda Beagan, *The Great Master of Ecstasy* (Bridgend: Seren, 2009), p. 53.

15 Ibid., p. 54.

16 Lloyd Jones, *Y Dŵr* (Talybont: Y Lolfa, 2009), p. 127.

17 Mihangel Morgan, *Pantglas* (Talybont: Y Lolfa, 2011), p. 151.

18 Ibid., p. 245.

19 Ibid., p. 246.

20 R. S. Thomas, 'Reservoirs', *Collected Poems 1945–1990* (London: Dent, 1993), p. 194.

21 Sally Spedding, *A Night with No Stars* (London: Allison & Busby, 2004), p. 286

Select Bibliography

∽

Primary sources

Alexie, Sherman, 'The sin eaters', *The Toughest Indian in the World* (New York: Atlantic Monthly Press, 2000), 76–120.

Atwood, Margaret, 'The sin eater', *Dancing Girls* (1977; London: Virago, 1984), pp. 213–24.

Baring, Max [Charles Messent], *A Prophet of Wales: A Story* (London: Greening & Company, 1905).

Beagan, Glenda, *The Great Master of Ecstasy* (Bridgend: Seren, 2009).

Bennett, Anna Maria, *Anna: or Memoirs of a Welsh Heiress: interspersed with anecdotes of a Nabob*, 4 vols (London: William Lane, 1785; 2nd edn, London: William Lane, 1786).

——, *Ellen, Countess of Castle Howel*, 4 vols (London, 1794; 2nd edn, 2 vols, Dublin: Jones, Colbert, Fitzpatrick & Milliken, 1794).

'Beuno', 'Legend of Iolo ap Hugh', 'Legend of Bala Lake', *The Cambrian Quarterly Magazine and Celtic Repertory*, i (1829), 40–3, 53–4.

Bloch, Robert, 'The dark isle', *Weird Tales* [May, 1939], repr. in Peter Haining (ed.), *Great Welsh Fantasy Stories* (Llanrwst: Gwasg Carreg Gwalch, 2000; first published as *The Magic Valley Travellers* (London; Victor Gollancz, 1974)), pp. 240–67.

Brand, Christianna, *What Dread Hand: A Collection of Short Stories* (London: Michael Joseph, 1939; repr. Hornchurch: Ian Henry Publications, 1977).

Brutus [David Owen], *Wil Brydydd y Coed* (1863–5; Caerdydd: Gwasg Prifysgol Cymru, 1949).

Chetwynd-Hayes, R. (ed.), *Welsh Tales of Terror* (London: Fontana, 1973).

Clark, Emily, *Ianthé, or the Flower of Caernarvon*, 2 vols (London: printed for the author, 1798).

Conran, Tony, *Welsh Verse* (1976; Bridgend: Poetry Wales Press, 1986).

Dalton, Trevor, *The Possession Legacy* ([Denia, Costa Blanca]: Libros International, 2006)

David, Peter (scripter) and Rich Buckler (penciler), *The Death of Jean DeWolff*, from *The Amazing Spider-man* series, originally published in magazine form as *Peter Parker, The Spectacular Spider-man* (1985; New York: Marvel Comics, 1990).

Davies, Gwen (ed.), *Sing Sorrow Sorrow: Dark and Chilling Tales* (Bridgend: Seren, 2010).

Davies, Rhys, *The Withered Root* (1927; Cardigan: Parthian, 2007).

——, *Print of a Hare's Foot* (London: Heinemann, 1969).

——, *Collected Stories*, ed. Meic Stephens, 3 vols (Llandysul: Gomer Press, 1996–8).

DeMatties, J. M. (scripter) and Bob Budinasky (penciler), *Ghost Rider*, i, 80 and 81 (New York: Marvel Comics, 1983).

Denton, Bradley, 'The sin-eater of the Kaw', *Fantasy & Science Fiction*, 76/6 (1989), 6–39.

Downes, Joseph, *The Mountain Decameron*, 3 vols (London: Richard Bentley, 1836).

[Earle, William], *Welsh Legends: A Collection of Popular Oral Tales* (London: J. Babcock, 1802).

——, *The Welshman, a Romance*, 4 vols (London: Earle and Hemet, 1801).

Edwards, Dyfed, *Dant at Waed* (Talybont: Y Lolfa, 1996).

Elfyn, Menna and John Rowlands (eds), *The Bloodaxe Book of Modern Welsh Poetry: Twentieth-century Welsh-language Poetry in Translation* (Tarset: Bloodaxe Books, 2003).

Elis, Islwyn Ffowc, *Y Gromlech yn yr Haidd* (Llandysul: Gwasg Gomer, 1970).

Ellis, Alice Thomas [Anna Haycraft], *The Sin Eater* (London: Duckworth, 1977).

——, *Fairy Tale* (1996; Harmondsworth: Penguin, 1997).

Elwyn [Henry Elwyn Thomas], *Ifor Owain: Nofel am Gymru yn Amser Cromwel* (Gwrecsam: Hughes a'i Fab, 1911).

Emson, Thomas [Dyfed Edwards], *Zombie Britannica* (Kirtlington: Snowbooks, 2010).

Etheridge, Ken, *Songs for Courage* (Llandysul: Gomerian Press, 1940).

Evans, Caradoc, *My People* (1915; Bridgend: Seren, 1987).

——, *Capel Sion* (1916; Bridgend: Seren, 2002).

Evans, Evan [Ieuan Prydydd Hir], *Some Specimens of the Poetry of the Antient Welsh Bards. Translated into English* . . . (London: R. and J. Dodsley, 1764).

Evans, Margiad, *Country Dance* (1932; Cardigan: Parthian, 2006).

——, *Creed* (Oxford: Basil Blackwell, 1936).

[Evans, Robert], *The Stranger; or, Llewellyn Family: A Cambrian Tale*, 2 vols (London: Minerva Press, 1798).

Fisher, Catherine, *Darkhenge* (London: Bodley Head, 2005).

Forest, Regan, *Bridge across Forever* (New York: Silhouette Books, 1993).

Gardner, Craig Shaw, *Buffy the Vampire Slayer: Return to Chaos* (Lonon, Sydney, New York: Pocket Books, 1998).

Gaskell, Elizabeth, 'The doom of the Griffiths', *Harper's Magazine* (1858), repr. in Laura Kranzler (ed.), *Gothic Tales* (London: Penguin, 2000), pp. 103–38.

Godwin, William, *Imogen: A Pastoral Romance* . . . *From the Ancient British* (London: William Lane, 1784).

[Gray, James], *Cona; or The Vale of Clwyd* (London: Longman, Hurst, Rees, Orme and Brown, 1814).

Gray, Thomas, *The Complete English Poems of Thomas Gray*, ed. James Reeves (London: Heinemann, 1973).

Green, Septimus G., *A Vision of Time, the Sin Eater, Cecilia, and Other Poems* (London: Erskine Macdonald, 1920).

Guest, Lady Charlotte, *The Mabinogion Translated from the Red Book of Hergest*, 3 vols (1838–49; London: T. Fisher Unwin, 1902).

Gwanas, Bethan, *Gwrach y Gwyllt* (Llandysul: Gwasg Gomer, 2003).

Gwenallt [D. Gwenallt Jones], *Ysgubau'r Awen* (Aberystwyth: Gwasg Aberystwyth, 1935).

Haining, Peter (ed.), *Great Welsh Fantasy Stories* (Llanrwst: Gwasg Carreg Gwalch, 2000); first published as *The Magic Valley Travellers* (London: Victor Gollancz, 1974).

[Hatton, Julia Ann] Ann of Swansea, *Cambrian Pictures; or, Every One Has Errors*, 3 vols (London: E. Kerby, 1810).

Heseltine, Nigel, *Tales of the Squirearchy* (Carmarthen and Dublin: The Druid Press, 1946).

Hooson, I. D., *Cerddi a Baledi* (Dinbych: Gwasg Gee, 1936).

Howell, Ann, *Anzoletta Zadoski. A Novel*, 2 vols (London: Minerva Press, 1796).

[Hughes, Annie Harriet] Gwyneth Vaughan, 'Breuddwyd nos Nadolig', *Cymru*, 29 (1905), 245–8.

Hughes, Richard, *A Moment of Time* (London: Chatto & Windus, 1926).

Hughes, Tristan, *Send My Cold Bones Home* (Cardigan: Parthian, 2006).

Jones, Angharad, *Y Dylluan Wen* (Llandysul: Gwasg Gomer, 1995).

Jones, Evan, *The Bard; or, the Towers of Morven. A Legendary Tale* (London: printed for the author, 1809).

Jones, Gerry, *The Sin Eater* (1971; London: New English Library, 1972).

Jones, Glyn, *The Collected Stories of Glyn Jones*, ed. Tony Brown (Cardiff: University of Wales Press, 1999).

Jones, [D.] Griffith, *Ofnadwy Ddydd* (Abercynon: Cwmni'r Cyhoeddiadau Modern Cymreig, 1966).

——, *Y Clychau* (Llandybïe: Llyfrau'r Dryw, 1972).

Jones, Gwyn, *The Walk Home* (London: Dent, 1962).

——, *Collected Stories of Gwyn Jones* (Cardiff: University of Wales Press, 1998).

Jones, Mary, *Resistance* (Belfast: Blackstaff Press, 1985).

Jones, Lloyd, *Y Dŵr* (Talybont: Y Lolfa, 2009).

Jones, Thomas Gwynn, *Caniadau* (Wrecsam: Hughes a'i Fab, 1934).

Kava, Alex, *A Necessary Evil* (Richmond: Mira, 2006).

[Kelly, Isabella], *The Abbey of St Asaph*, 3 vols (London: Minerva Press, 1795).

Lansdell, Sarah, *The Tower; or the Romance of Ruthyne*, 3 vols (London: printed for the author, 1798).

Lewis, Caryl, *Martha, Jac a Sianco* (Talybont: Y Lolfa, 2004).

Lewis, Gwyneth, *The Meat Tree* (Bridgend: Seren Press, 2010).

Lewis, Matthew G., *The Castle Spectre: A Drama. In Five Acts* [1797] (London: I. Bell, 1798).

Lewis, Roy, *Dawns Angau* (Talybont: Y Lolfa, 1981).

Llewellyn, Alun, *The Deacon* (London: G. Bell & Sons, 1934).

Llwyd, Richard, *Beaumaris Bay, a Poem: with Notes, Descriptive and Explanatory* (Chester: J. Fletcher, n.d. [1800]).

Low, Glenn, *Sin Eater* (Chicago: Novel Books, 1960).

[Lucas, Charles], *The Castle of Saint Donats: or, the History of Jack Smith*, 3 vols (London: William Lane, 1798).

Machen, Arthur, *The Great God Pan and The Hill of Dreams* (1894; Mineola, NY: Dover Publications, 2006).

——, 'The shining pyramid' [1895], repr. in R. Chetwynd-Hayes (ed.), *Welsh Tales of Terror* (London: Fontana, 1973), pp. 46–70.

——, *The Three Impostors* (London: John Lane, 1895; repr. Mineola, NY: Dover Publications, 2007).

——, 'A fragment of life', *The House of Souls* (London: Grant Richards, 1906; repr. US: Blackmask, 2007), pp. 3–75.

——, *The Hill of Dreams* (1907; Mineola, NY: Dover Publications, 2006).

——, *The Bowmen and Other Legends of the War* (London: Kent, Simpkin, Marshall, Hamilton, 1915).

——, *The Great Return* (London: The Faith Press, 1915).

——, *Far Off Things* [1922], in *The Autobiography of Arthur Machen* (London: The Richards Press, 1951).

——, *The Secret Glory* (London: Martin Secker, 1922).

Merrill, Lew [Victor Rousseau Emanuel], 'The Sin-eater', *Spicy Mystery*, 12/4 (1942), 18–29, 90–2.

Meuryn [Robert John Rowlands], *Chwedlau'r Meini: Gwib i Fro'r Cysgodion* (Dinbych: Gwasg Gee, 1946).

Miller, Deborah J., *The Sin Eater* (Dingwall, Ross-shire: Sandstone Press, 2007).

Morgan, Elena Puw, *Y Wisg Sidan* (Dinbych: Clwb Llyfrau Cymraeg, 1939).

Morgan, Mihangel, *Pantglas* (Talybont: Y Lolfa, 2011).

Motley, James, *Tales of the Cymry: With Notes Illustrative and Explanatory* (London, Swansea and Llanelly: Longmans, Hughes, Cambrian Office and Thomas, 1848).

Neilson, Francis, *The Sin-eater's Hallowe'en: A Fantasy in One Act and Two Scenes* (1923; New York: B. W. Huebsch, 1924).

Owen, Daniel, *Gwen Tomos* (1894; Wrecsam: Hughes a'i Fab, 1907); trans. T. Ceiriog Williams and E. R. Harries (Wrexham: Hughes & Son, 1963).

Owen, Frances Mary, *Across the Hills* (London: Kegan Paul, Tench & Co., 1883).

Owen, Gerallt Lloyd, *Cerddi'r Cywilydd* (Caernarfon: Gwasg Gwynedd, 1972).

Parry-Williams, T. H., *Ugain o Gerddi* (Aberystwyth: Gwasg Aberystwyth, 1949).

Peacock, Thomas Love, *The Misfortunes of Elphin* (1829), in *Novels of Thomas Love Peacock*, ed. Barbara Lloyd Evans (London: Pan, 1967).

Pendarves, G. G. [Gladys Gordon Trenery], 'The sin eater', *Weird Tales* [1938]; repr. *Weird Tales* [1952]; repr. *Lost Fantasies*, 9 (1979), 7–29.

Prichard, Caradog, *Un Nos Ola Leuad* (1961; Talybont: Y Lolfa, 2008); *One Moonlit Night*, trans. Philip Mitchell (Edinburgh: Canongate, 1995).

Price, Angharad, *O! Tyn y Gorchudd* [2002], trans. Lloyd Jones, *The Life of Rebecca Jones* (Llandysul: Gwasg Gomer, 2010).

Pryce, Malcolm, *Aberystwyth Mon Amour* (London: Bloomsbury, 2001).

Pryce-Jones, David, *Shirley's Guild* (1979; London: Capuchin Classics, 2009).

Raine, Allen [Anne Adaliza Beynon Puddicombe], *Garthowen: A Story of a Welsh Homestead* (London: Hutchinson, 1900).

——, *Hearts of Wales: An Old Romance* (London: Hutchinson, 1905).

——, *Queen of the Rushes: A Tale of the Welsh Revival* (1906; Dinas Powys: Honno Press, 1998).

——, *Where Billows Roll* (London: Hutchinson, 1909).

Rhys, Ernest, *Welsh Ballads and Other Poems* (London, Carmarthen and Bangor: David Nutt, W. Spurrell and Jarvis and Foster, 1895).

[Richards, Thomas], *Tales of Welsh Society and Scenery*, 2 vols (London: Longman, Rees, Orme, Brown, and Green, 1827).

Rickman, Phil, *Candlenight* (London: Macmillan, 1991; London: Pan Books, 1993).

——, *Crybbe* (London: Macmillan, 1993; US edn, *Curfew*, New York: Putnam, 1993).

Rivers, Francine, *The Last Sin Eater: A Novel* (Wheaton, Illinois: Tyndale House, 1998).

Robinson, Mary, *Walsingham, or, The Pupil of Nature*, 4 vols (London: T. N. Longman, 1797); repr. facs. edn, with intro. by Peter Garside (London: Routledge/Thoemmes Press, 1992).

——, *Angelina; A Novel*, 3 vols (London: Hookham & Carpenter, 1796).

——, *Memoirs of the late Mrs Robinson, written by herself. With some posthumous pieces*, ed. Maria Elizabeth Robinson, 4 vols (London: Richard Phillips, 1801; first two vols repr. as *Perdita: The Memoirs of Mary Robinson*, ed. M. J. Levy (London: Peter Owen, 1994)).

Roberts, William, *Ffrewyll y Methodistiaid* [*c*.1747], ed. A. Cynfael Lake (Caerdydd: Gwasg Prifysgol Cymru, 1998).

Rollins, Elizabeth, *The Sin Eater* (Beverly, Mass.: Corvid Pres, 2003).

[Ryves, Elizabeth], *The Hermit of Snowden* [*sic*]: *or Memoirs of Albert and Lavinia* (London: Logographic Press for Literary Society, 1789).

Schmidt, Gary D., *The Sin Eater* (New York: Lodestar Books, 1996).

[Sharp, William] Fiona Macleod, *The Sin-eater and other Tales* (Edinburgh and Chicago: Patrick Geddes and Stone & Kimball, 1895).

Smith, Guy N., *The Knighton Vampires* (London: Piatkus, 1993).

Spedding, Sally, *A Night with No Stars* (London: Allison & Busby, 2004).

Stephens, Nella, *The Robber Chieftain, or, Dinas Linn*, 4 vols (London: A. K. Newman, 1825).

Thomas, Bertha, *Picture Tales from Welsh Hills* (London: T. Fisher Unwin, 1912); repr. in *Stranger within the Gates*, ed. Kirsti Bohata (Dinas Powys: Honno, 2008).

Thomas, Dylan, *The Collected Stories*, ed. Walford Davies (London: Dent, 1983).

Thomas, Gwyn, *The Dark Philosophers* (1946; Cardigan: Parthian, 2006).

Thomas, Gwyn, *Drychiolaethau* (Caernarfon: Gwasg y Bwthyn, 2010).

Thomas, [Henry] Elwyn, *The Forerunner* (London: Lynwood & Co., 1910).

Thomas, R. S., *Collected Poems 1945–1990* (London: Dent, 1993).

Tomos, Angharad, *Hen Fyd Hurt* (Talybont: Y Lolfa, 1982).

——, *Yma o Hyd* (Talybont: Y Lolfa, 1985).

Trezise, Rachel, *In and Out of the Goldfish Bowl* (2000; Cardiff: Parthian Books, 2002).

Vulliamy, C. E. [Colwyn Edward], *The Proud Walkers* (London: Chapman & Hall, 1955).

Walter, Elizabeth, *The Sin-eater and other Scientific Impossibilities* (London: The Harvill Press, 1967).

Wardle, Charlotte, *St Ælian's, or the Cursing Well. A Poem in Five Cantos* (London: printed for the author, 1814).

Waters, Sarah, *The Little Stranger* (London: Virago, 2009).

Watkins, Ivor, *Demon* (London: Macdonald, 1983; London: Futura Publications, 1994).

Webb, Mary, *Precious Bane* (London: Jonathan Cape, 1924).

Whisper, A [Eleanor Nepean], *Ffynon, the Sin-eater* (London: Holden and Hardingham, 1914).

Wilkins, Charles, *Kilsanos: A Tale of the Welsh Mountains* (Cardiff: Daniel Owen, 1894).

Williams, Raymond, *People of the Black Mountains 2: The Eggs of the Eagle* (London: Chatto & Windus, 1990).

Williams, Sarah (Sadie), *Twilight Hours: A Legacy of Verse* (London: Strahan & Co., 1868).

Williams, Taliesin, *The Doom of Colyn Dolphyn. A Poem; with notes illustrative of various traditions of Glamorganshire* (London: Longman, Rees, Orme, & Co.,1837).

Williams, William Frederick, *Fitzmaurice: A Novel*, 2 vols (London: J. Murray and S. Highley, 1800).

——, *The Witcheries of Craig Isaf*, 2 vols (London: Minerva Press, 1805).

Wynne, Ellis, *Gweledigaethau y Bardd Cwsc* (1703; Caerdydd: Gwasg Prifysgol Cymru, 1960); trans. Robert Gwyneddon Jones, *Visions of the Sleeping Bard* (London and Caernarfon: Simpkin, Marshall & Co. and The Welsh National Press Company, 1897).

Secondary sources

Aaron, Jane, 'Postcolonial change', *New Welsh Review*, 67 (2005), 32–6.

——, 'Twentieth-century and contemporary Welsh gothic', *Literature Compass*, 7/4 (2010), 281–9, *www3.interscience.wiley.com/journal/ 123338358*, accessed 6 October 2012.

—— and Chris Williams (eds), *Postcolonial Wales* (Cardiff: University of Wales Press, 2005).

[Anon.], 'Defodau angladd', *Cymru Fu; yn cynwys Hanesion, Traddodiadau, yn nghyda Chwedlau a Dammegion Cymreig* (Wrexham: Hughes & Son, 1862).

[Anon.], 'Druidism and popular Welsh occultism', *The Platonist* (1890s; repr. Largs, Scotland: The Banton Press, 1991).

Aubrey, John, *Remains of Gentilisme and Judaisme* (1686–7; London: Folklore Society, 1881); repr. in *John Aubrey, Three Prose Works*, ed. J. Buchanan-Brown (London: Centaur Classics, 1972).

Bagford, John, 'A letter to the publisher, written by the ingenious Mr. John Bagford, in which are many curious remarks relating to the City of London, and some things about Leland', in John Leland, *Antiquarii De Rebus Britannicis Collectanea*, vol. i, ed. Thomas Hearne (London: William and John Richardson, 1770).

Baldick, Chris, *In Frankenstein's Shadow: Myth, Monstrosity and Nineteenth-century Writing* (Oxford: Clarendon Press, 1987).

Ballin, Malcolm, *Welsh Periodicals in English: 1882–2000* (Cardiff: University of Wales Press, 2012).

Benjamin, Walter, 'What is epic theatre?' (1939), *Understanding Brecht* (London: New Left Books, 1977).

Bohata, Kirsti, 'Apes and cannibals in Cambria: images of the racial and gendered other in Gothic writing in Wales', *Welsh Writing in English: A Yearbook of Critical Essays*, 6 (2000), 119–43.

——, *Postcolonialism Revisited* (Cardiff: University of Wales Press, 2004).

——, '"Psycho-colonialism" revisited', *New Welsh Review*, 69 (2005), 31–9.

——, '"Unhomely moments": reading and writing nation in Welsh female Gothic', in Diana Wallace and Andrew Smith (eds), *The Female Gothic: New Directions* (Basingstoke: Palgrave Macmillan, 2009), pp. 180–95.

Botting, Fred, *Gothic* (London: Routledge, 1996).

Bracegirdle, Cyril, *Dr William Price: Saint or Sinner?* (Llanrwst: Gwasg Carreg Gwalch, 1997).

Brantlinger, Patrick, *Rule of Darkness: British Literature and Imperialism 1830–1914* (Ithaca, NY: Cornell University Press, 1988).

Bromham, Ivor J., '"Ann of Swansea" (Ann Julia Hatton: 1764–1838)', *Glamorgan Historian*, 7 (1971), 173–86.

Castle, Terry, *The Female Thermometer: Eighteenth-Century Culture and the Invention of the Uncanny* (Oxford: Oxford University Press, 1995)

Charnell-White, Cathryn A., *Bardic Circles: National, Regional and Personal Identity in the Bardic Vision of Iolo Morganwg* (Cardiff: University of Wales Press, 2007).

Coles, Gladys Mary, *Mary Webb* (Bridgend: Seren, 1990).

Colley, Linda, *Britons: Forging the Nation 1797–1837* (New Haven and London: Yale University Press, 1992).

Conran, Tony, *The Cost of Strangeness* (Llandysul: Gwasg Gomer, 1982).

Constantine, Mary-Ann, *The Truth against the World: Iolo Morganwg and Romantic Forgery* (Cardiff: University of Wales Press, 2007).

Cunningham, Valentine, *Everywhere Spoken Against: Dissent in the Victorian Novel* (Oxford: Clarendon Press, 1975).

Davies, Andrew, '"The Gothic novel in Wales" revisited: a preliminary survey of the Wales-related Romantic fiction at Cardiff University', *Cardiff Corvey: Reading the Romantic Text*, 2 (1998), *www.cf.ac.uk/encap/corvey/articles/cc02_n01.html*, accessed January 2008.

——, 'The reputed nation of inspiration: representations of Wales in fiction from the Romantic period, 1780–1830' (unpublished Ph.D. thesis, Cardiff University, 2001).

Davies, Rhian, 'Scarred background: Nigel Heseltine (1916–1995), a biographical introduction and a bibliography', in *Welsh Writing in English: A Yearbook of Critical Essays*, ii (2006–7), 69–101.

Davies, Norman, *The Isles: A History* (London: Macmillan, 1999).

Davison, Carol Margaret, *Gothic Literature 1764–1824* (Cardiff: University of Wales Press, 2009).

Deane, Seamus, *Strange Country: Modernity and Nationhood in Irish Writing since 1790* (London: Oxford University Press, 1997).

Dearnley, Moira, *Distant Fields: Eighteenth-century Fictions of Wales* (Cardiff: University of Wales Press, 2001).

E.S.A. [Ernest Silvanus Appleyard], *Welsh Sketches*, 3rd ser. (London: James Darling, 1853).

Egan, David, *Coal Society: A History of the South Wales Mining Valleys 1840–1980* (Llandysul: Gomer Press, 1987).

Fanon, Frantz, *Black Skin, White Mask* (1952; London: Pluto Press, 1986).

——, *The Wretched of the Earth*, trans. C. Farrington (New York: Grove Press, 1963).

Freud, Sigmund, 'From the history of an infantile neurosis' [1918] and 'The "Uncanny"' [1919], *The Standard Edition of the Complete Psychological*

Works of Sigmund Freud: An Infantile Neurosis and Other Works (1917–1919), XVII, ed. James Strachey (1955; London: Vintage, 2001), pp. 3–123 and 219–56.

Gimbutas, Marija, *The Civilization of the Goddess* (San Francisco: Harper San Francisco, 1991).

Gomme, George Laurence, *Ethnology and Folklore* (London: Kegan Paul, Trench, Trubner & Co., 1892).

Gordon, Avery F., *Ghostly Matters: Haunting and the Sociological Imagination* (1997; new edn, Minneapolis: University of Minnesota Press, 2008).

Gossedge, Rob, 'Tales of the *Boneddigion*: Nigel Heseltine's gentry context', *Almanac: Yearbook of Welsh Writing in English*, 13 (2008–9), 55–80.

Gramich, Katie (ed.), *Mapping the Territory: Critical Approaches to Welsh Fiction in English* (Cardigan: Parthian, 2010).

Graves, Robert, *The White Goddess: A Historical Grammar of Poetic Myth* (1948; New York: Farrar, Straus and Giroux, 1966).

Green, Miranda J., *Exploring the World of the Druids* (London: Thames & Hudson, 1997). Gruffydd, Eirlys, *Gwrachod Cymru* (Caernarfon: Gwasg Gwynedd, 1980).

Hansen, Jim, *Terror and Irish Modernism: The Gothic Tradition from Burke to Beckett* (Albany, NY: SUNY Press, 2009).

Harris, John, 'Queen of the Rushes: Allen Raine and her public', *Planet*, 97 (1993), 64–72.

Henderson, James, 'The Gothic novel in Wales', *National Library of Wales Journal*, 11 (1959–60), 244–54.

——, 'An edition of the poems of Ann of Swansea (Ann Julia Hatton, née Kemble, 1764–1838) including unpublished material' (unpublished M.Phil. thesis, University of Glamorgan, 2005).

Herbert, Trevor and Gareth Elwyn Jones (eds), *People & Protest: Wales 1815–1880* (Cardiff: University of Wales Press, 1988).

—— and —— (eds), *The Remaking of Wales in the Eighteenth Century* (Cardiff: University of Wales Press, 1988).

Hogle, Jerrold E. (ed.), *The Cambridge Companion to Gothic Fiction* (Cambridge: Cambridge University Press, 2002).

Hughes, William and Andrew Smith, 'Introduction: defining the relationships between Gothic and the postcolonial', *Gothic Studies*, 'Postcolonial Gothic' special no., 5/2 (2003), 1–6.

Hume, I. and W. T. R. Pryce (eds), *The Welsh and their Country* (Llandysul: Gomer Press, 1986).

Jarvis, Matthew, *Ruth Bidgood* (Cardiff: University of Wales Press, 2012).

Jenkins, Geraint H. (ed.), *A Rattleskull Genius: The Many Faces of Iolo Morganwg* (Cardiff: University of Wales Press, 2005).

Jenkins, Philip, *The Making of a Ruling Class: The Glamorgan Gentry 1640–1790* (Cambridge: Cambridge University Press, 1983).

John, Angela V. (ed.), *Our Mothers' Land: Chapters in Welsh Women's History 1830–1939* (1991; Cardiff: University of Wales Press, 2010).

Jones, Alun R. and Gwyn Thomas (eds), *Presenting Saunders Lewis* (Cardiff: University of Wales Press, 1983).

Jones, Darryl, 'Borderlands: spiritualism and the occult in fin de siècle and Edwardian Welsh and Irish horror', *Irish Studies Review*, 17/1 (2009), 31–44.

Jones, David J. V., *Rebecca's Children: A Study of Rural Society, Crime and Protest* (Oxford: Clarendon Press, 1989).

Jones, Dot, *Statistical Evidence relating to the Welsh Language 1801–1911* (Cardiff: University of Wales Press, 1998).

Jones, Edmund, *A Relation of the Apparitions of Spirits, in the Principality of Wales* (1780; repr. as *The Appearance of Evil*, ed. with an intro. by John Harvey (Cardiff: University of Wales Press, 2003)).

Jones, Glyn, *The Dragon Has Two Tongues: Essays on Anglo-Welsh Writers and Writing* (London: J. M. Dent, 1968).

Jones, Ieuan Gwynedd, *Mid-Victorian Wales: The Observers and the Observed* (Cardiff: University of Wales Press, 1992).

Jones, Sally Roberts, *Allen Raine* (Cardiff: University of Wales Press, 1979).

Jones, T. Gwynn, *Welsh Folklore and Folk-customs* (1930; repr. Cambridge: D. S. Brewer, 1979).

Joshi, S. T., *The Weird Tale* (Austin: University of Texas Press, 1990).

Killeen, Jarlath, *Gothic Literature 1825–1914* (Cardiff: University of Wales Press, 2009).

Knight, Stephen, *One Hundred Years of Fiction: Writing Wales in English* (Cardiff: University of Wales Press, 2004).

——, '"On Stony Ground": Rhys Davies's *The Withered Root*', in Katie Gramich (ed.), *Mapping the Territory: Critical Approaches to Welsh Fiction in English* (Cardigan: Parthian, 2010), pp. 11–34.

Koch, J. T. (ed.), *The Celtic Heroic Age: Literary Sources for Ancient Celtic Europe, Early Ireland & Wales* (Aberystwyth: Celtic Studies Publications, 2000).

Kristeva, Julia, *Powers of Horror: An Essay on Subjection* (New York: Columbia University Press, 1982).

Lewis, Saunders, *Tynged yr Iaith* (1962; Llandysul: Gwasg Gomer, 2012).

Lord, Peter, 'Y Bardd – Celtiaeth a chelfyddyd', in Geraint H. Jenkins (ed.), *Cof Cenedl VII* (Llandysdul: Gwasg Gomer, 1992).

——, *Winifred Coombe Tennant: A Life through Art* (Aberystwyth: Llyfrgell Genedlaethol Cymru, 2007).

Malchow, H. L., *Gothic Images of Race in Nineteenth-century Britain* (Stanford, Calif.: Stanford University Press, 1996).

Marx, Karl and Friedrich Engels, *Selected Works* (London: Lawrence & Wishart, 1968).

Mighall, Robert, *A Geography of Victorian Gothic Fiction: Mapping History's Nightmares* (Oxford: Oxford University Press, 1999).

Morgan, Owen (Morien), *Kimmerian Revelations: The Winged Son of Stonehenge and Avebury* (Pontypridd: Glamorgan Free Press Office, n.d.).

——, *The Light of Britannia . . .* (Cardiff and London: Daniel Owen, Whittaker, J. W. Boulton, n.d.).

Morgan, Prys (ed.), *Brad y Llyfrau Gleision* (Llandysul: Gwasg Gomer, 1991).

Mulvey-Roberts, Marie (ed.), *The Handbook to Gothic Literature* (Basingstoke and London: Macmillan, 1998).

Napier, James, *Folk Lore, or, Superstitious Beliefs in the West of Scotland within this Century* (1879; repr. Wakefield, Yorkshire: EP Publishing, 1976).

O'Connor, Laura, *Haunted English: The Celtic Fringe, the British Empire and De-Anglicization* (Baltimore: John Hopkins University Press, 2006).

Pennant, Thomas, *A Tour in Wales*, 2 vols (1778–81; London: Wilkie and Robinson, et al., 1810).

Piggott, Stuart, *The Druids* (London: Thames and Hudson, 1968)

Pittock, Murray, *Celtic Identity and the British Image* (Manchester and NY: Manchester University Press, 1999).

Prescott, Sarah, *Eighteenth-century Writing from Wales: Bards and Britons* (Cardiff: University of Wales Press, 2008).

Price, Cecil, *The English Theatre in Wales in the Eighteenth and Early Nineteenth Centuries* (Cardiff: University of Wales Press, 1948).

Puckle, Bertram S., *Funeral Customs: Their Origin and Development* (London: T. W. Laurie, 1926).

Punter, David, 'Scottish and Irish Gothic', in Jerrold E. Hogle (ed.), *The Cambridge Companion to Gothic Fiction* (Cambridge: Cambridge University Press, 2002), pp. 105–23.

—— and Glennis Byron, *The Gothic* (Oxford: Blackwell, 2004).

Roberts, Harri Garrod, 'The body and the book: Caradoc Evans's *My People*', *Welsh Writing in English: A Yearbook of Critical Essays*, 11 (2006–7), 188–209.

——, *Embodying Identity: Representations of the Body in Welsh Literature* (Cardiff: University of Wales Press, 2009).

Roberts, J., *Druidical Remains and Antiquities of the Ancient Britons, principally in Glamorgan* (Swansea: E. Griffiths, 1842).

Roberts, Peter, *The Cambrian Popular Antiquities; or, an account of some Traditions, Customs, and Superstitions of Wales* (London: E. Williams, 1815).

Sandys, Oliver, *Caradoc Evans* (London: Hurst & Blackett, 1945).

Sikes, Wirt, *British Goblins: Welsh Folk-lore, Fairy Mythology, Legends and Traditions* (London: Sampson Low, Marston, Searle & Rivington, 1880).

Smith, Dai, 'Psycho-colonialism', *New Welsh Review*, 66 (2004), 22–9.

Smith, Andrew and William Hughes (eds), *Empire and the Gothic: The Politics of Genre* (Basingstoke: Palgrave Macmillan, 2003).

Suggett, Richard, *A History of Magic and Witchcraft in Wales* (Stroud: The History Press, 2008).

Thomas, M. Wynn, *Internal Difference: Literature in Twentieth-century Wales* (Cardiff: University of Wales Press, 1992).

——, '"A Grand Harlequinade": the border writing of Nigel Heseltine', in *Welsh Writing in English: A Yearbook of Critical Essays*, ii (2006–7), 51–68.

——, *In the Shadow of the Pulpit: Literature and Nonconformist Wales* (Cardiff: University of Wales Press, 2010).

Trevelyan, Marie, *Folk-lore and Folk-stories of Wales* (London: Elliot Stock, 1909).

Trumpener, Katie, *Bardic Nationalism: The Romantic Novel and the British Empire* (Princeton, NJ: Princeton University Press, 1997).

Valentine, Mark, *Arthur Machen*, Border Lines series (Bridgend: Seren Books, 1995).

Wallace, Diana, *Female Gothic Histories* (Cardiff: University of Wales Press, 2013).

—— and Andrew Smith (eds), *The Female Gothic: New Directions* (Basingstoke: Palgrave Macmillan, 2009).

Walters, Huw, 'Bwyta pechod yng Nghwmaman', *Y Genhinen*, xxviii (1978), 96–9.

——, *Canu'r Pwll a'r Pulpud: Portread o'r Diwylliant Barddol Cymraeg yn Nyffryn Aman* (Abertawe: Cyhoeddiadau Barddas, 1987).

Williams, Raymond, *Who Speaks for Wales? Nation, Culture, Identity*, ed. Daniel Williams (Cardiff: University of Wales Press, 2003).

Williams, T. L., *Caradoc Evans* (Cardiff: University of Wales Press, 1970).

Index